CW01213431

Justin Bonello cooks
...for friends

PENGUIN BOOKS

Published by the Penguin Group
Penguin Books (South Africa) (Pty) Ltd, 24 Sturdee Avenue, Rosebank, Johannesburg 2196, South Africa
Penguin Group (USA) Inc, 375 Hudson Street, New York, New York 10014, USA
Penguin Group (Canada), 90 Eglinton Avenue East, Suite 700, Toronto, Ontario, Canada M4P 2Y3
(a division of Pearson Penguin Canada Inc)
Penguin Books Ltd, 80 Strand, London WO2R 0RL, England
Penguin Ireland, 25 St Stephen's Green, Dublin 2, Ireland (a division of Penguin Books Ltd)
Penguin Group (Australia), 250 Camberwell Road, Camberwell, Victoria 3124, Australia
(a division of Pearson Australia Group Pty Ltd)
Penguin Books India Pvt Ltd, 11 Community Centre, Panchsheel Park, New Delhi – 110 017, India
Penguin Group (NZ), 67 Apollo Drive, Mairangi Bay, Auckland 1310, New Zealand
(a division of Pearson New Zealand Ltd)

Penguin Books (South Africa) (Pty) Ltd, Registered Offices:
24 Sturdee Avenue, Rosebank, Johannesburg 2196, South Africa

www.penguinbooks.co.za

First published by Penguin Books (South Africa) (Pty) Ltd 2011
Copyright © Cooked in Africa Films 2011

ALL RIGHTS RESERVED
THE MORAL RIGHT OF THE AUTHOR HAS BEEN ASSERTED
ISBN 978-0-14-352829-6

Written by Justin Bonello, Helena Lombard and Bianca Coleman
Design and layout by twoshoes.co.za
Cover design by twoshoes.co.za
Photography by Louis Hiemstra and Duane Howard
Food styling by Jules Mercer
Illustrations by David Jackson
Printed and bound by 1010 Printing International Ltd, China

Except in the United States of America, this book is sold subject to the
condition that it shall not, by way of trade or otherwise, be lent, resold, hired out
or otherwise circulated without the publisher's prior consent in any form of binding
other than that in which it is published and without a similar condition including
this condition being imposed on the subsequent purchaser.

CONTENTS

STRANDLOPER • PG 6
HOOK LINE & SINKER ★ SEARED BLACK PEPPER YELLOW FIN TUNA
WEST COAST KREEF CHOWDER ★ BRAAI'D WEST COAST HOTNOT FISH
PERIWINKLE ★ WEST COAST BLACK MUSSEL POT ★ KERRIE VIS

BOS KOS • PG 34
THE STORY OF THE KASSIE ★ CHICKEN IN A KASSIE ★ SMOKED FILLET IN A KASSIE
FLAT BREAD IN A KASSIE ★ THE BUTTER CLUB ★ BILTONG
BILTONG, LEEK AND ASPARAGUS QUICHE ★ TOMATO LAMB POTJIE WITH GNOCCHI
BOEREWORS KING ★ SMILEYS ★ PEPPERCORN OSTRICH FILLET
MUSHROOM AND SMASHED BABY POTATO SALAD ★ STUFFED FILLET
STUFFED MUSHROOMS ★ JUANITA'S POTATO BREAD ★ POTATO POTJIE
BOTTOMLESS APPLE CRUMBLE

LET'S GOOI • PG 82
THAI MUSSELS ON POT BREAD ★ BUNNY (CHOW) ★ FISH PARCELS
TROUT THREE WAYS ★ CRAB IN PUMPKIN LEAVES ★ PREGO ROLL
CHICKEN IN CRUSTY BREAD ★ LULA IN ÁGUA NEGRA ★ FISH BAKED IN SALT
FRUITY PANCAKE MOUNTAIN ★ WILD CHILD SMOOTHIES

PARK OFF • PG 126
ONE PAN BREAKFAST ★ PIES ON THE BRAAI ★ REALLY SCRUMPTIOUS BURGERS
YIN & YANG GAZPACHO ★ VICIOUS WA ★ PASTA PUTTANESCA
STUFFED STICK BREADS ★ FRITTERS ★ KEBABS ★ THAI SEAFOOD SALAD
SALAD DRESSING WITH A BITE ★ BUTTERMILK & PAPRIKA SPATCHCOCK CHICKEN
WARM TOMATO SALAD ★ GENIE'S ROASTED BUTTERNUT & BEETROOT SALAD
OLIVE OIL ★ GARTH'S TART ★ MESSY CHOCOLATE AND BERRY PIE
MESSY CHOCOLATE SUSHI ★ MELKTERT

9.5km turn right
The Pride of Malawi
KUCHE KUCHE
MOWA WATHU WATHU
net: 500ml
IMPORTANT

INTRODUCTION

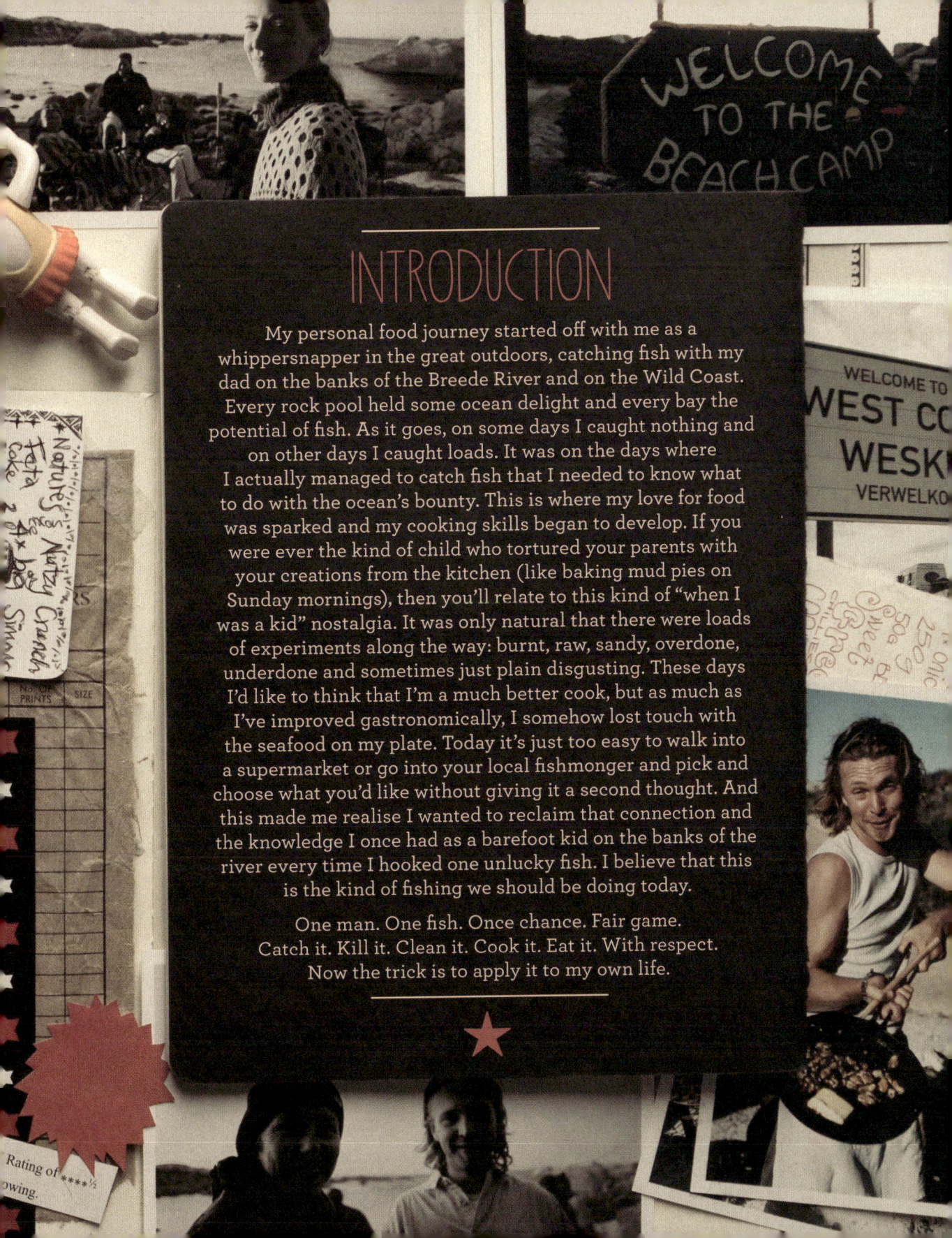

My personal food journey started off with me as a whippersnapper in the great outdoors, catching fish with my dad on the banks of the Breede River and on the Wild Coast. Every rock pool held some ocean delight and every bay the potential of fish. As it goes, on some days I caught nothing and on other days I caught loads. It was on the days where I actually managed to catch fish that I needed to know what to do with the ocean's bounty. This is where my love for food was sparked and my cooking skills began to develop. If you were ever the kind of child who tortured your parents with your creations from the kitchen (like baking mud pies on Sunday mornings), then you'll relate to this kind of "when I was a kid" nostalgia. It was only natural that there were loads of experiments along the way: burnt, raw, sandy, overdone, underdone and sometimes just plain disgusting. These days I'd like to think that I'm a much better cook, but as much as I've improved gastronomically, I somehow lost touch with the seafood on my plate. Today it's just too easy to walk into a supermarket or go into your local fishmonger and pick and choose what you'd like without giving it a second thought. And this made me realise I wanted to reclaim that connection and the knowledge I once had as a barefoot kid on the banks of the river every time I hooked one unlucky fish. I believe that this is the kind of fishing we should be doing today.

One man. One fish. Once chance. Fair game.
Catch it. Kill it. Clean it. Cook it. Eat it. With respect.
Now the trick is to apply it to my own life.

★

STRAN

OLOPER

Chapter One

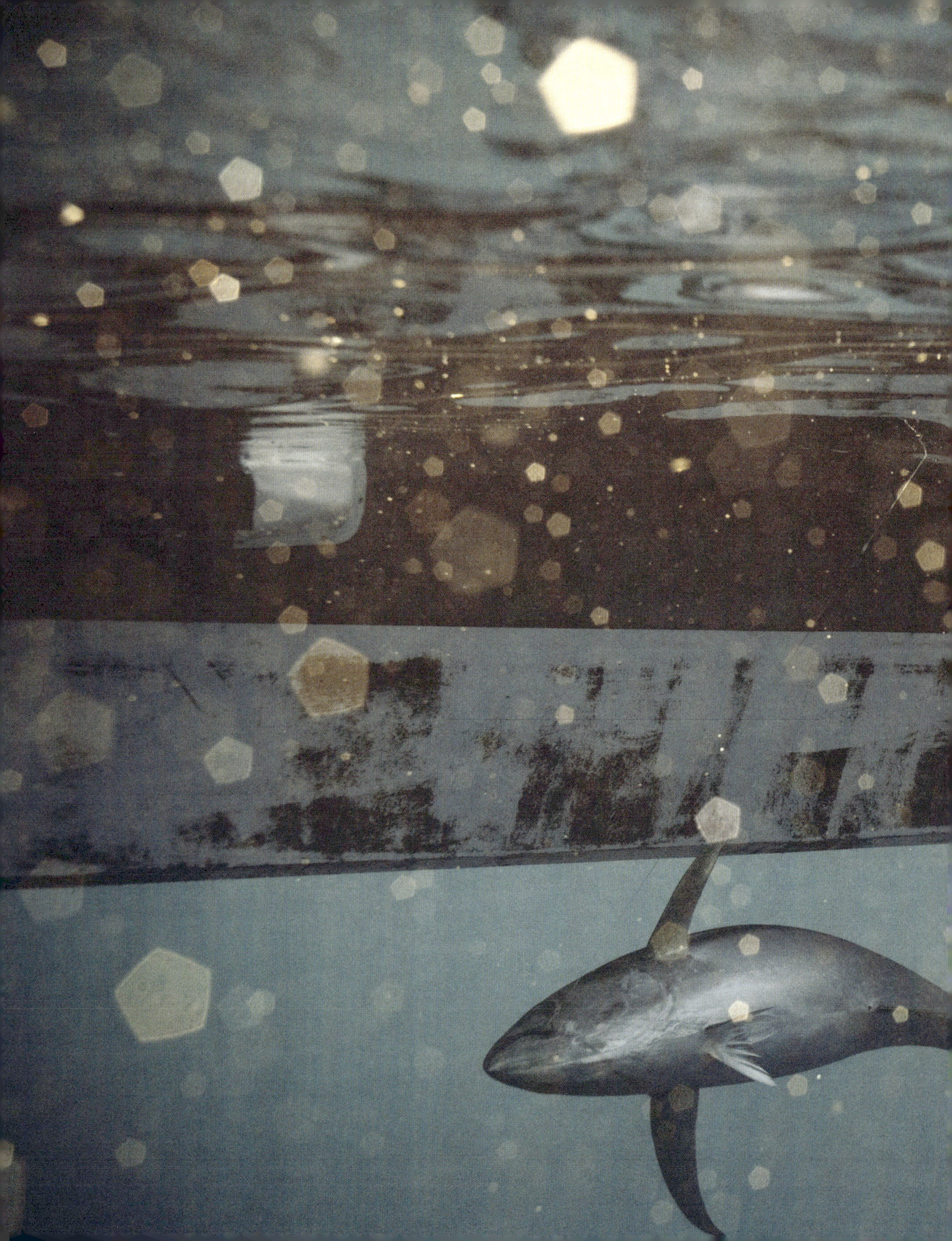

HOOK, LINE AND SINKER

To rectify my lack of knowledge and to get back in touch with real fishing I went to sea with fish assassin, whale rescuer and close friend Gareth Beaumont on his boat *Tyler* to the rich fishing grounds 27 nautical miles off Cape Point, a region known as the Canyon. Our mission? To catch one of the fastest fish in the deep blue: *Thunnus albacares* (commonly known as yellow fin tuna).

The first fish of the day was a long fin tuna, caught by yours truly, but this little guy was too small, and was lucky enough to be tagged, released and sent on his merry way. The second fish wasn't so lucky and with Gareth shouting instructions – 'bend your knees, rock back, stand up, wind!' – I caught my very first yellow fin tuna. Weighing in at over 40 kg, it was the biggest fish I've ever caught, and possibly one of the most exhilarating experiences of my life!

On the way back to shore, two things struck me straight off the bat. The first was to respect death. As much as I was shaking from the adrenalin of this experience, I didn't expect to be affected by the reality of killing tuna (incidentally, the most humane way of doing this is by cutting a chunk out of its head and sticking a wire down its spine, killing it instantly) or the amount of blood on my hands afterwards. The second thing was knowing where my fish came from. Before you buy fish, you've got to ask yourself 'was this hauled in by a trawler or caught using long-line and how does it affect the environment?' Catching and killing my own tuna gave me new respect for the seafood I eat.

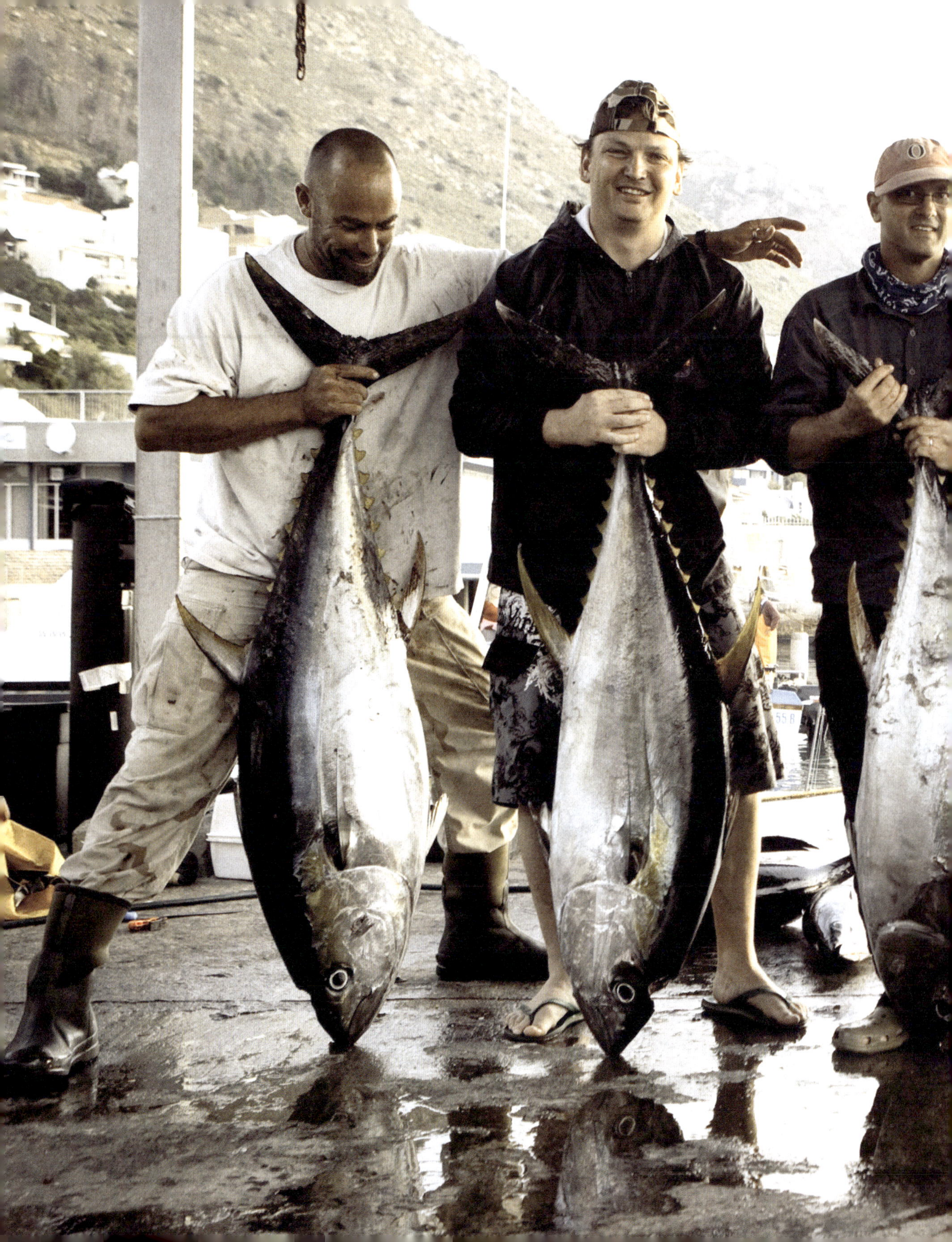

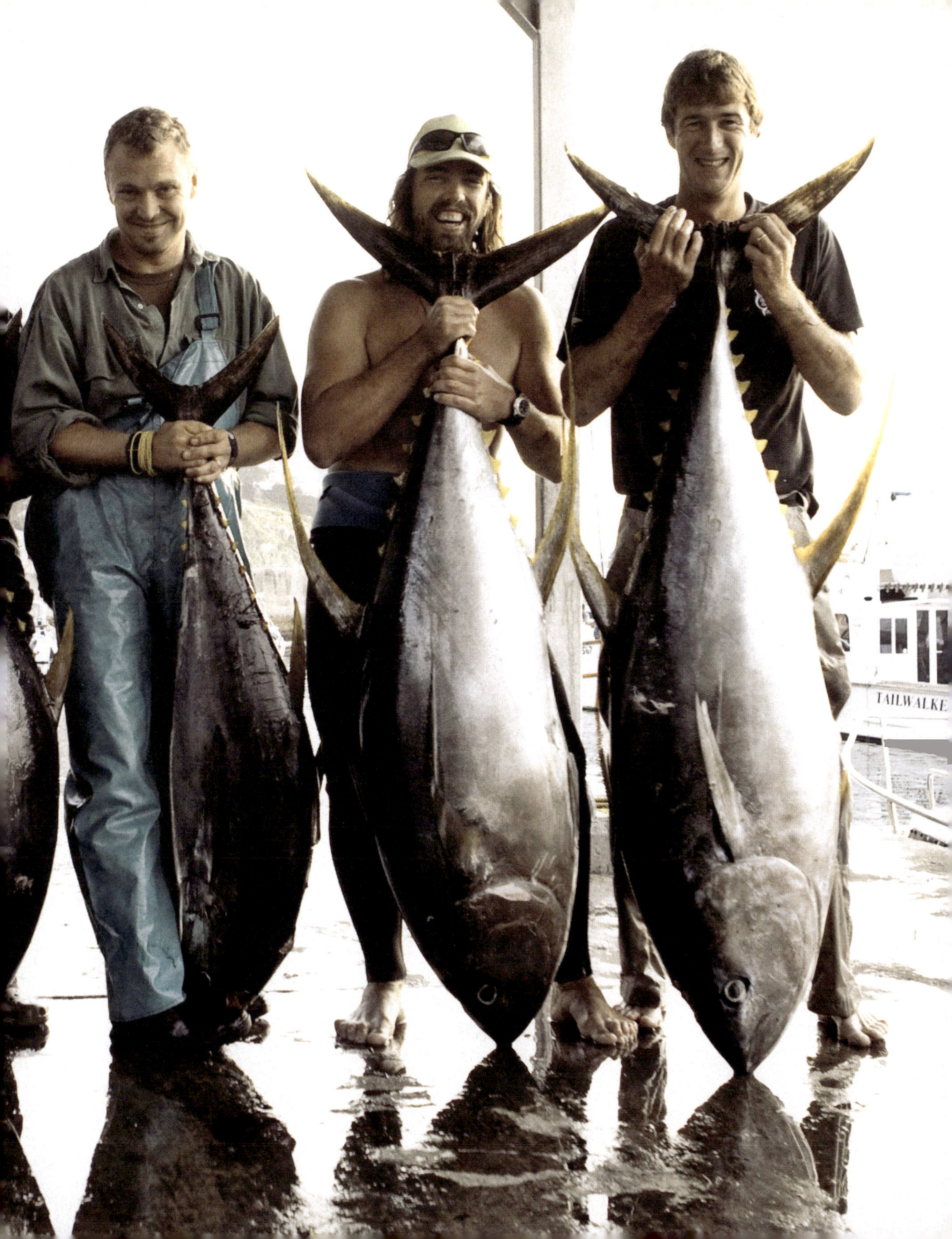
TAILWALKE

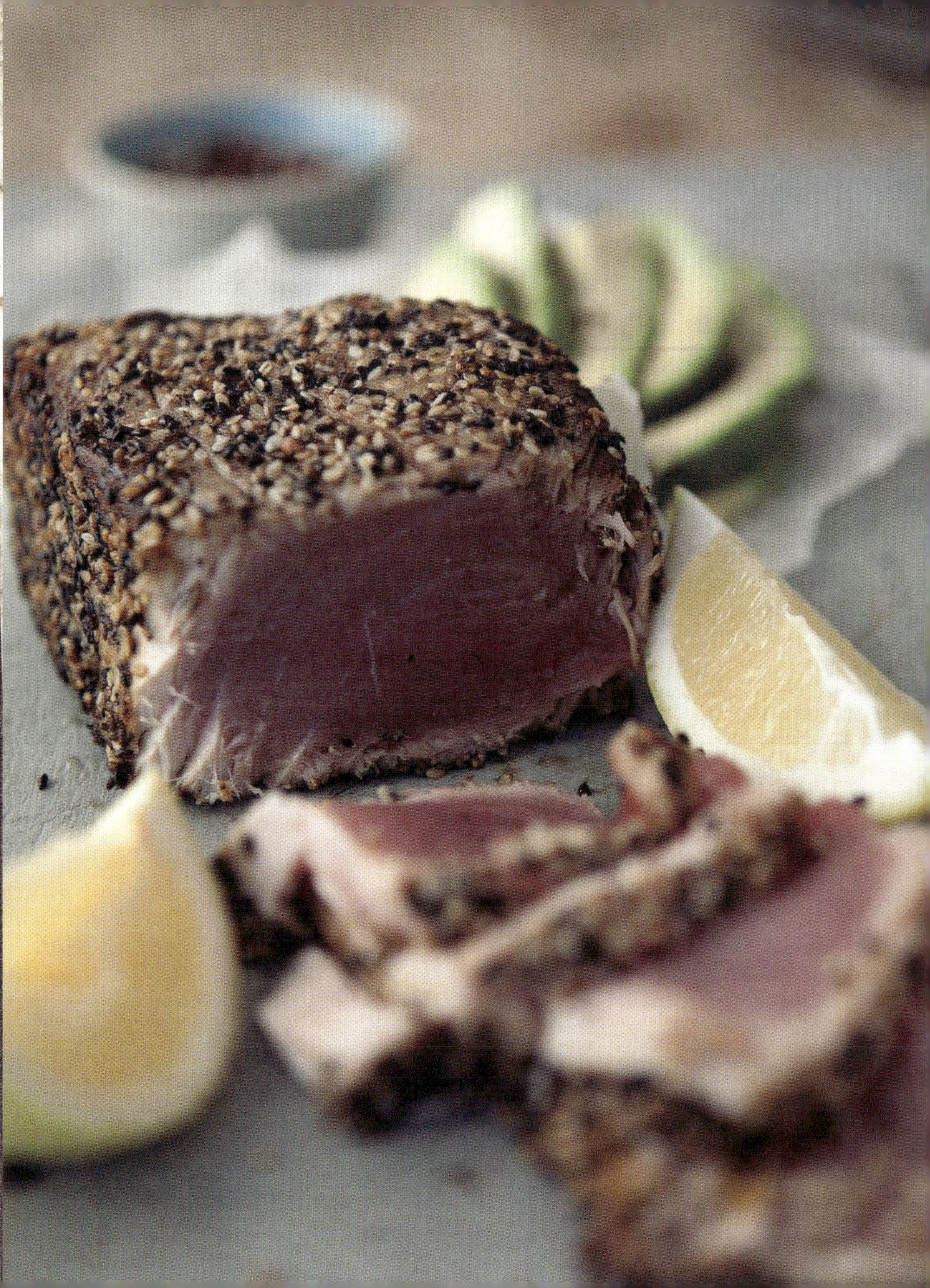

SEARED BLACK PEPPER YELLOW FIN TUNA

As much as I enjoy fishing, I'll admit the *kuier* after the action and the stories told around the fire are always better. In typical Bonello-Beaumont style, that's exactly what we did. This is finger food at its best!

You'll need:
- 1 loin yellow fin tuna – pole or fishing rod caught only
- soy sauce
- a handful coarse black pepper
- olive oil
- avo
- real French mayonnaise
- a bunch of flat leaf parsley
- lemon juice

Take the tuna loin, dip it into soy sauce, and while it's still moist, roll it in the crushed black pepper until it has an even coating all over. Now heat some olive oil in a non-stick pan and drop your tuna into it. Turn it every second time you blink (about every 30 seconds) until it's seared on all sides. Whatever you do, don't overcook it – that's sacrilege!

Remove the tuna from the heat and while it's resting peel your avo and cut into slices. Now using a sharp knife (if it's not sharp, it'll tear the tuna) cut the loin into thick slices – about 1 cm wide. If it's like sashimi in the middle, you're right on the money!

Top a slice of tuna with some avo, a dollop of that darn good mayo, parsley and a good splash of lemon. Alternatively, you can dip it into a honey soya sauce (see below).

Best served with crisp dry white wine and stories of 'the one that got away', while the sun is setting.

★ Honey and Soya Sauce // This is very straightforward. All you need is good quality honey, soya sauce and a splash of port. Mix it up according to your taste. Done.

REAL MAYONNAISE: TRY YOUR HAND AT MAKING YOUR OWN, IT'S ACTUALLY REALLY EASY

I'm not quite sure what's happened to us. We've become so used to a lifestyle of convenience that we've forgotten where our food comes from, and how simple it actually is to make something like mayonnaise. These fast-paced lives we lead are slowly robbing us of the joys of growing, farming and later preparing our own food – so take back the stolen knowledge and make your own mayo.

You'll need:
- 1 egg yolk
- half a lemon
- canola oil

To avoid getting a tired, cramped hand, use an electric beater, or just toughen up. Crack the egg and separate the white from the yolk. Pour the yolk into a bowl and start whisking – you're going to whisk till the bitter end. Add one or two squeezes of lemon juice and then one drop of canola oil. Add a little more oil, and then a little more. Stop when it starts looking like thick paint. Well done! You've made your own mayonnaise!

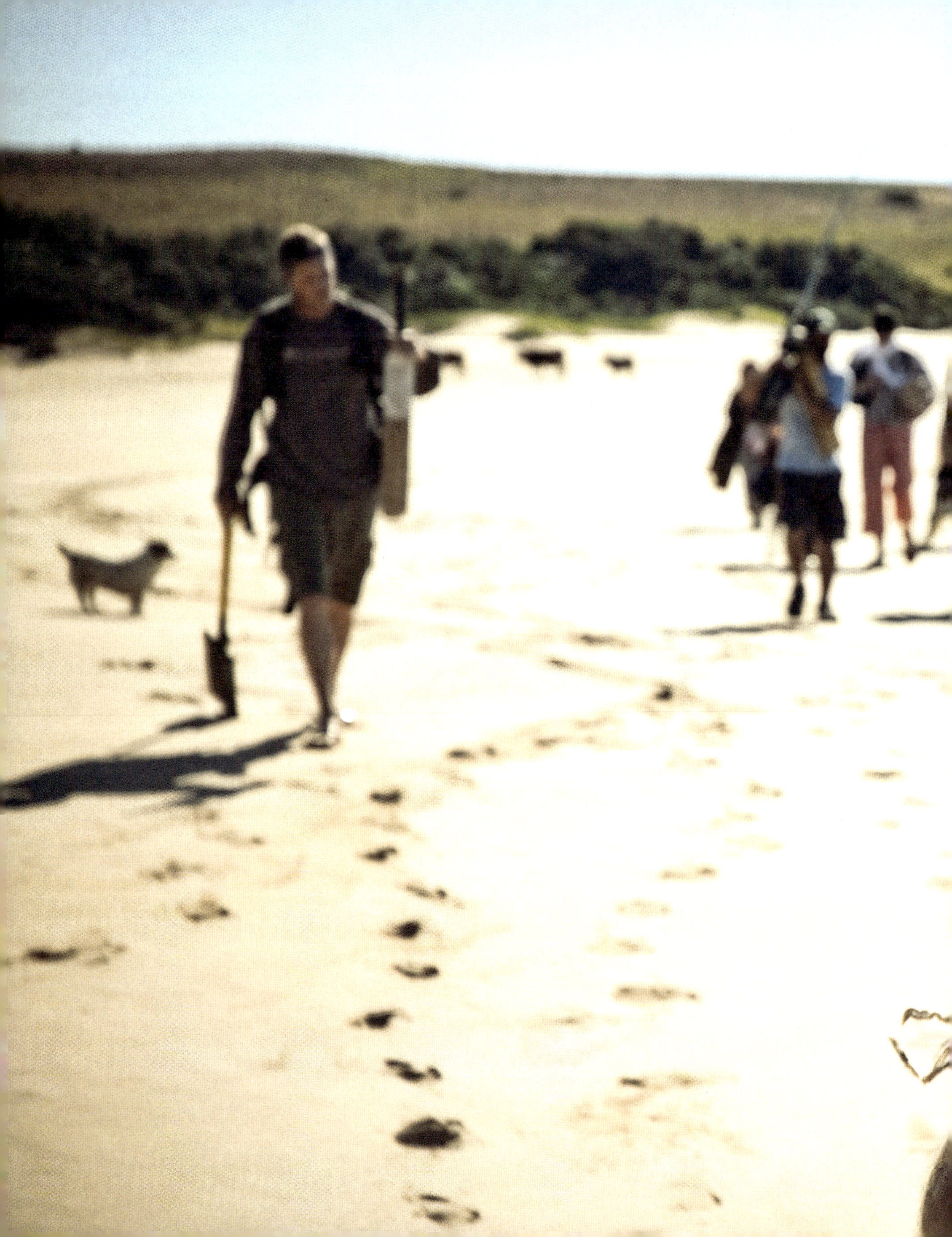

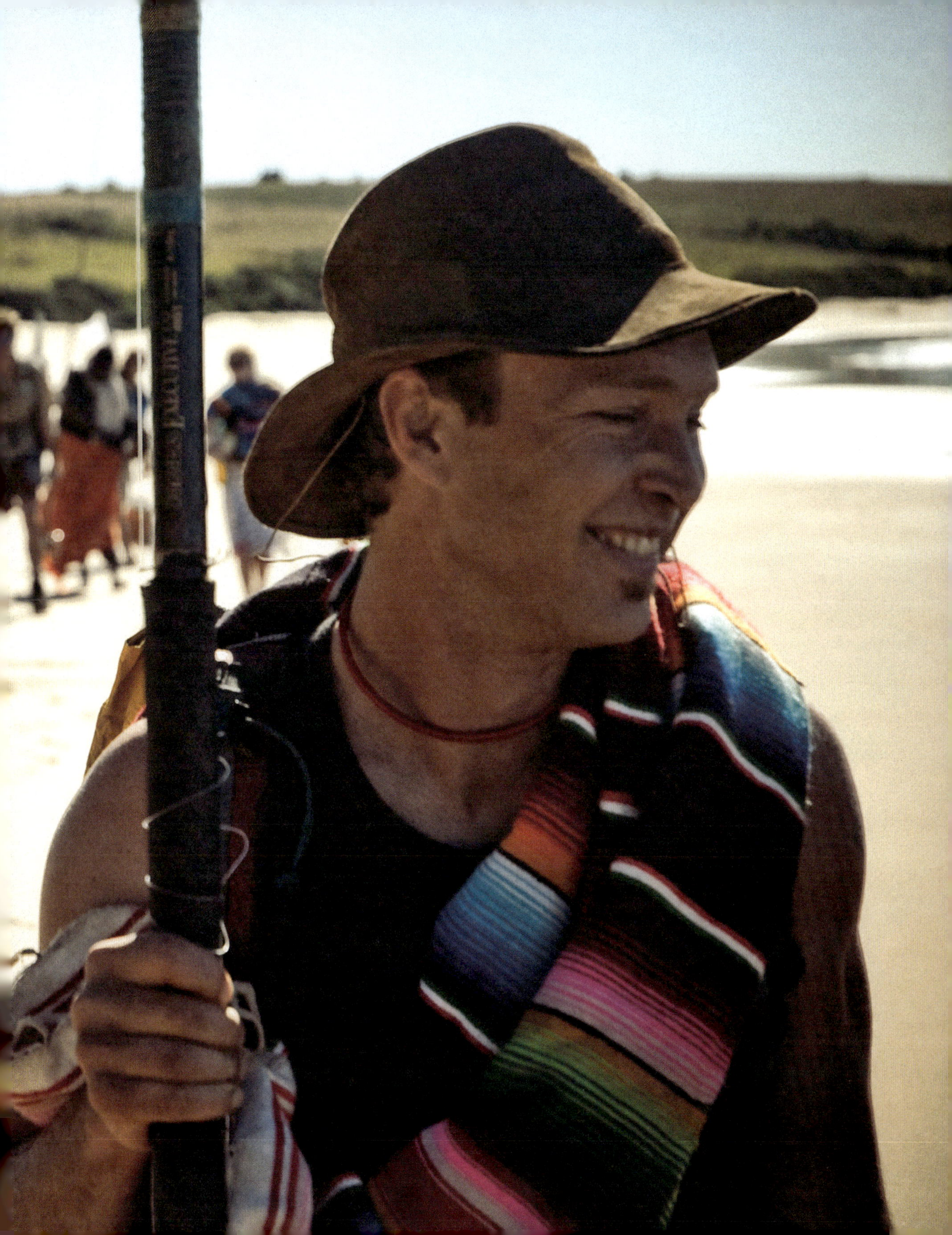

WEST COAST KREEF CHOWDER

Making this takes a while, so I'm going to skip telling you about its origin, and all the adventures we had that weekend at the Beach Camp, so you can just get on with it.

> First up, make a big fire. You're going to cook loads of stuff on it, so you need all the heat and all the space you can get.

Heat up a potjie over the fire, chuck in all the mussels and a good splash of white wine (pour a glass for yourself too – this is hard work and you deserve it). Put the lid on and steam until the mussels open. Remove from the heat and set aside.

Next up, whack the fish on a grid and braai until cooked, turning every so often so it doesn't burn. Now would also be a good time to clean the crayfish and braai them – about 5 minutes, shell side down, just until the flesh changes from translucent to white. Don't overcook crayfish!

★ Take all your seafood to a big table and get your friends to help.

Mussels // Clean the mussels by pulling out the beard and taking the mussel off the shell. Chuck the shells back into the ocean, along with any mussels that aren't open – chances are they were already dead.

Kreef and Fish // Pull off the kreef heads and put into a bowl. Take the tails, pull out all that lovely sweet meat and chuck it into another bowl. Add the tail shells to the bowl with the kreef heads. Please remember to crack open the kreef legs and suck out the meat. Next, flake the fish and mix it in with the kreef meat making sure to remove any sharp bones. Chuck the fish skeleton, bones and skin in with the kreef shells.

A lot of the flavour of fish and seafood is contained in the skin, shell and bones. They are going to go into your stock so you can get every last bit of flavour out of them.

You'll need:

> 3 or 4 kreef (crayfish) – cleaned, preferably fresh and only when in-season
> 2 whole fish – scaled and gutted (any kind, but try to stick to something that's local to where you are – I used the Hottentot Gareth caught) – about 1 & a bit kg
> a whole lot of black mussels (probably enough to fill a medium-sized potjie)
> white wine

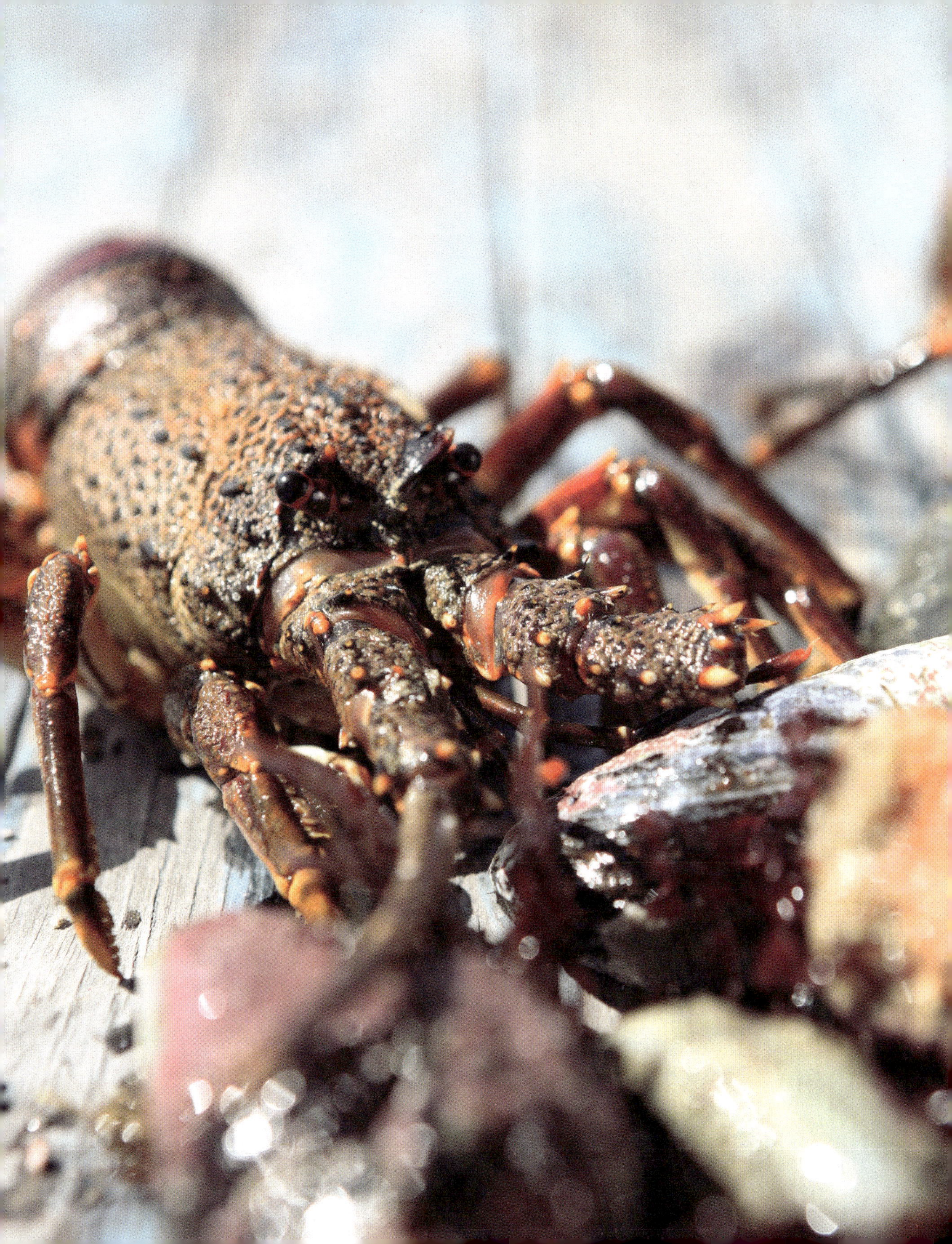

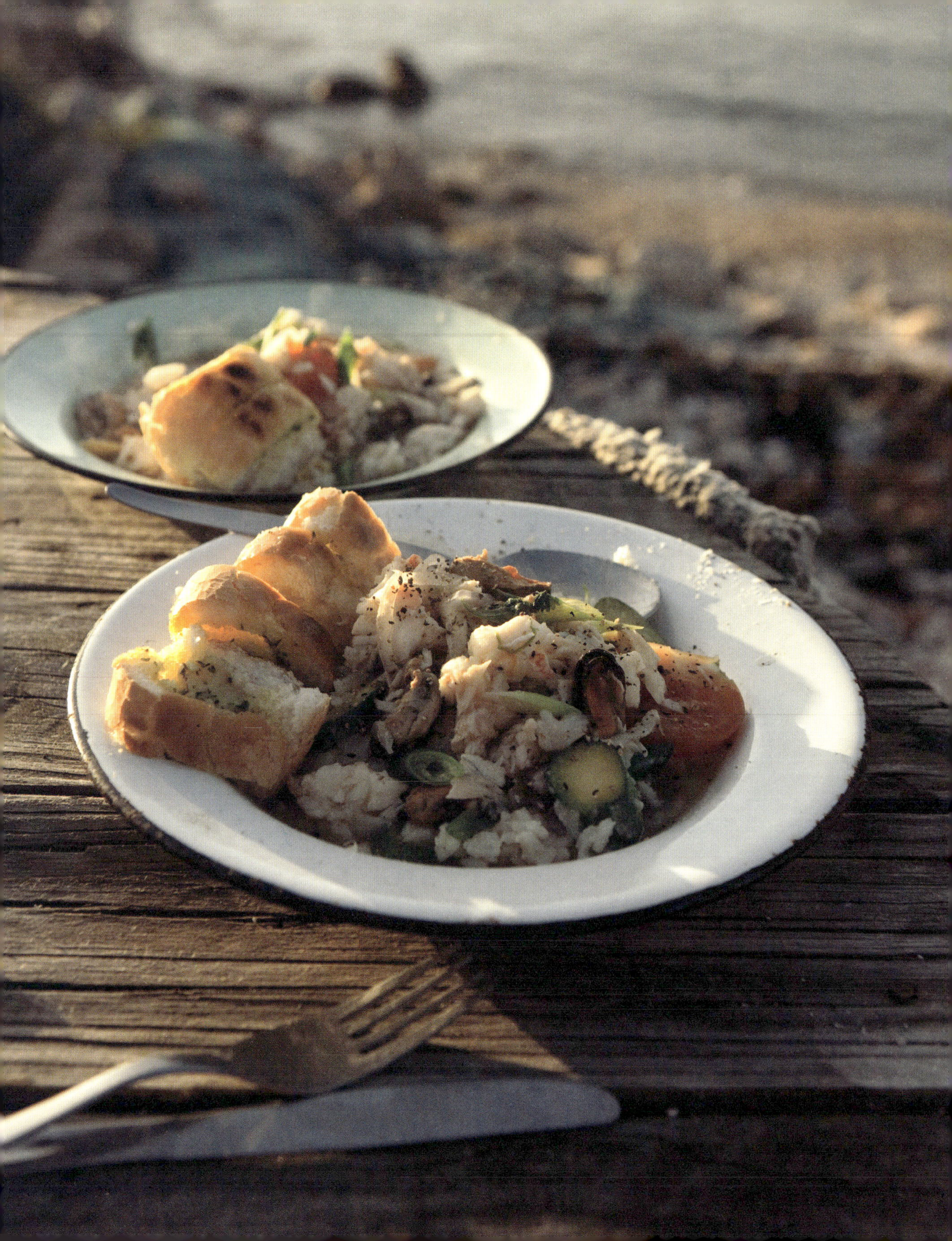

You'll need:
> a bunch of carrots
> a couple of celery stalks – leaves and all
> a whole whack of leeks
> a couple of cloves of garlic – crushed
> a couple of bay leaves
> crayfish heads and shells
> fish bones, skin and heads
> black pepper
> Maldon salt
> water
> splash of white wine

Last bits and bobs . . .
> about 6 large tomatoes – chopped
> 2 red onions – sliced
> crayfish meat
> fish
> mussels
> fresh basil

★ Stock

This forms the basis of the soup, so you need to get as much flavour out of it as possible.

Chop the vegetables roughly and toss into a potjie with the garlic, bay leaves, kreef heads and shells, fish bones, heads and skin, black pepper and crushed salt. Top it up with water and a splash of wine. Then, using the back of a wooden spoon, crunch the kreef shells to release all their flavour. At the hour mark, taste the stock and adjust the seasoning if necessary. Next, strain the stock through a sieve and then through a triple layer of muslin (seriously) and put it back on the fire. The idea with the straining is to get rid of all impurities so that you end up with a nice clear stock.

★ Last bits and bobs . . .

Add the tomatoes, red onion, crayfish meat and fish to the stock and let it simmer for about 20 minutes. Add the mussels and leave them to warm up while you go gather your starving friends (if they're not lined up already).

I like to serve the chowder over rice garnished with fresh basil with chunks of warm garlic bread on the side.

The west coast is synonymous with fishing and fishermen and R&R. It's where you head out of the city for a weekend of kreefing, diving, fishing, drinking and kuiering in a rough, raw and relatively unspoilt environment. About 15 km north-west of Vredenburg is Paternoster, one of the oldest fishing towns along the west coast and famous for its crayfish, its long white beaches and wind, and it's where I went when I wanted to hang out with some local fishermen to find out how they fish, survive and how they prepare their food. Pietie Louw, one of the locals, took me to sea in his little crayfish bakkie (boat). Unfortunately, kreef were out of season so we did the next best thing and caught hotnot. Funnily enough, hotnot is not that well known or eaten other than on the west coast where it's really plentiful and provides sustenance for the locals out of the crayfish season. For a change I caught fish. Lots of them. Seems like local knowledge and generations of experience all added up to Bonello actually catching. (I have this hoodoo, when the cameras roll, the fish disappear.)

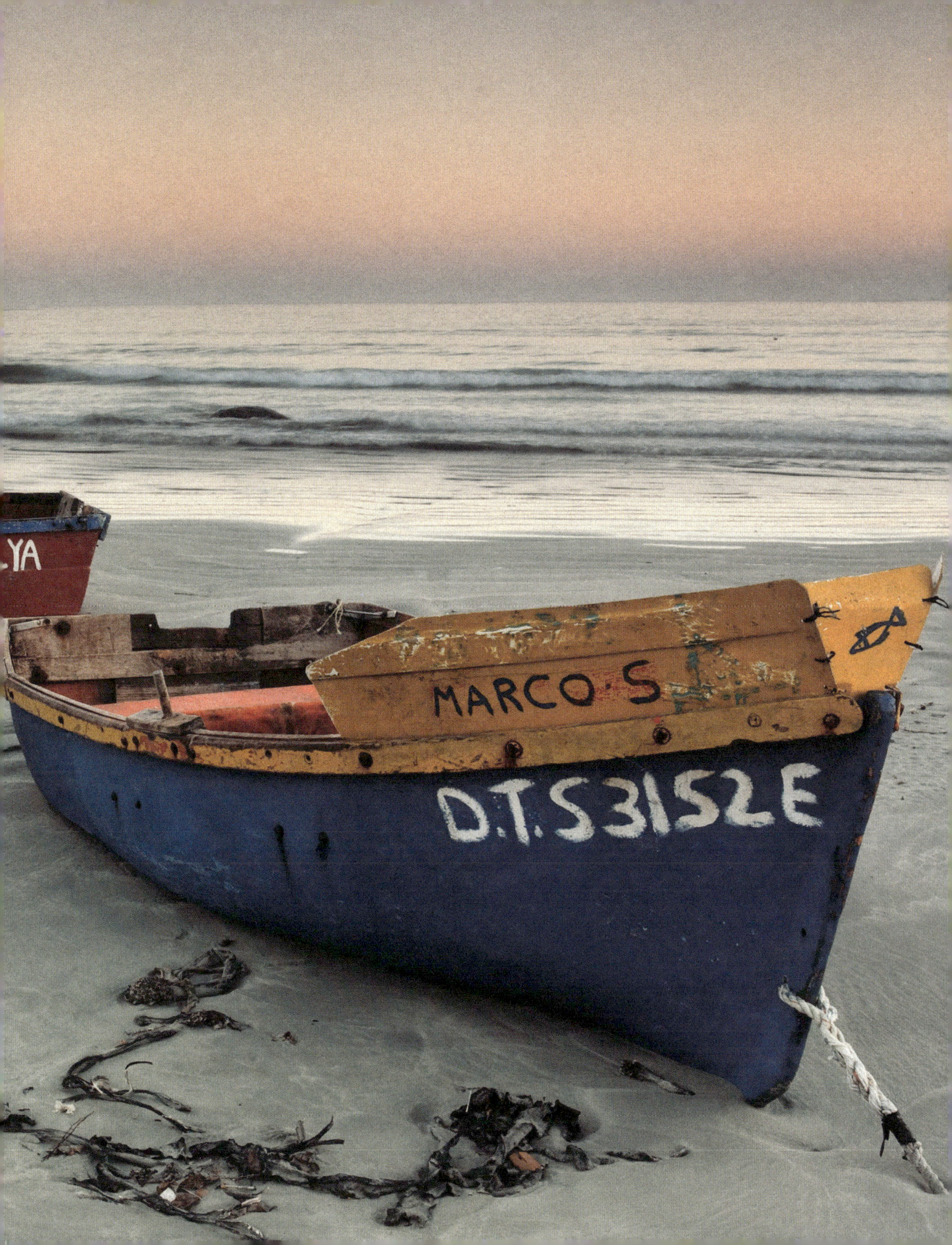
YA
MARCO S
D.T.S3152E

BRAAI'D WEST COAST HOTNOT FISH

We took our bounty back to Pietie's house where his wife was going to prepare it her way. In an old fashioned and comforting traditional division of labour, Pietie did the dirty man work of cleaning, gutting and butterflying (or *vlekking*, as it's known on the West Coast) the fish before his wife took over in the kitchen.

Method of Preparation

She seasoned it well with salt, white pepper and fish spice. (I'm not a fan of the ready-made packet spices but this time I wasn't in charge of the kitchen.) She then liberally scattered onion rings, sliced tomato and grated cheese over and inside the fish.

Pietie folded it closed and popped it inside the griddle over medium coals to let all those flavours permeate the flesh while the men stood around the fire in the time honoured ritual of drinking beer, talking about rugby and the one that got away.

When the fish was golden and crispy, and the cheese had melted into a gooey mess we ate on the stoep with our fingers. It's often the simple things in life – and food – that bring the most satisfaction.

I cannot say that I have ever had better fish. Caught by yours truly, moments later prepared by Pietie and his wife – brilliant.

> ★ **Hottentot** (*Pachymetopon blochii*) is a member of the seabream family and is endemic to southern African coastal waters. It is one of the more abundant seabream species in the Western Cape and is associated with rocky reefs and kelp beds. It is an important species in traditional line fishery which operates from small boats within the inshore zone along the South African coastline, but it is also targeted by recreational line fishers and spear fishers. The minimum size limit is 22 cm for both recreational and commercial fishers.
> (Source: www.wwfsassi.co.za – the South African Sustainable Seafood Initiative)

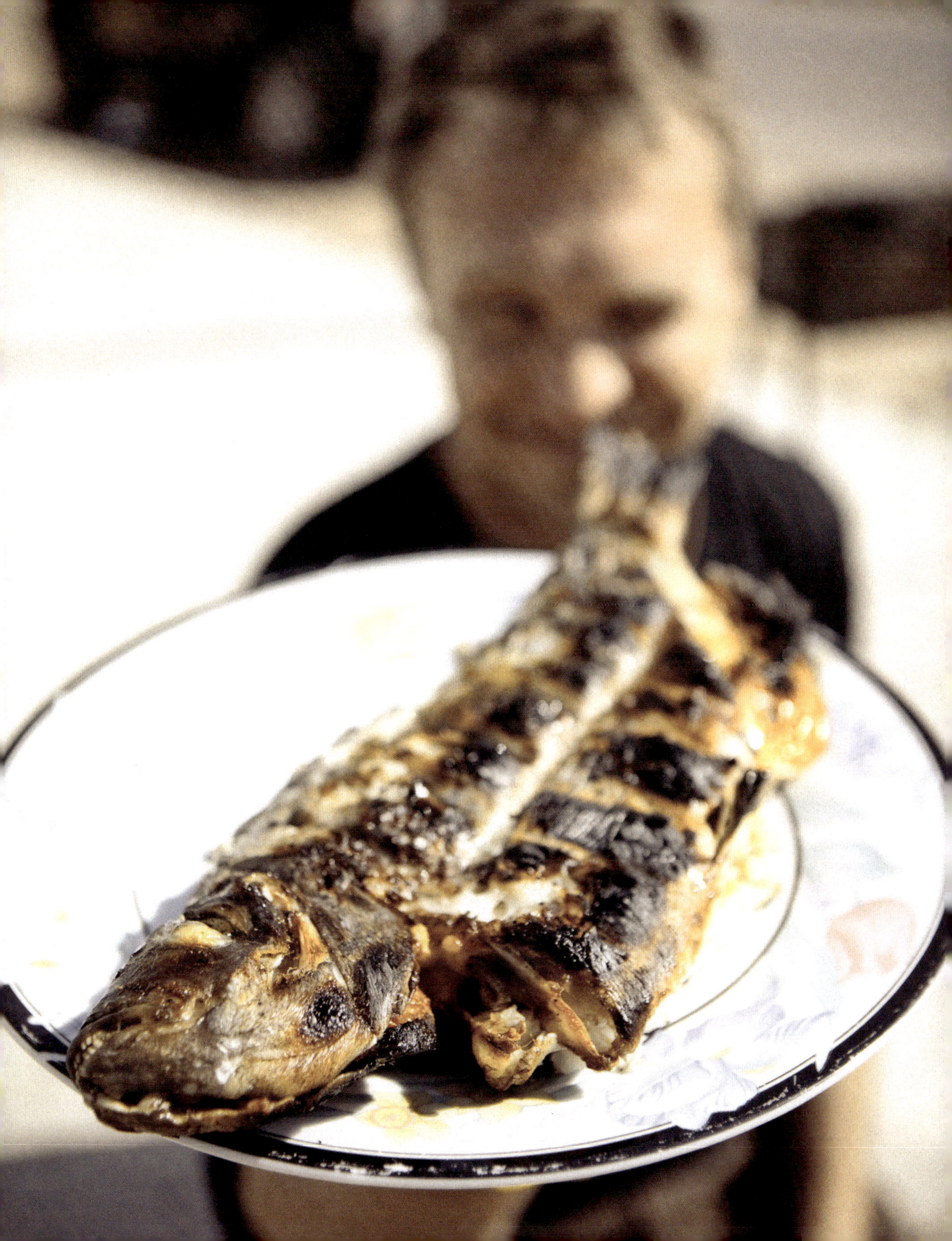

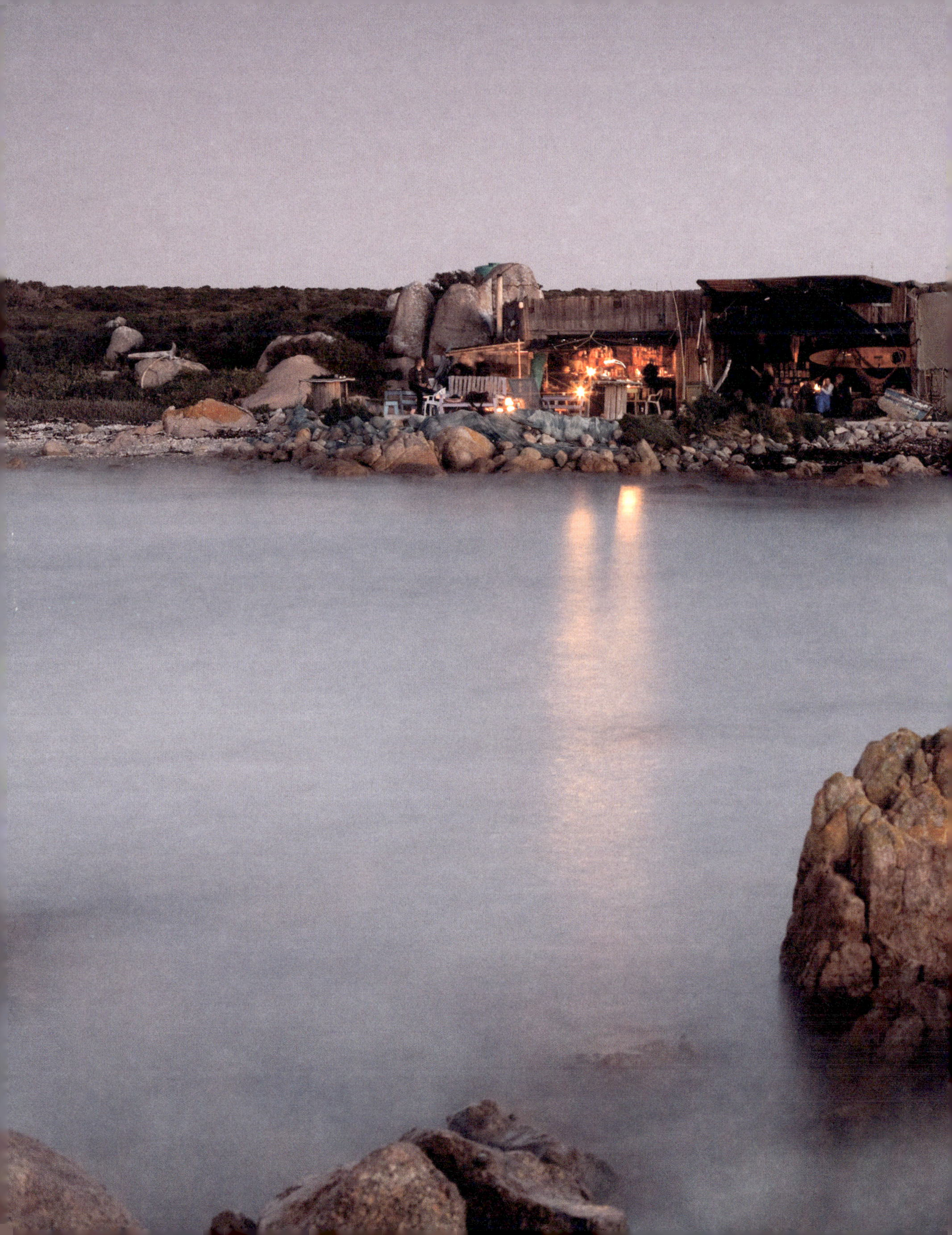

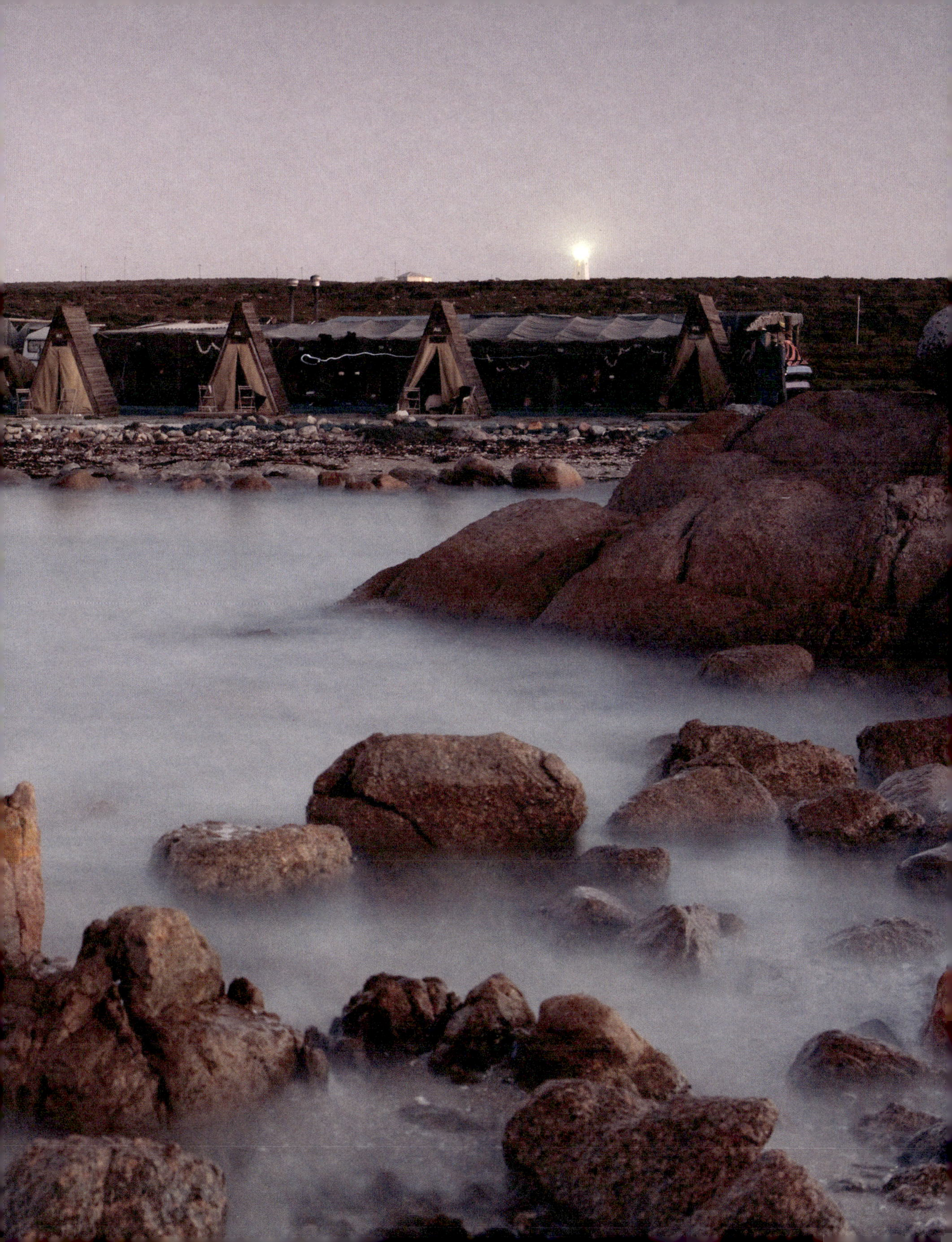

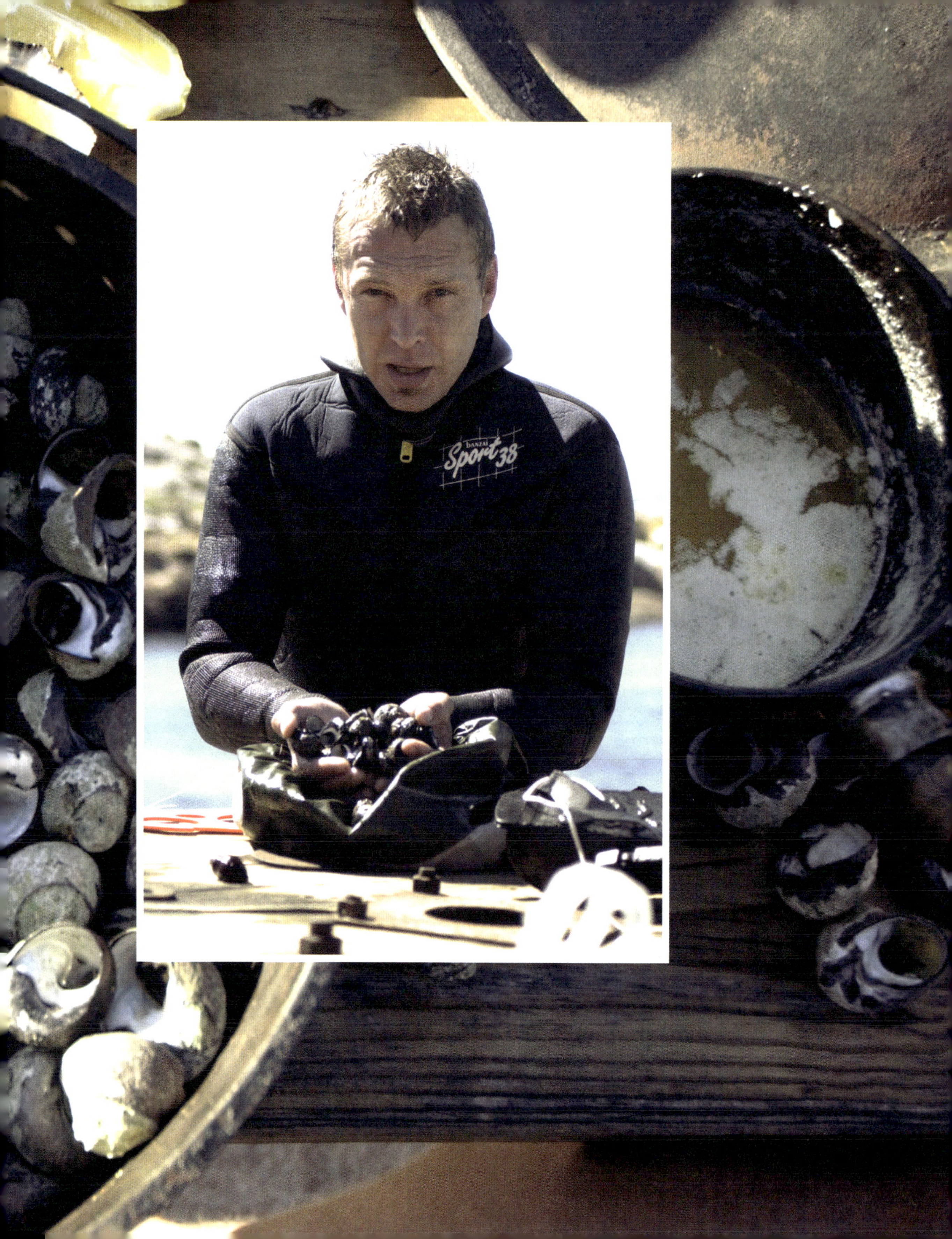
BANZAI
Sport 38

PERIWINKLE

The Beach Camp in the Cape Columbine Nature Reserve is one the best places to go when I need to get my groove back, especially on weekends because it's only a two-hour drive from Cape Town. I've always loved this space, have shot the giant catapult and woken up with a thick head in the bar at three in the morning more times than I can remember. The only downer is the green loos... good old eco long drops. By the end of a weekend I'd rather go in the bush than face whatever's lurking behind those toilet doors. Toilets aside, this tented spot is right on the water's edge near Paternoster, has no electricity and is exactly the kind of laid-back vibe that I enjoy.

One weekend my plan was to dive *alikreukel* (*Periwinklis giganticus* to us; *Turbo sarmaticus* to scientists) aka a giant sea snail, for a light lunch, but sometimes harvesting turns out to be more about hope than it does about actual food. I couldn't find what I was looking for – in fact, I found just about everything except *alikreukel*! So, with my reputation as 'bush cook' on the line, I settled for something else – as one does when dependent on catching one's own food. And so I went from giant to tiny and found an abundance of periwinkle. Being the smaller cousin of *alikreukel*, they taste pretty much the same, but they are a lot trickier to eat. If you're the kind of person who has the patience to crack open one pistachio at a time, then you'll be just fine. It's not the kind of thing you'll eat every day, but when you do it'll give you bush cook kudos.

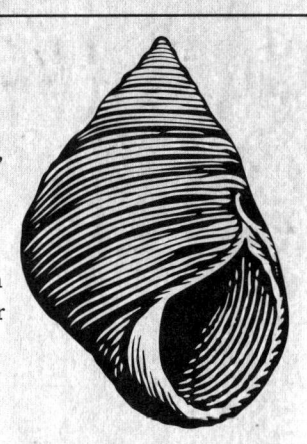

You'll need:

- a potjie (Dutch oven) – preheated on a fire
- a whole lot of periwinkles – I had about 150
- dry white wine
- garlic butter dipping sauce
- lemon butter dipping sauce
- vinegar – in dipping bowl
- a couple of pins (yes, really!)

Whack the whole lot of snails into the pot, add a couple of splashes of wine and put the lid on. While it's steaming, make the garlic and lemon butter dipping sauces (see pages 46-47).

The periwinkles should be done after about a beer (but not if you're a slow drinker). Remove them from your potjie and put straight into a bowl. If you think you're going to tuck in straight away, you're smoking your socks. The real work starts now and you might start feeling that you're in the Land of Lilliput!

★ PERFORMING THE OPEN HEART SURGERY

Take a pin, dig behind the foot of the snail and pull out the meat. Remove the plastic looking disc and the *derms* (guts) and dip the tiny bit that's left into either of the butters or the vinegar or just give it a good squeeze of lemon. If you're like me, you'll get a handful ready and then stuff them into your mouth all in one go.

> **PS** If you actually made this recipe – WELL DONE! You now have bush cook kudos.

WEST COAST BLACK MUSSEL POT

The West Coast is known for many things – from the friendly people to the endless beaches and rugged coastline. And of course it is home to one of South Africa's culinary treasures: the West Coast black mussel. On the scale of taste explosions, not a lot comes close to the full flavour of the black mussel – especially if you make it in a potjie over a fire, serve it with freshly baked bread and eat it with good friends . . . you get the picture.

But first, you need to . . . Flex your muscles and get your own.

Mussels are really easy to harvest. You don't need bait. You don't need to sit around and hope for a bite on the other end of the line. All you need is a knife or screwdriver, tackies (so you don't cut your feet on the rocks), and either a big hat, a bucket or even a pillowcase for your pickings, and you need a permit (obtainable in SA from the post office). Make sure to check with the local fishermen whether there's a red tide. Wait for low tide, trek down to the rocks and pick as many as you can find, keeping in mind the bag limit of your permit. Here's what you do.

- ★ Pretend you're a *klipspringer* and make your way towards the water's edge.
- ★ Have your screwdriver or knife ready (hopefully it was safely tucked away in a *lappie* in your hat, bucket or pillowcase).
- ★ Look around for mussels – if you're at a good spot they're easy to find.
- ★ Using the blade of your knife, slip it in behind the back of the mussel and cut through the beard (the strands that attach the mussel with super glue-like strength to the rocks). No knife? Grab the mussel and twist it off the rock. Works just as well.
- ★ Chuck the mussel in your hat, bucket or pillowcase.
- ★ Repeat these steps until your hat, bucket or pillowcase is filled to the bag limit.
- ★ Keep an eye on the waves – you don't want to be lost at sea. If you see a big one approaching, run like hell! (Which reminds me, it's probably a good idea to let your wife, husband, boyfriend or girlfriend know what you'll be getting up to.)

Once you've got enough mussels, go back to the shore and tend to your scraped knuckles.

First, heat up a potjie, chuck in the mussels, the parsley and a good splash of white wine. Put the lid back on and steam the mussels until they open. You can eat some of the mussels straight from the shell just like that – really simple and delicious. But keep some for the main act. Throw away the ones that didn't open. Clean the mussels by pulling off the beards and removing them from the shells.

Heat up another potjie, add a generous knob of butter, a good squeeze of lemon, black pepper, crushed salt, the garlic and the cleaned mussels. If you want mussels with a bit of a bite, add some chilli and grated ginger. Let it simmer for a moment, give it a good stir, then tuck in.

Best served with fresh potato bread (page 77) which is ideal for soaking up any juice left behind in the potjie. *Lekker.*

You'll need:
- a couple of hatfuls of mussels
- a handful of fresh parsley
- a splash of dry white wine
- butter
- lemon
- black pepper
- salt
- a couple of cloves of garlic – crushed
- fresh chopped chilli
- a chunk of ginger – peeled and grated

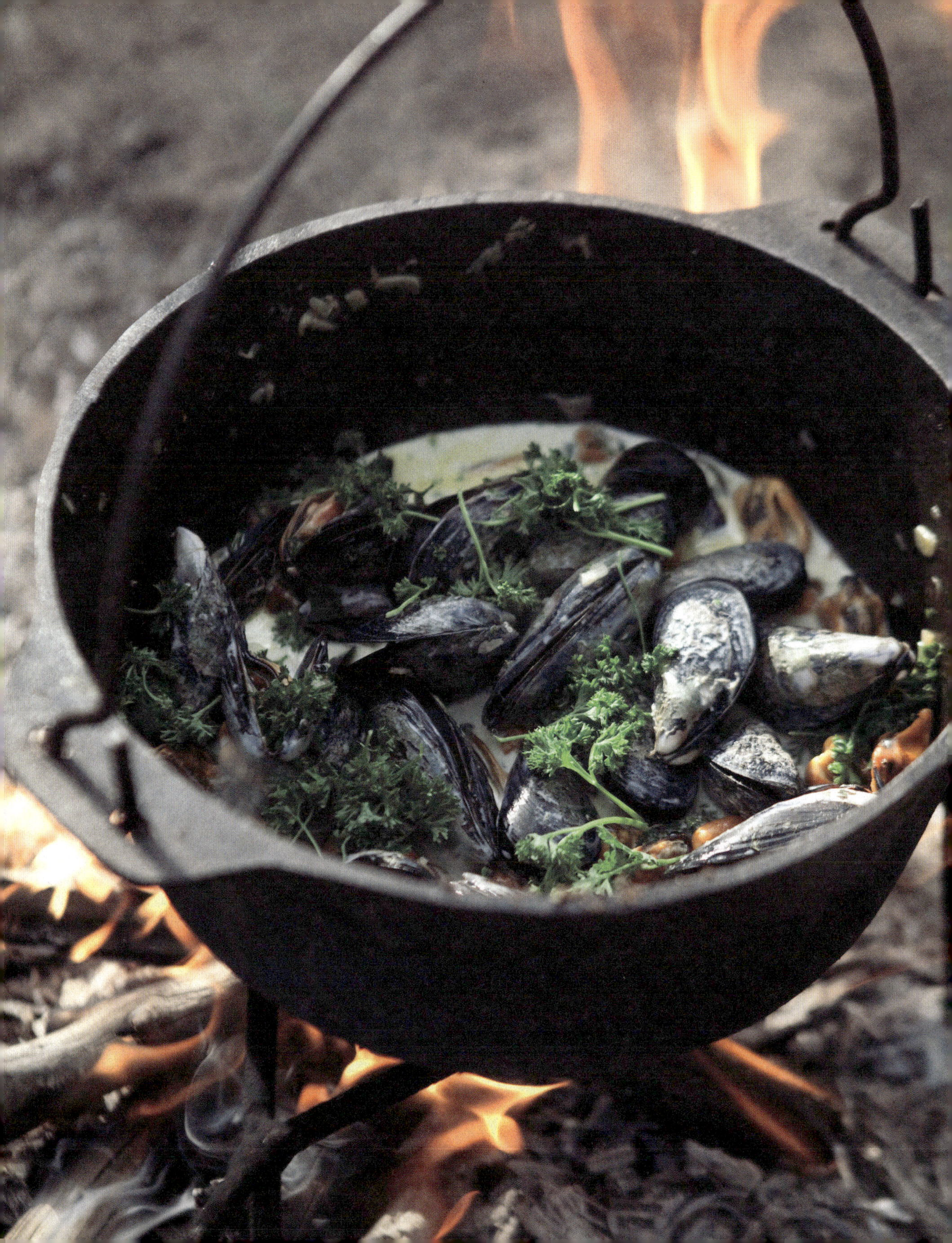

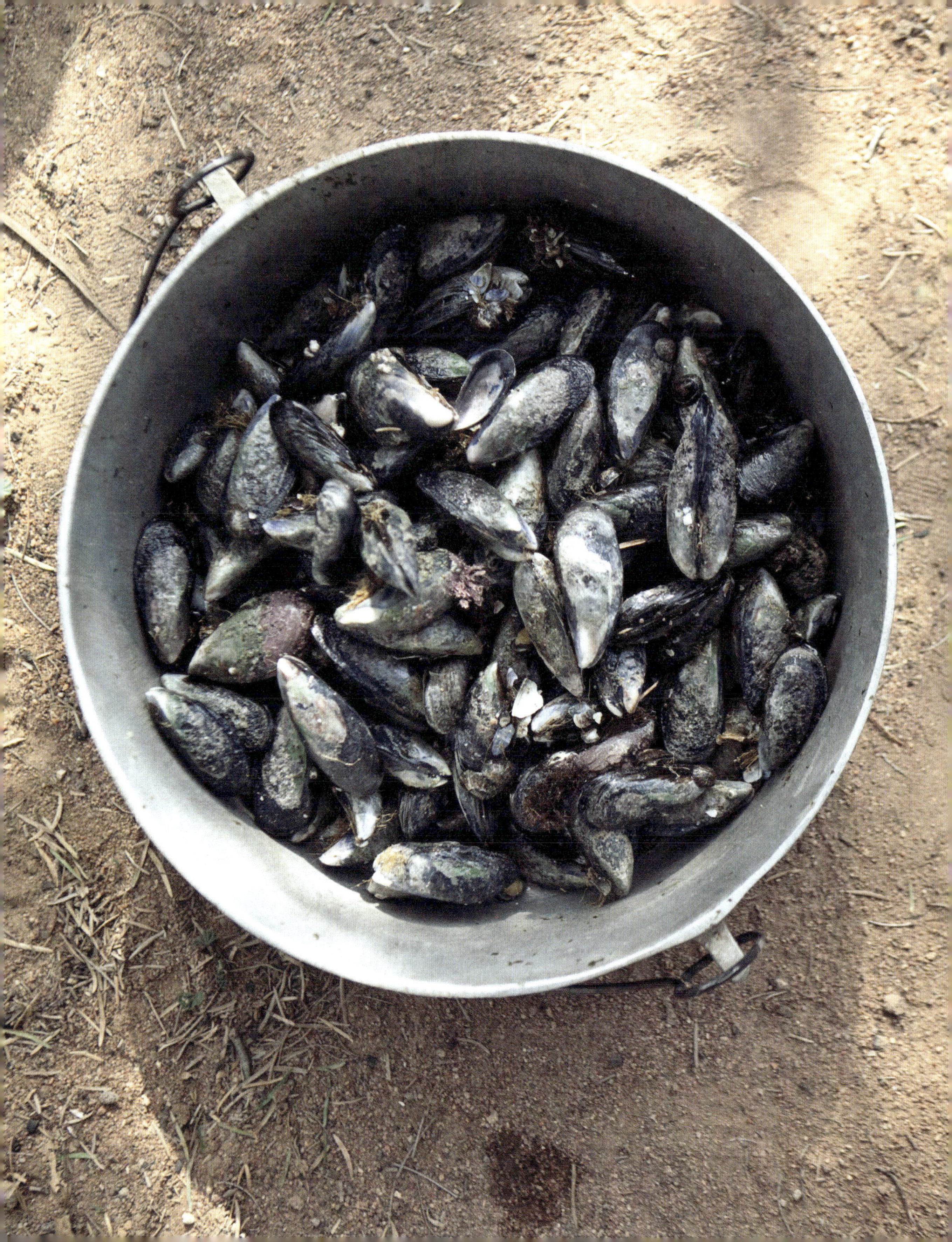

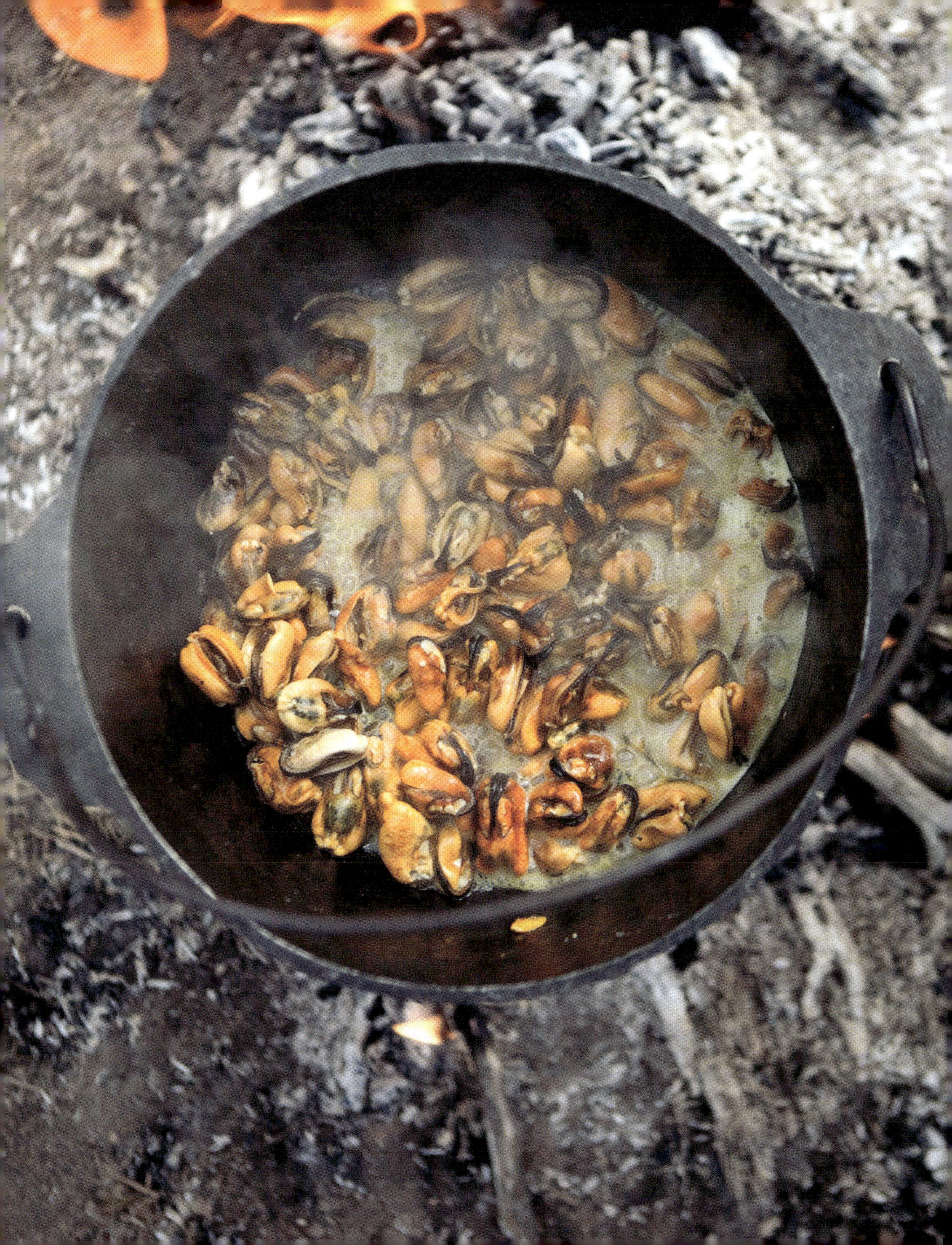

KERRIE VIS

Kerrie Vis (curried fish) arrived in South Africa waaaaay back when the Cape of Good Hope was founded. The original recipe arrived on a ship, courtesy of the Spice Islands in the east. This is one of the oldest and probably the most popular Cape dishes, and has a humble history in Cape Malay cooking, where every family has their own (closely guarded) recipe for the perfect curried fish. Although the idea of pickling fish to preserve it (in the days before refrigerators and other mod cons) is quite common, adding spices and curry to the mix is what makes this truly South African.

★ The first thing you've got to do is cut the fish into cubes and then sprinkle over the curry and turmeric, rubbing it into the fish with your hands. Heat up a non-stick pan, add a large amount of oil and carefully place your fish in the hot pan (be careful not to fry your fingers). The fish will be fully cooked after about 10 minutes, so once it's done set it aside.

★ Next, pour the vinegar into a large pot and bring it to the boil. Add the onion and let it cook for about a minute, then add the apricot jam and stir around until it's dissolved. Keep tasting until you've got a sweetness level you like that fights the acidity of the vinegar. Slice the chillies in half (lengthways) and chuck them in. Go wash your hands immediately – you don't want any part of your body (think eyes, nose, or even worse) to burn later on! Add a small handful of black peppercorns and the bay leaves then remove from the heat and chuck in the fish.

★ Spoon into the glass jars while it's still warm, and screw on the tops. Let the jars chill in the fridge while you get on with life. After a couple of days, it's time to eat. Serve with fresh bread rolls and a green salad.

If you use proper preserving jars (like the Consol ones) the fish should last up to 3 months, but once you've opened it, rather be safe and eat it within a couple of days.

Just a word of warning:
If your glass jars have metal tops, put some greaseproof paper on top of the fish before screwing on the cap. Metal and vinegar are not good friends. And remember to sterilise the jars thoroughly before bottling the fish.

You'll need:
- 1 kg yellowtail (or any other firm white fish) – skinned and cleaned (or leave the skin if you like – it contains a lot of flavour)
- curry powder (the amount depends on the quality of the powder and how strong you like it. I use about 6 tablespoons)
- 2 tablespoons turmeric
- sunflower oil for frying
- 750 ml white wine or grape vinegar
- 2 onions – cut in half and sliced very thinly
- apricot jam
- a whole whack of chillies
- a small handful of whole black peppercorns
- a couple of bay leaves
- Consol glass jars (with lids)

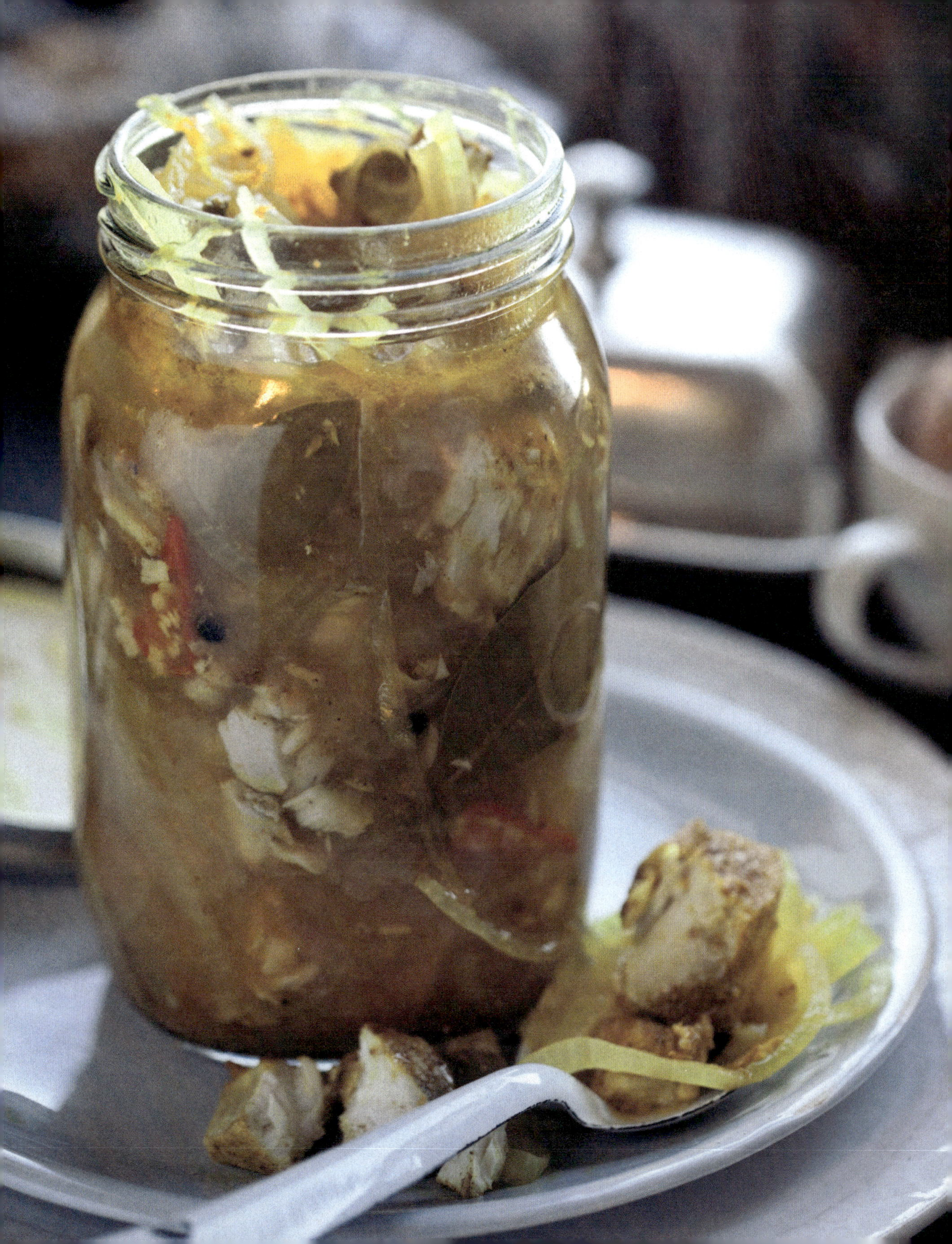

BOS

CHAPTER 2

KOS

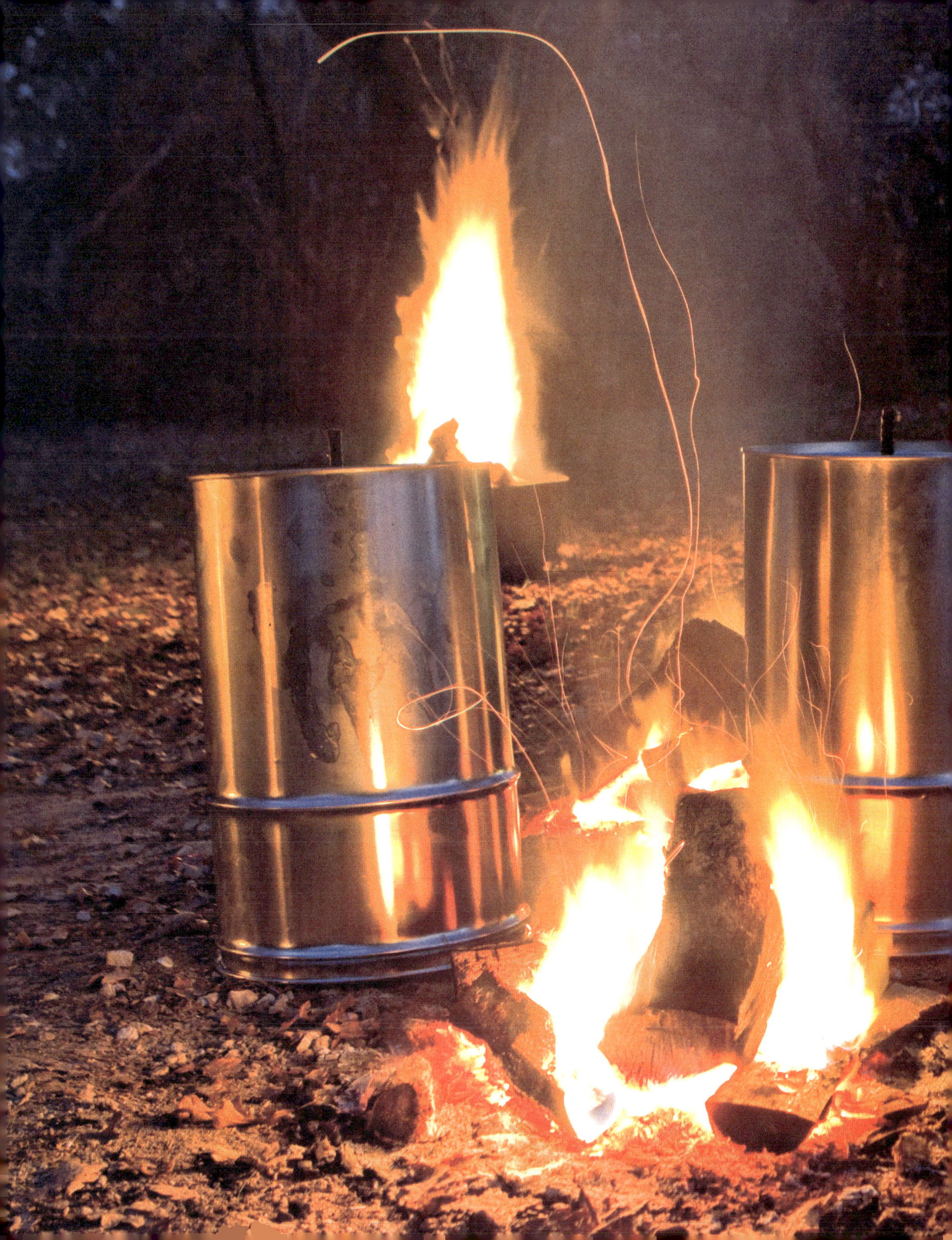

THE STORY OF THE KASSIE

(Dedicated to a man named Kassie on a farm in Grabouw)

The last time I got excited about making my own oven was when I figured out how to take an empty dustbin and convert it into a pizza oven. That was until I received an email forwarded to me by my friend Graham Brookman and, let me tell you, I'm completely bos-befok over this latest discovery.

When I shot *Cooked Season 5*, my crew and I travelled to Jeanne Groenewald's free-range chicken farm in Grabouw. I was going to cook my chicken in a very clean, empty paint drum as per the email sent by my mate Graham. In fact, I did just that and they were beautiful. Then I met a bloke by the name of Kassie and he converted it from 'just another cooking drum' into a Rolls Royce oven fit for even the most novice of bush cooks. In his honour, I decided to call it *The Kassie*. He added a smoking spit, a smoking grid and a pole with 'stuff' (for want of a better description) welded on to it for me.

Now the beautiful thing about the Kassie is that it is the most perfect and versatile little oven. I've used mine to smoke fish, roast chicken and bake bread, and I'm sure there's a world of other dishes waiting to be kassied.

Just a word of warning. I love the Kassie almost as much as I love my wife, but it drove my crew crazy when we travelled with it. Not even David Bowie on full blast could drown out the insistent rattling coming from the boot. But what Raylene and Megan will fail to tell you is that even though the rattling drove them to stick their heads out of the Defender window, it was the best chicken they'd ever tasted.

THE IDIOT'S GUIDE TO USING THE CHICKEN KASSIE

What I really love about food is that once you understand the basic principles – of timing, of alchemy, of combinations – you don't need a fancy expensive oven to cook your grub. If I can make pizza in a dustbin, why not chicken in a drum? Truth be told, however, the original idea for the kassie came from my best mate Graham – I just made it better.

You'll need:
- 1 x drum
- 1 x steel pole
- 1 x hammer
- 1 x jelly mould

There are two ways to make your kassie. The first means you have to get your hands on an old 25-litre paraffin drum. Then you have to clean it thoroughly and cut the top off. Etc. Me? I chose to use a brand new paint drum because the top was already cut off and it gave me a lid that I could use. (And, let's face it, the last thing I wanted to do was poison all my friends because I gave them grub cooked in an old, not so clean, paraffin drum.) If you opt for the paint drum, make sure it isn't plastic coated – for obvious reasons.

You're also going to need one stainless steel jelly mould – the diameter of this should be a tad smaller than your drum and the mould should have a hole in the middle.

One fence pole. This is not so easy to find, but lady luck was on my side and I found a couple of (discarded) poles on the side of the road, near a construction site. These are usually best collected at night. Just a (nother) word of warning, if you do use an old pole, clean it thoroughly. If it's rusted, dip it in some cooking oil and burn it clean.

★ NEXT STEP

Take your hammer (or in my case a piece of hardwood) and your fence pole and bang a hole through the top/bottom of your drum. Try to get as close to the middle as possible. Pull the drum off the pole and set both aside. You've just made a Chicken Kassie.

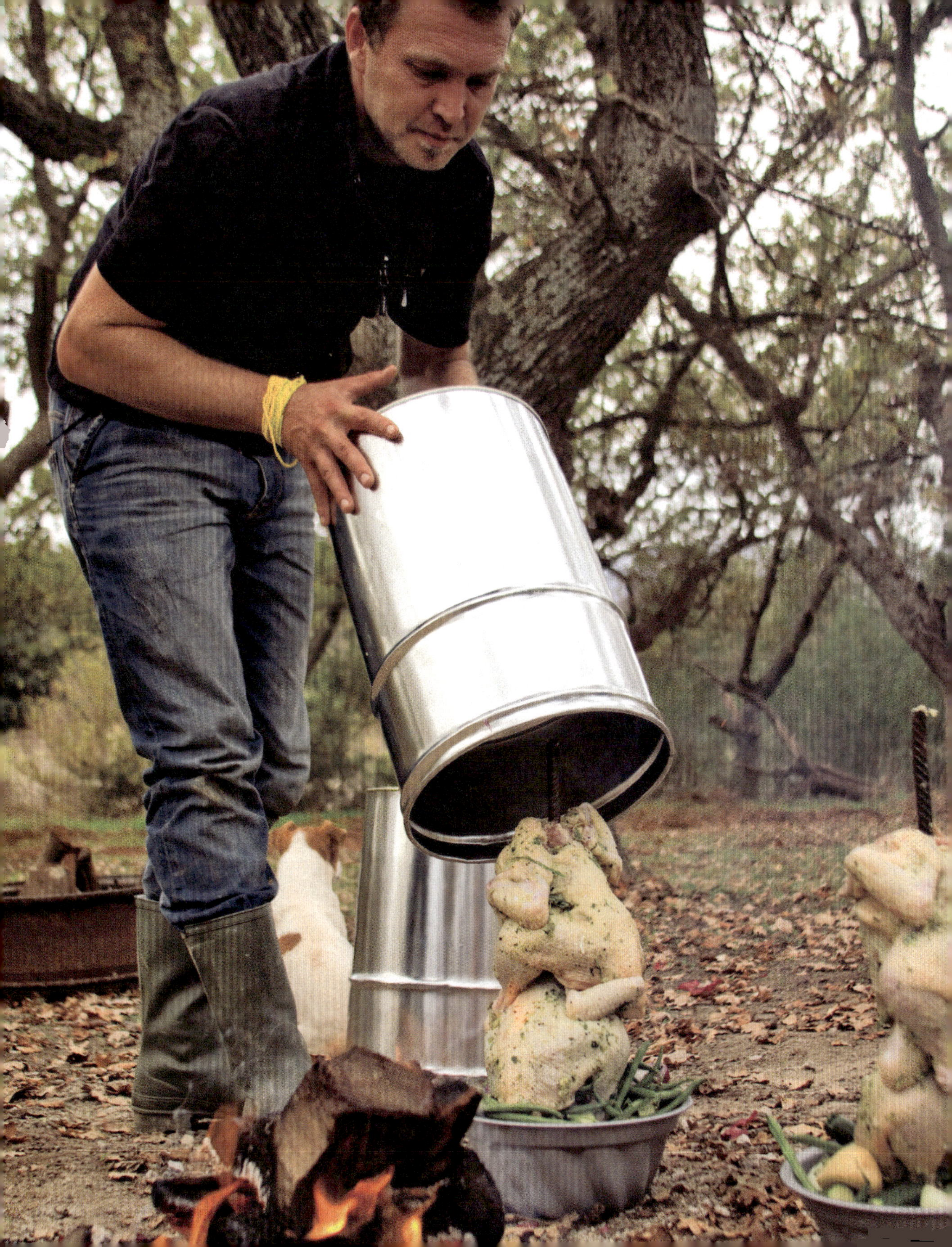

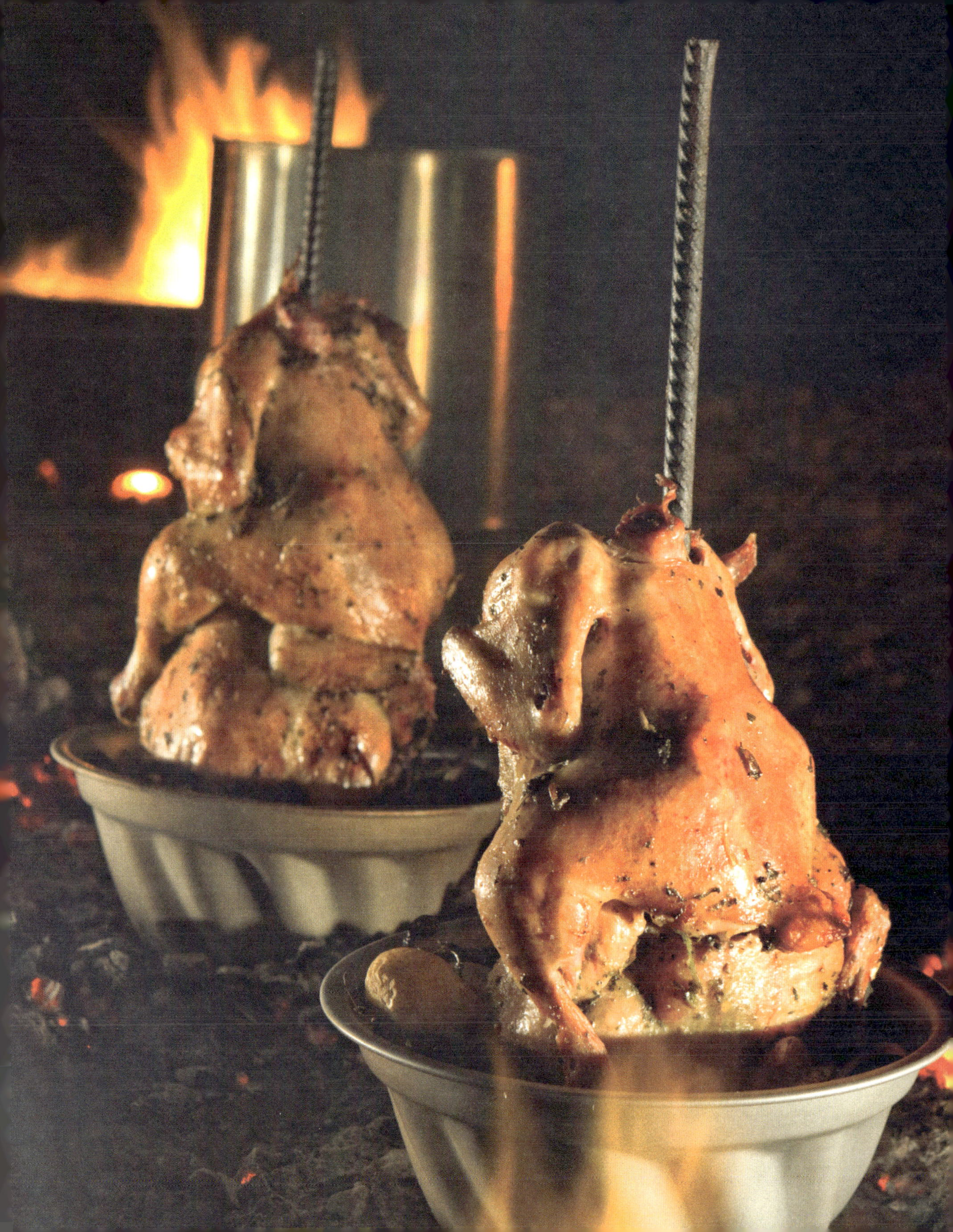

CHICKEN IN A KASSIE

★ THE CHICKEN HERB RUB

Once you've built your kassie, and if you still have all your fingers intact, it's time to get your herb rub and chicken ready.

Mix it all up (not the chickens, idiot) into a nice thick paste, then grab the youngest guy around and get him to rub the herb mix all over and inside the bird. Young lads need all the practice they can get when it comes to rubbing birds the right way, so get him to really massage those breasts and stroke those thighs. Once the bird looks happy you're almost ready to slide it over the pole.

You'll need:
> 2 free-range chickens
> a couple of pinches of dried sage
> fresh parsley – chopped
> crushed Maldon salt and pepper
> fresh tarragon

★ ALMOST THERE – THE JELLY MOULD

You've got to think of your jelly mould as kind of like a potjie. Chuck in the veggies that are going to take a while to cook (things like potato and butternut) and later on layer in your faster cooking vegetables like green beans, baby marrows, onions and mushrooms. There really are no rules when deciding which vegetables to choose – just chop up and add whatever you feel like eating with your roast chicken.

★ KASSIE TIME

Find a spot where your wife won't mind you burning stuff, and moer the pole into the ground, then slide over the jelly mould (think of it as a bad pole dancer, collapsing in a heap on the ground) and thread your chickens over the pole, so that the base of the first one rests on the jelly mould. Now close her up, sliding the drum over the whole lot. Build a fire all around and on top of the kassie so that the chicken will cook evenly on all sides.

Leave your chicken to slow cook for about 1 to 1½ hours (or in my case, as long as it took to catch a chicken in the dark), but remember to stoke up your fire every so often to keep a constant heat.

You can check up on your bird every now and then by pushing aside the coals and then lifting the drum off with anything that's going to stop you from burning your fingers.

The chicken at the top takes longer to cook, but the bottom one should bronze up nicely. Once it's cooked, serve with a mountain of roast veg from the jelly mould.

I'm going to let you figure out how to get the chicken off the pole without getting blisters on your fingers. Good luck!

★ There are two ways to check if your chicken is cooked. One is to prick the chicken in one of the thicker parts (think breast) – if the juice runs clear it's cooked. The other is if the thigh/leg comes/falls out of the socket easily when you try and pick it up.

SMOKED FILLET IN A KASSIE

You'll need:
- a decent sized fillet

The rub:
- coriander seeds
- mustard seeds
- Maldon salt
- cracked mixed peppercorns
- crushed garlic
- olive oil

Take equal quantities of coriander seeds, mustard seeds, Maldon salt, mixed peppercorns and crushed garlic. Chuck them into a mortar and pestle and bash them until you've got a nice crumbly rub. Rub the fillet with olive oil and then rub the rub all over the fillet. Be generous!

FLAME IT

My office wife, Raylene, taught me the best way to do a fillet – and I just perfected it. Make a fire like you normally would. When the coals get to the stage where they're almost ready to be spread out and braaied on, it's time to flame grill the fillet on the braai. Here's the trick: put the fillet on the grid, and drizzle a little sunflower oil over it. The oil will drip off the edges on to the flames below, which in turn kick up and lick the fillet. Not only are these flames very hot, but they seal the meat completely. I turn the meat every two minutes and cook it on all sides, adding a drizzle of oil every time.

SMOKE IT

Once the fillet is cooked to your liking (I think rare to medium rare is best) let it rest for about 5 to 6 minutes, then cut it into slices about 2 cm thick. Now you're going to take your kassie, a foil baking tin and some of the remaining coals from your fire and move to a safe spot in your garden. Carefully chuck the coals into the tin and place it on the ground. Stick the pole of the kassie through the tin and into the ground.

Put the fillet slices on the different smoking grids. Now the magic is going to happen: take a handful of wood shavings and scatter them over the coals. I use oak shavings, but there are many varieties, each with its own unique flavour, so play around and see which you like best. Slide the drum over the whole lot.

After a while, you'll see smoke coming out of the top of the kassie, almost like a chimney. If it starts looking like a mini-version of the Salt River industrial area you're doing it right. If not, either your coals aren't hot enough or you didn't add enough shavings. The whole smoking process shouldn't take more than 5 minutes. The word for smoked fillet cooked this way is *umami* – and if you ever figure out a way to bottle it, you'll be a gazzilionaire.

★ Tip // For those of you who're Weber kings – here's how to do it. When you've sliced the fillet into 2 cm thick rounds, kill the fire in the Weber a bit by putting the lid on and closing the air intakes. When the fire's mellowed out, put the fillet rounds on the grid, chuck a handful of oak sawdust on the coals, put the lid on, open the air intakes, and wait 5 minutes. *Lekker*.

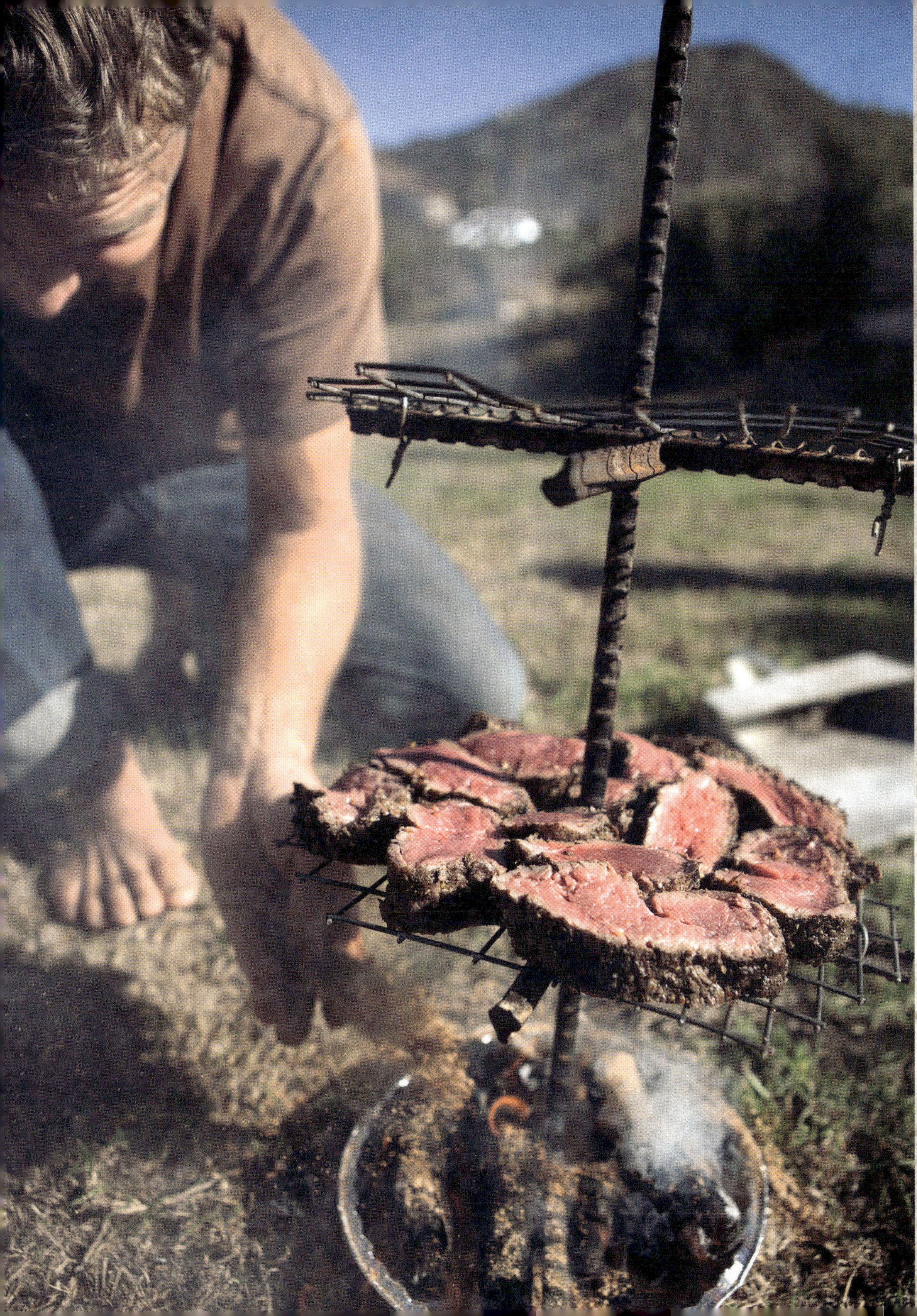

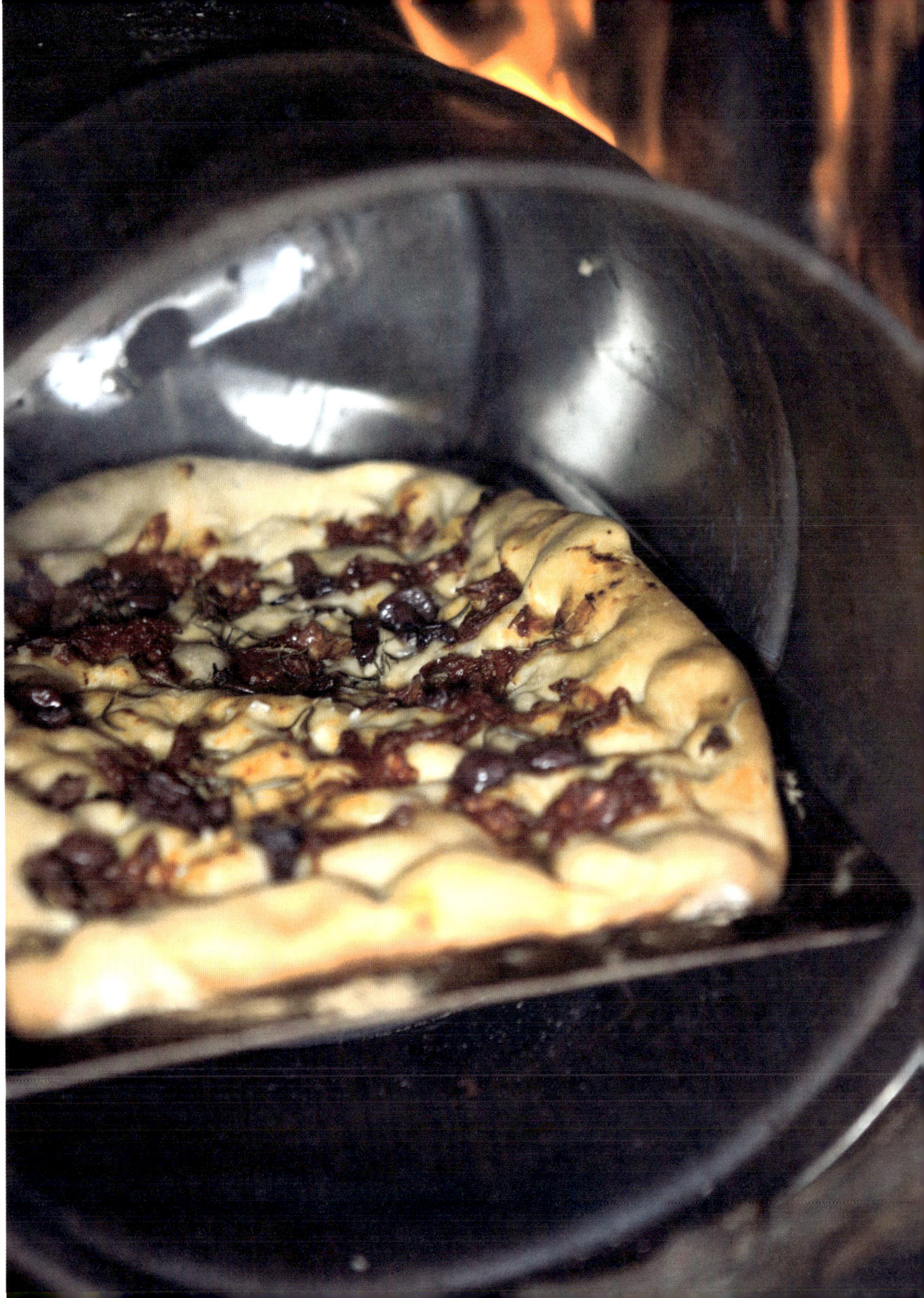

FLAT BREAD IN A KASSIE

After being victorious at cooking chicken and fish and smoking fillet in my kassie, I was determined to see if I could bake bread in it as well, thereby turning it into the most versatile bush oven on the planet ever. Here's how I did it.

★ **BASIC BREAD DOUGH** // You're going to start off by making a basic bread dough. First activate the yeast. Mix the sugar, yeast and warm water together, then sprinkle a tablespoon of flour on top (this prevents the yeast mixture from getting a dry crust) and leave in a warm spot for 10 minutes or until frothy. Sieve the flour into a bowl, add the salt and then, using clean fingertips, rub in the butter.

Next, beat the eggs lightly with a fork and add to the yeast mixture. Make an indentation in the flour, pour in the yeast and egg mixture and knead it well until you have soft, pliable dough. Brush the dough with sunflower oil, place in big bowl, cover in cling wrap or a damp tea towel, and let it rise in a warm spot for about 40 minutes, or until it has doubled in size. Knead the dough one more time (this step is called knocking it down), and then you're ready.

You'll need:
> 10 ml dried yeast
> 4 ml sugar
> 100 ml warm water
> 400 g flour
> 4 ml salt
> 60 g butter
> 2 eggs
> sunflower oil

For the filling:
> sundried tomatoes – soaked in olive oil, salt and pepper
> olives
> fresh rosemary – removed from the stalks
> crushed salt
> olive oil

Once your dough is ready, get your hands on the oldest baking tray you can find. Make sure the tray can slide into the drum when it's lying on its side.

Roll out the bread dough until it's about 1 cm thick. Sprinkle flour on to the baking tray, and put the dough on the tray. Using your fingers, poke small potholes into your dough. If it starts looking like a typical South African tar road, you're on the right track. Now you're going to fill the holes, the first half with a small handful of lubricated sundried tomatoes and then the rest with the olives. (De-pit the olives by squashing them with the back of a knife. The pit should pop out.) Sprinkle the top of the dough with rosemary, a little crushed salt and a drizzle of olive oil.

Put your baking tray into the drum, place a couple of coals inside the drum under the tray and attach the lid. If you forgot the lid at home (like I did) use some tinfoil to close it up. Place your kassie on the fire and build a small fire around the drum. Your bread should be done after about 20 minutes, but if you're feeling nervous check from about the 15 minute mark.

★ Serve warm and give your mates a selection of flavoured butters to spread on (pages 46-47) or, even better, serve with Kassie Chicken (page 41) and dip the bread into all those lovely juices that collect in the jelly mould. Don't have a kassie? You can do this in an oven at 180°C for 15-30 minutes.

THE BUTTER CLUB

It might be high in kilojoules and fat, but butter is one of your best friends when it comes to adding flavour to your cooking and your food. And, let's face it, if food isn't mouth-wateringly delicious, there's no point in eating! For that reason, it only seems right to have a page totally dedicated to the magic of butter. Welcome to the Butter Club. Please leave your diet at home and wipe your feet before entering.

★ **Hard Butters //** The beauty of flavouring your own butter is that it's simple to do and there are virtually no rules about what you can put into it. Add chunks of flavoured butters to anything from a slice of toast to your favourite steak. The butter will melt into it and get all those delicious flavours out. You can buy some of these ready-made, but you won't be doing yourself any favours. Hard butters can be wrapped and frozen and pulled out when you need a wow factor.

★ **Herbed Butter //** Have an excess of fresh herbs in the garden? Make a parsley butter . . . a tarragon butter . . . a rosemary butter . . . you get the idea? Just mush it together with the back of a fork and put it in the fridge to set and then freeze for later use.

What I'm really trying to get across is that in this space there are no rules. Experiment with butter and develop your own favourites. PS: If you buy flavoured butter, you're denied membership of the club, so rather just turn the page.

★ **Marmite Butter**

Using the back of a fork, mush one teaspoon of marmite into a fifth of a big block of butter. This is great on toast or on top of mushrooms, and for those of you with Marmite fetishes it's damn good on almost anything. Sometimes, I even toss a knob of it on to hot veggies and mix it around. Clearly, this is my second favourite butter.

★ Anchovy Butter

Using the back of a fork, mush together six anchovy fillets, a crack of black pepper, a pinch or two of crushed red pepper and a big pinch of fresh chopped parsley into a fifth of a big block of butter. This is really lekker on fish or freshly baked bread. And is my numero uno favourite. I've been known to toss a knob on to fresh pasta and eat it just like that – you figure out where you'd like it best.

★ Rosemary and Orange Zest

Mush together a couple of knobs of butter, the zest of half an orange and a sprig of rosemary. Weird? Yes! But delicious on lamb.

★ DIPPING BUTTERS

These are delicious melt-in-the-mouth sauces that you can serve with seafood or bread, drizzled over chicken or as an accompaniment to fillet. Dipping sauces will turn even the most tasteless meal into a mouth-watering feast.

My favourite dipping butter is made with lemon and black pepper. All you've got to do is melt some butter in a small pan on a very low heat, squeeze in the juice of half a lemon and add some cracked black pepper. Be careful not to burn it. Goes especially well with seafood.

The same can be done with a lot of crushed garlic, chopped chilli and ginger or fresh herbs.

It's that easy!

BIL'TONG

Biltong is about as South African as you can get. It's right up there with hitching up the caravan and dragging your wife and kids kicking and screaming down to the coast for your annual holiday. The thing is, what was once a way of preserving venison by our forefathers has become without a doubt our favourite snack and no road trip or rugby game would be complete without it. The Americans make something called jerky, but that's not biltong. They smoke it and do all sorts of nasties to it. Here in SA, biltong as we know it is mildy spiced, salted and air cured meat, and like most South Africans, I believe that you mustn't mess with our meat. After all, a good biltong is like a good prosciutto. You'd be surprised to learn how easy it is to make at home, and it will be nothing like that over-salted-over-spiced-dried-out piece of flavoured cardboard you buy in the shops. You just have to take control of your biltong destiny.

★ First, you need to score some meat.

Typically, lamb, pork and chicken are not used to make biltong (although there are some crazy cats out there who do). In the biltong world, game and beef (and ostrich) are used, with the best cuts to use being silverside, topside, flank, etc, with the best, most soft and delicate biltong being made from fillet. (Biltong made from fillet is often called *ouma se biltong* (grandmother's biltong) and in my head I have this image of a toothless granny sucking on the best 'tong.) Tell the butcher you're making biltong – and he'll suggest good cuts of meat. Game by its nature doesn't have a lot of fat so it does stand the risk of becoming a bit dry, but beef with a nice bit of fat on it is just the berries. There is one rule of thumb: use the best meat you can afford. Cheaper cuts are full of sinew and stuff and don't make lekker 'tong.

Once you've got your meat, cut it into strips about 20 cm long and 3 cm thick (the length of the strips will depend on the size of your biltong box) and cut it with the grain. In cooler, drier climates, you can afford to cut it slightly thicker; in warmer, moist climates, cut it slightly thinner. This is to avoid the meat spoiling while it's curing (especially in warm, moist climates) – the thicker the cut, the longer it'll take to cure.

★ Next, season it.

You'll need:
> salt
> white pepper
> peppercorns – crushed
> garlic
> brown sugar
> chilli flakes
> coriander seeds
> Worcestershire sauce
> vinegar

Do this by first making a spice mixture. In a bowl, mix equal quantities of salt, white pepper, roughly crushed pepper corns, garlic, brown sugar and chilli flakes. To this add triple the amount of dry roasted coriander seeds (some crushed, some whole). Don't be too heavy handed with the salt – there is nothing worse than over-salted, over-spiced biltong). Over time you'll be able to refine the spice mixture to suit your palate.

Place a single layer of meat strips in a glass or stainless steel bowl and dress with a sprinkling of the spice mixture and a light drizzle of Worcestershire sauce and vinegar. You can use any vinegar – I'm still experimenting with balsamic, apple and red wine vinegar... and even mixing them to see what happens. Put another layer of meat across that and repeat the process (meat, spice, vinegar, Worcestershire sauce) until you've used up all the meat.

Leave overnight in the fridge or a very cool spot to soak up the flavours.

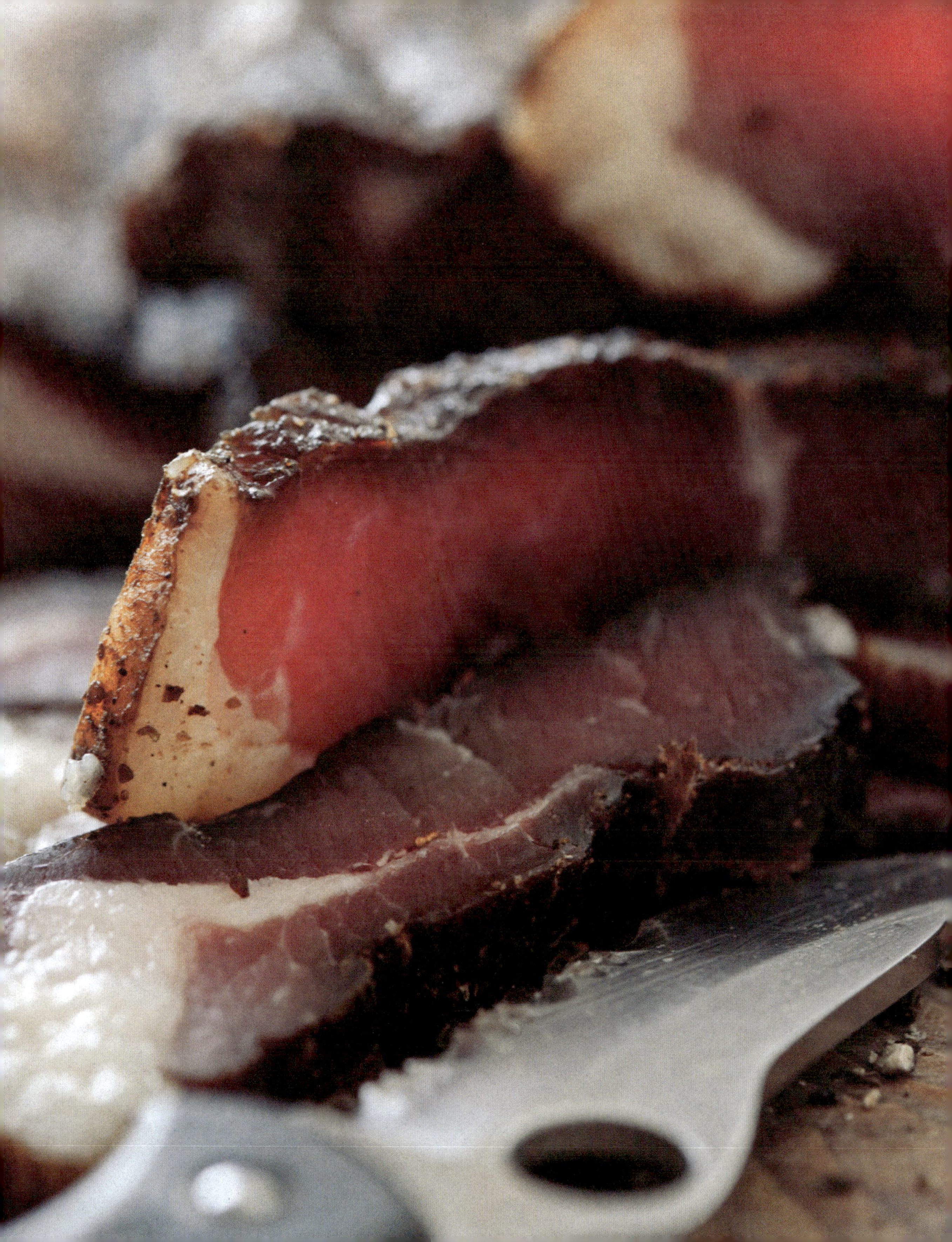

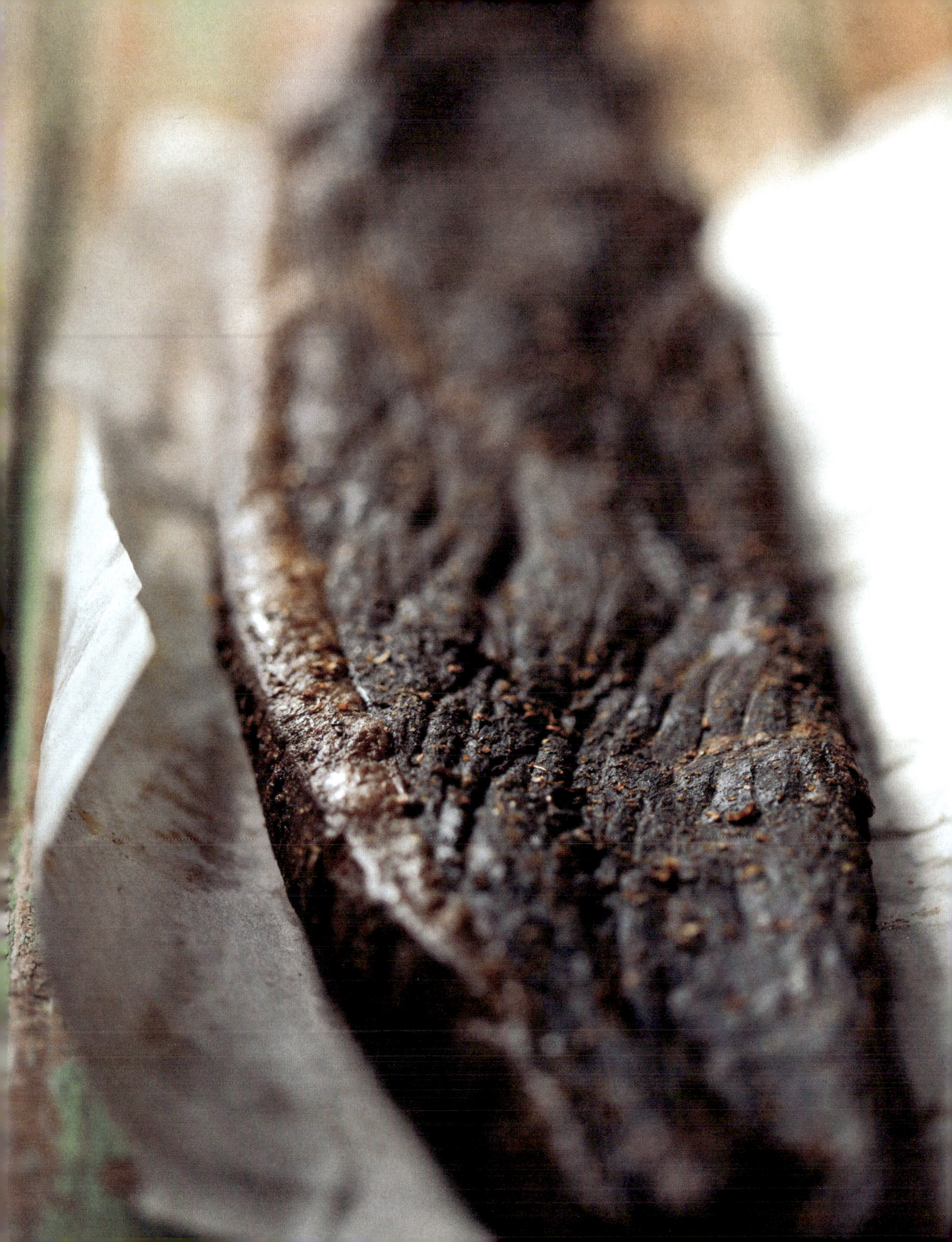

DRYING YOUR 'TONG

To dry your own 'tong all you need is your own drying box, which must be big enough to hang the meat inside. The drying process needs warm dry air, in the form of a light bulb or two and a fan. Make sure you cover the air holes with some kind of fine netting to stop the flies and other nasties getting in; here in Africa flies are for free and ants like our stuff and, before you know it, they ruin your biltong.

Hang up the spiced, marinated strips of meat with the thickest part at the top, and not touching one another. Leave to dry for 3 to 6 days, depending on how you like it. The length of time it takes to dry your own homemade biltong and to become the envy of your friends and neighbours will also depend on how you like it – thick or thin? Wet and fatty? Dry and lean? Just make sure you cut the meat to match the length of the box otherwise you'll have a whole lot of short pieces and wasted space.

Eventually, you'll be able to tell if your biltong is ready by simply giving it a squeeze. You'll know by its texture and squishiness if it's ready to munch on or not.

To build your 'tong box you'll need

★ 1 large wooden box ★ 1 x sheet of wood with holes drilled in it – to fit in the box ★ thin metal rods ★ small hooks made from metal paper clips ★ fine netting ★ drill ★ 2 x hinges ★ string ★ light fitting ★ electrical cord ★ desk fan

Make a wooden box with a hinged door. Cut out the inside of the door, and fix mesh in the frame. Next, fix a row of metal rods across the top of the box by drilling holes as close as you can to the top of the box, and sliding the metal rods through them. Make some holes in the side of the box for ventilation. Cover these holes with fine netting to stop the flies from getting in. Attach the light bulb fitting to the base of the box, and fit a shelf above this with plenty of ventilation holes in it.

Next, pierce each piece of meat with a knife or skewer and thread through a loop of string or a paper clip hook. Tie to or hook over the metal rods, spaced evenly apart. Close the lid tightly, switch the light and fan on and leave to dry until desired consistency. Simple.

BILTONG, LEEK AND ASPARAGUS QUICHE

I made this as a little tucker for my mates en route to the Grand View Lodge on the edge of the world's second biggest canyon, The Fish River Canyon of Namibia. You might think quiche is *ou tannie kos* meant to be served with tea, gossip and church music, but it's not. Not only is it delicious, but it's also an easy way to stretch your culinary buck. I love a biltong quiche, but there are literally no rules when you make a quiche – almost any filling will do, just not soggy ones. The principle behind the quiche is simple: pastry crust filled with an egg custard flavoured with whatever you have in the fridge or cooler-box.

★ **For the pastry crust //** Mix it all up until you have a stiff dough. If you're feeling naughty, add half a cup of grated Parmesan to the mix. Once your dough is ready, grease a round baking tin with butter. Take a ball of the dough and press it down with your fingers until you have an even base all round and up the edges of the baking tin. Blind bake for 5 minutes at 180°C to set the pastry. This will prevent the pastry from going soggy when you add the custard mixture. To stop the pastry from rising while you're blind baking it, weigh it down with dried beans. I didn't have any, so I just used a couple of baby potatoes – so much of my cooking life is *boer maak 'n plan*.

★ **For the filling //** Crack the eggs into a bowl, pour in the cream and milk and whisk it up until you've got a rich custard. Grate in a handful of pecorino cheese and mix it around loosely. (The pecorino has a lovely dark and salty flavour that goes well with the biltong.)

Trim the asparagus stalks and cook for a couple of minutes in salted water. Drain off the hot water, and refresh the asparagus in iced water for a minute or two to stop them cooking before chopping them up. Add the asparagus and chopped leeks to the custard and then take a handful of moist biltong and sprinkle on top.

Pour the custard into the blind-baked pastry case and bake it in the oven at 180°C for half an hour or until golden on top.

For the pastry crust:
› 300 g flour
› 4 ml salt
› 100 g butter
› a splash of water

For the filling:
› 3 free-range eggs
› 250 ml cream
› 250 ml milk
› pecorino cheese – grated
› a bunch of asparagus
› a couple of leeks – chopped
› a handful of moist biltong – torn into pieces
› crushed salt and black pepper to taste

★ When you think it's cooked, you can do the wobble test to check if the custard has set. Take the quiche out of the oven with oven gloves and give it a gentle shake. If the centre wobbles, it needs more time in the oven. The quiche is ready when the custard is firm but not dry.

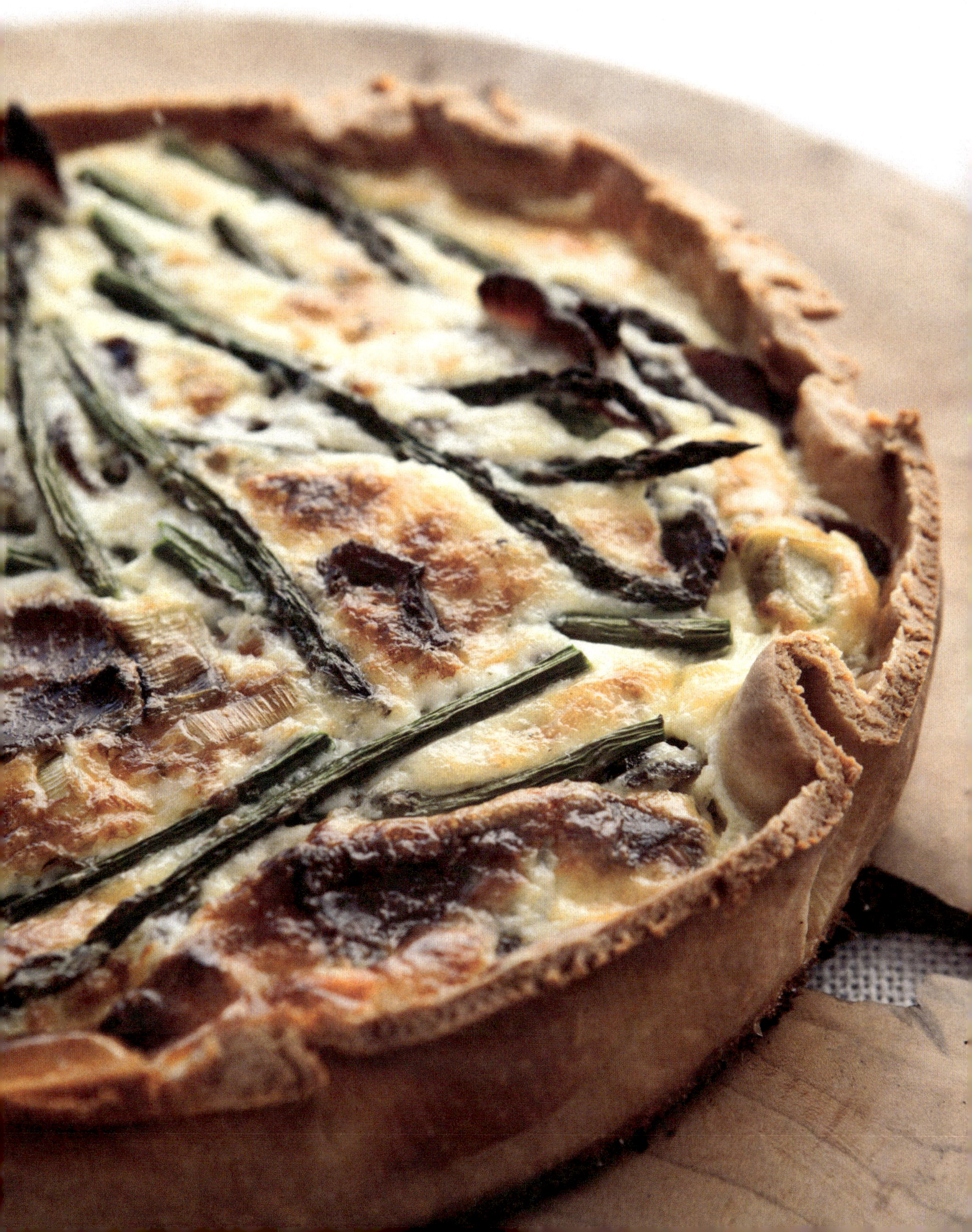

TOMATO LAMB POTJIE WITH GNOCCHI

> This is probably the only potjie I'll make this year.

This has got to be one of my favourite potjies of all time because I get to blend the spirit of adventure with my love of food. Potjie has been around since Adam and so has gnocchi, so I took my new culinary skill (courtesy of chef Michael Broughton) and combined it with an old-school potjie recipe and the result is a dish that I think is bloody amazing!

POTJIE 101

★ Once the potjie is simmering, do not disturb! Don't remove the lid and don't stir it around. It's like a sleeping child – just leave it alone.

★ Keep the heat constant. Do this by either removing or adding coals once the potjie starts to cook. You don't want it to boil and you don't want it to cool down. The heat should be juuuust right.

★ Make a feeder fire close to the potjie for the coals you're going to use. It'll eliminate frustration and using up an entire packet of firelighters.

★ Be the potjie king. Make sure you have one secret ingredient. You want your friends to beg for the recipe, just so you can laugh at them and walk away.

★ Stock up on beers and snacks. Making a potjie takes forever; you've got to keep everyone happy so they won't notice. A good idea is to play the Trivial Pursuit Master Edition – that should take a good four hours.

For the Potjie:
- 2-3 kg free range Karoo lamb knuckles
- 1 onion – chopped
- 3-4 garlic cloves – crushed
- 2-3 leeks – sliced
- 2 tins good quality baby tomatoes
- 1 punnet fresh baby tomatoes – whole
- 300-500 ml organic beef stock (this gives the basic flavour to your potjie, so only the best will do)
- splash of red wine
- sweet basil – both dried and fresh
- oregano – dried
- salt and pepper to taste
- a handful grated pecorino or parmesan cheese

Dust the lamb in seasoned flour, seal and brown in a three-legged potjie, scoop out and set aside. Chuck in the onion, garlic and leeks and fry until soft, then return the sealed lamb to the potjie, add the tomatoes and pour in the beef stock and a splash of red wine (it should cover about two thirds of the meat). Add the dried herbs, salt and pepper, give it one stir and put the lid on. Let your potjie simmer until the meat falls off the bones (anything from three to five hours, depending on the patience of your guests). While the potjie is on the go, make a potato gnocchi, unless you had the jitters and made it the night before.

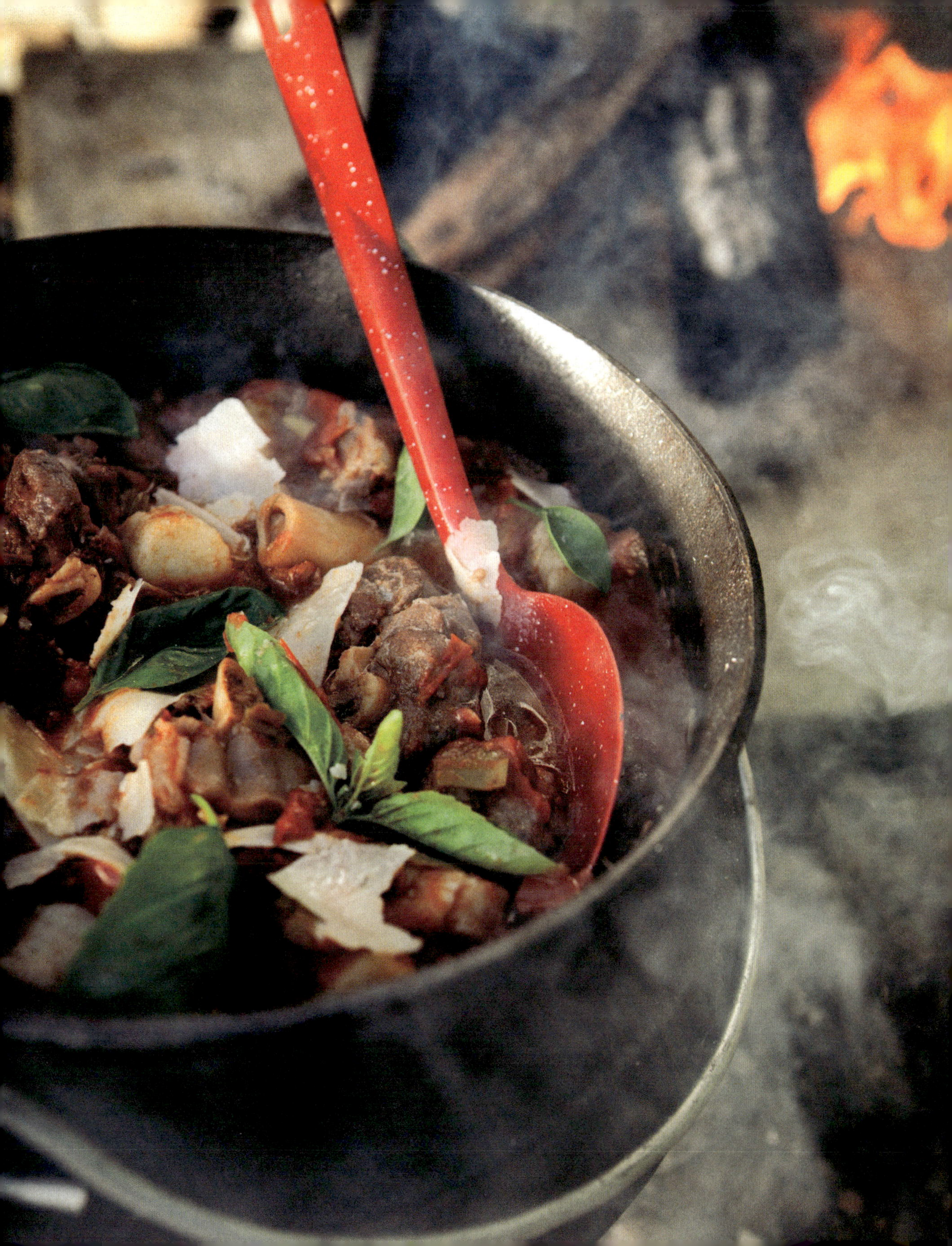

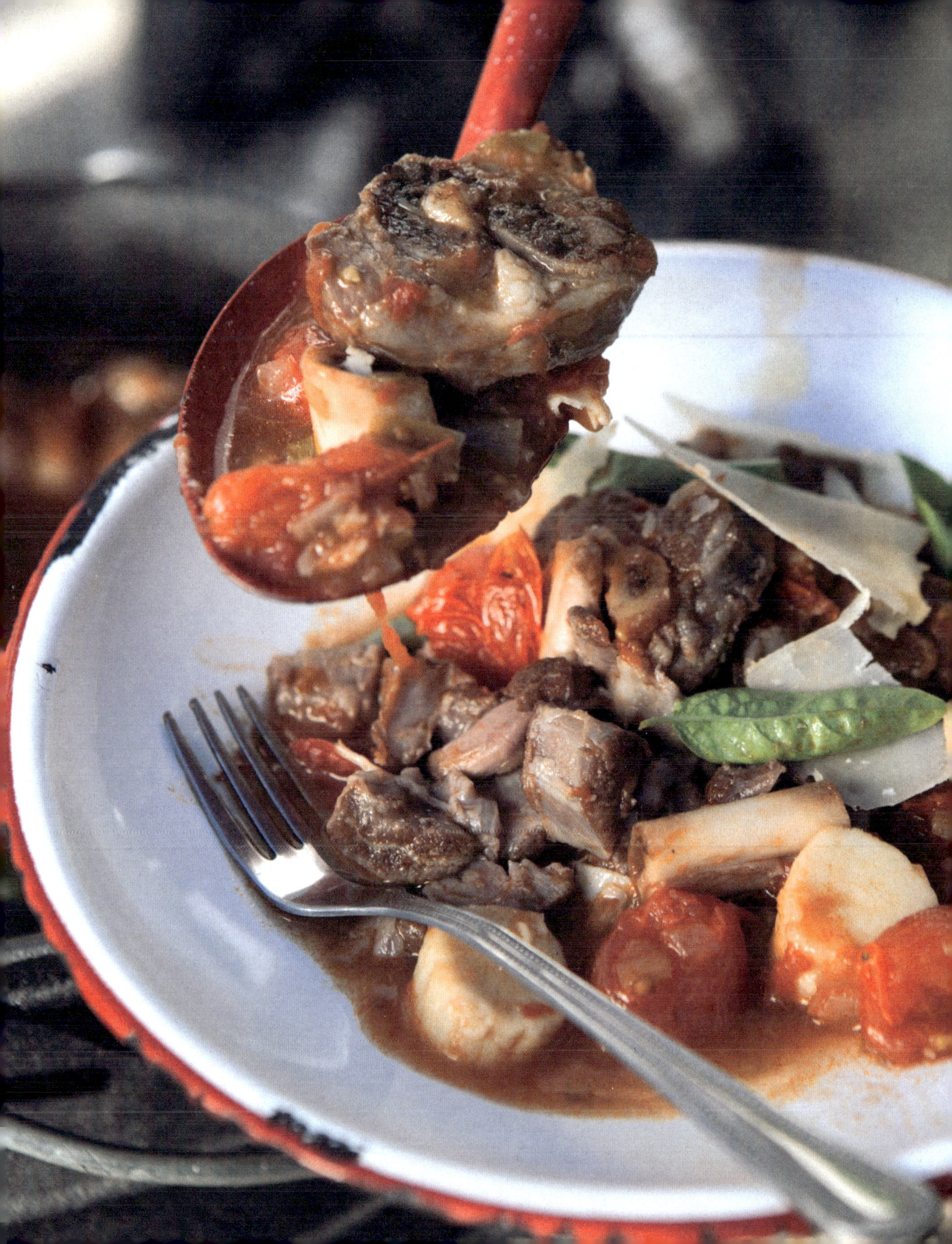

Rule Number 1 when making gnocchi:

Potatoes and water don't get along, so bake the potatoes on a bed of coarse sea salt (skin and all). Once done, cut the potatoes in half and, using a spoon, scoop the fluffy insides into a mixing bowl. Keep the discarded skins on the side for later – you're going to make really tasty potato snacks to tide over your famished friends (good for a peace offering when they start behaving like children of the corn).

For the Gnocchi:
> 1 kg warm dry mashed potato
> 300 g '00' flour
> 2 free-range egg yolks
> 1 teaspoon salt

CRISPY POTATO SKINS | Don't waste the potato skins. While your friends are (patiently) waiting for the potjie, toss the skins in some olive oil, crushed salt, black pepper and rosemary sprigs. Whack them on to a baking tray and into the oven until they've gone crisp and golden. Serve with sour cream for dipping. It's a great snack to keep the wolves at bay.

Put the potato through a Mouli (or just use a sieve) to mash it up nicely. And now the nasty bit. You want the potato to be as hot as your hands can handle because it gets the gluten in the flour working. You might end up with fried fingers, but it's essential.

Add the flour a little bit at a time, then the egg yolks and salt. Think of something that really grates you, and while keeping your hand as stiff as possible, mix the flour into the potato by jabbing (and swearing if you have to). What you're looking for is a wettish but workable and pliable dough that almost sticks to your fingers (If you've made dough for steamed bread before, it's the same kind of consistency.) Once it's mixed, roll it into sausage-like shapes (about 3 cm in diameter) and double wrap in cling film. To ensure it's watertight, go the extra mile and tie the ends with string.

Poach in simmering water for 15 - 30 minutes, shock in a bowl of iced water, and put in the fridge until needed. About 20 minutes before you'd like to eat, unwrap the gnocchi, slice into medallions, submerge in the potjie and leave to simmer and suck up all those juicy rich lamb and tomato flavours. Serve with cracked black pepper and torn leaves of fresh basil and grate cheese to taste on top.

PS | Tell anyone about this and I'll have to kill you. Keep it your secret – it's possibly the best potjie in the world.

BOEREWORS KING

As South Africans, we can all agree that boerewors is part of our genetic make-up. Whether we're gathering for the rugby, the soccer or just a weekend away, chances are there's a roll of boerewors in the cooler-box waiting to be slapped on the grid. But most of us have no clue what the butcher's put into this South African culinary great, and chances are we'd rather not know. It doesn't have to be this way. Making your own sausage is not that hard and you'll know exactly what's gone into it.

You'll need:

This recipe will make about 3.5 kg of boerie. If you want less, change the quantities proportionally.

1 kg beef, 1 kg veal or lean pork, 1 kg mutton

500 g spek (bacon)

a couple of good pinches of crushed salt

ground black pepper

a small handful of coriander seeds – roasted and crushed

a small pinch of ground cloves

a small pinch of ground nutmeg

about 1/4 cup red wine vinegar or red wine

5-6 cloves of garlic – crushed and minced

a good pinch of fresh thyme – chopped finely

a pinch of mustard seeds

6 cups of toasted bread crumbs

sausage casings (that fit on to your sausage funnel)

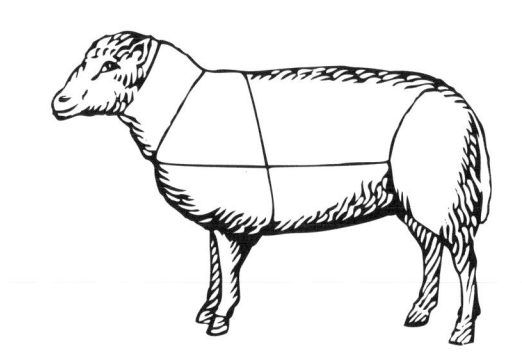

Ask your butcher for about 5 metres of sausage casings. Make sure the diameter of the casing matches that of the sausage funnel, or you'll be making another trip to the butcher.

Making your own boerie might seem a bit daunting, but there are just three (relatively) easy steps:

SPICE

Add the spices and the vinegar or wine to the sliced meat and allow it to marinate in the fridge before mincing – ideally, overnight. This will ensure that the spices are evenly distributed when you grind the meat.

MINCE

You can get your butcher to mince the meat for you, but I prefer to do it myself with my old-school mincer. This way, I can control how chunky the sausage is. There are a couple of things to keep in mind. Be sure that the meat has been in the fridge for an hour or two before mincing; cold meat is more likely to be minced rather than mashed. If you want less chunky sausage, run it through your mincer twice.

--- **Two Big Notes** ---

★ Make sure your mincing machine, hands and work surface are cleaner than the average South African hospital.

★ Once you've minced your meat, cook up a little taster to check that you're happy with the amount of seasoning and that it's not too dry. Once the meat is in the casing you won't be able to change the flavour or add juiciness.

STUFFING

I use a sausage funnel (or stuffing horn) but some of those fancy electric mincers have a special attachment. For my sanity, I'll only explain the sausage funnel.

First thing, you've got to flush the sausage casing by rinsing it in warm water three times and then running water through it. This helps to clean the sausage casing out and makes it easier to roll it on to the sausage funnel. Once rinsed, I measure out metre-long lengths of sausage casing, cut them, and place them in a bowl of warm water. This keeps them lubricated for rolling on to the funnel.

Next, find the end of a casing and slip it over the end of the funnel. Slide the casing over the funnel and leave a little casing hanging over the edge because you're going to have to tie a knot in a couple of moments. Now attach the funnel to the old-school mincer, making sure you remove the mincing blade at the same time (otherwise you'll end up mincing your meat twice). Put your mince in the top of the mincer funnel, and start cranking the handle. The corkscrew device in the mincer will force the mince through the funnel into the casing.

When the mince starts coming out of the funnel, ease the casing off the funnel at the same speed as the mince comes out. You should end up holding a nice sausage in your hand. Regulate the amount of mince going into the casing by holding the casing on the funnel with your thumb and forefinger. Increasing or decreasing finger pressure on the casing will determine how tightly and consistently the sausage is stuffed. Help it along a little by pulling (not yanking) the casing slowly – you don't want it to explode! If the casing bursts, tie it off and start again. When you're done, you can either twist off sausages into lengths that you like, or as in the case of boerewors, just leave one long sausage.

> Refrigerate until the casings are dry; this will help the flavours in the sausage to develop. Cook when you're ready using the method that makes you the braai master.

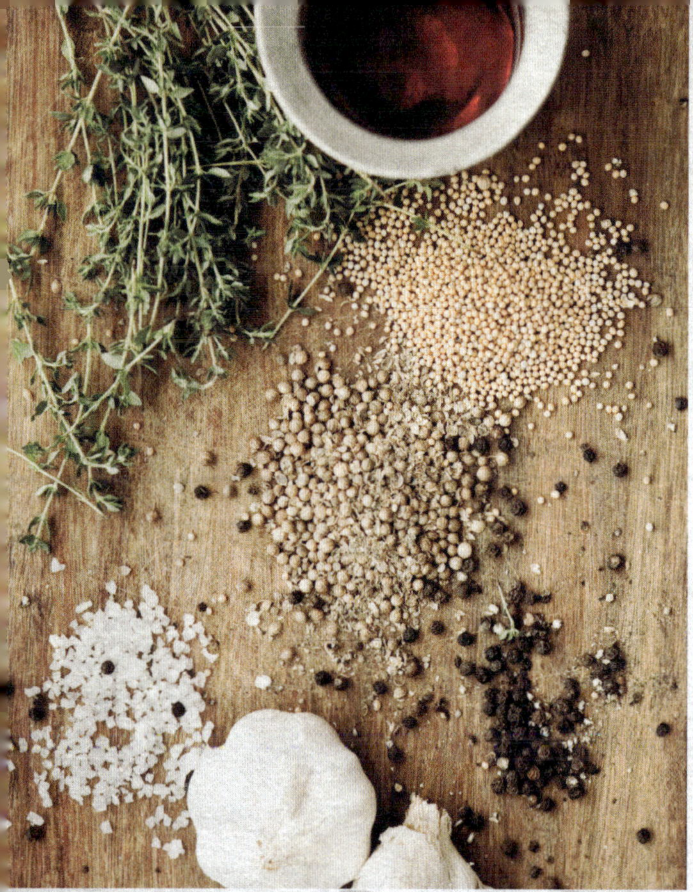
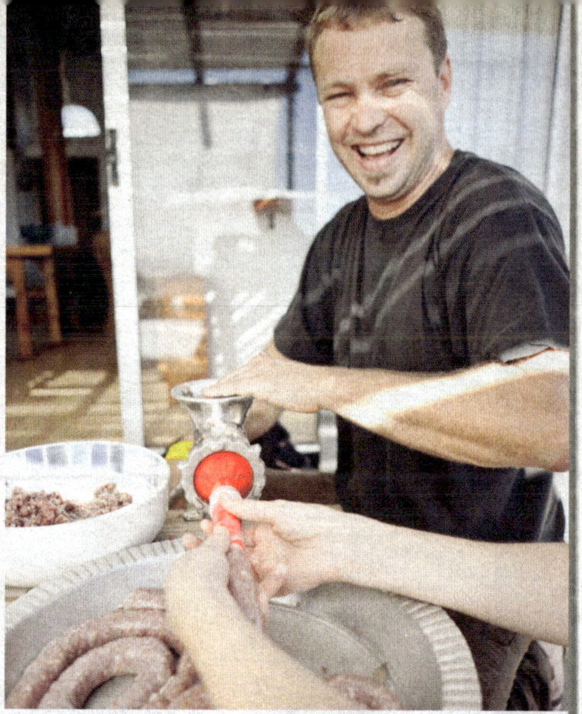
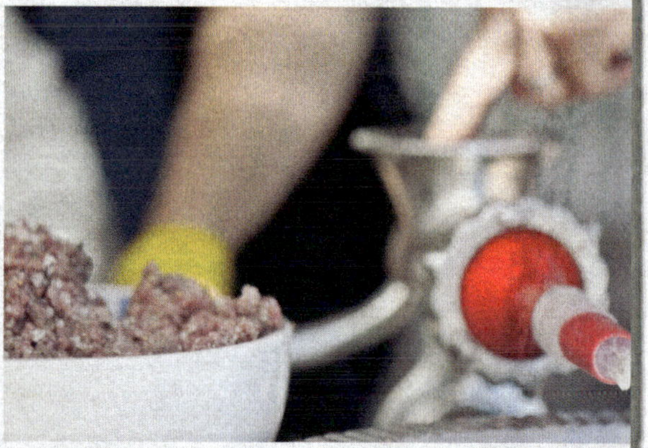
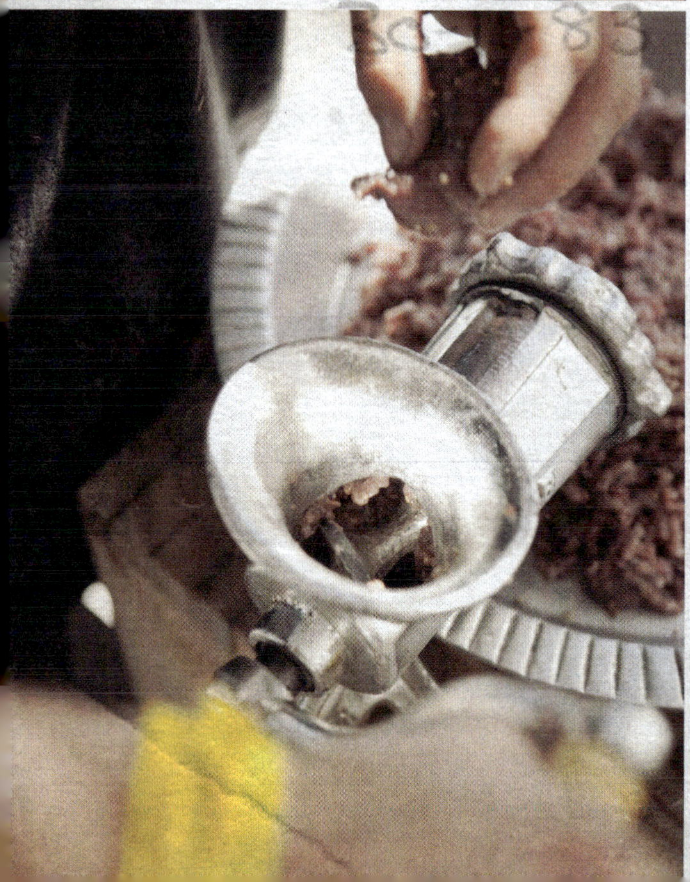
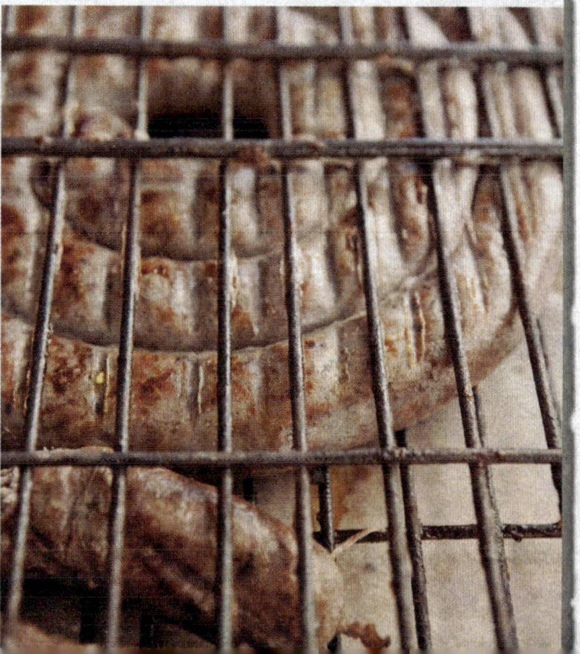
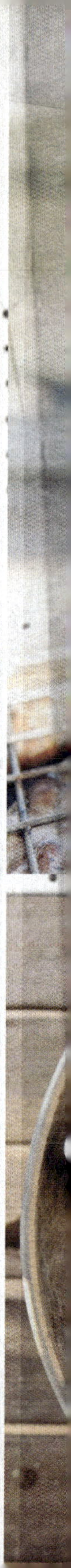

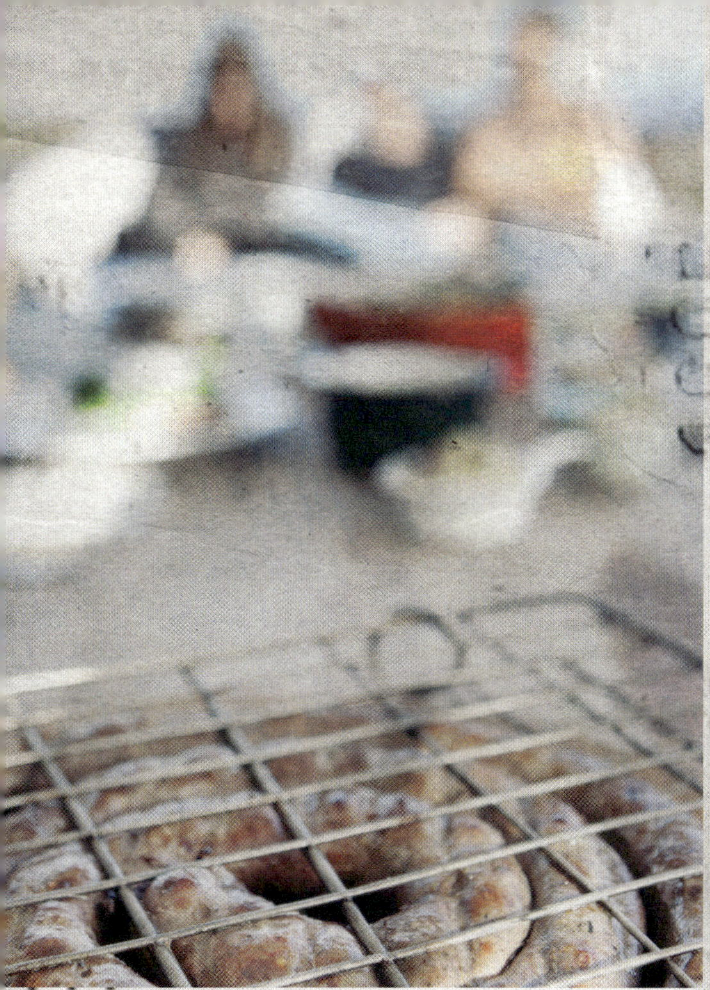

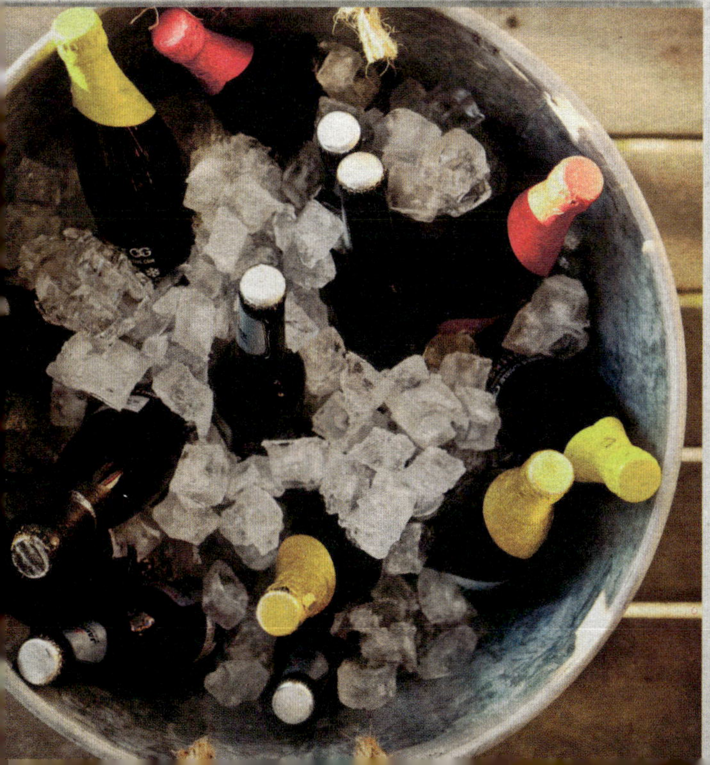

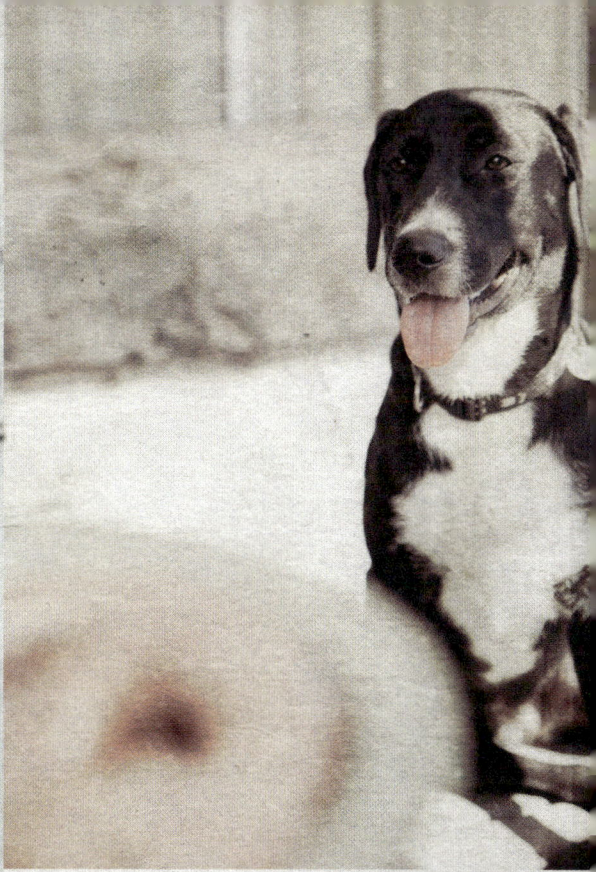

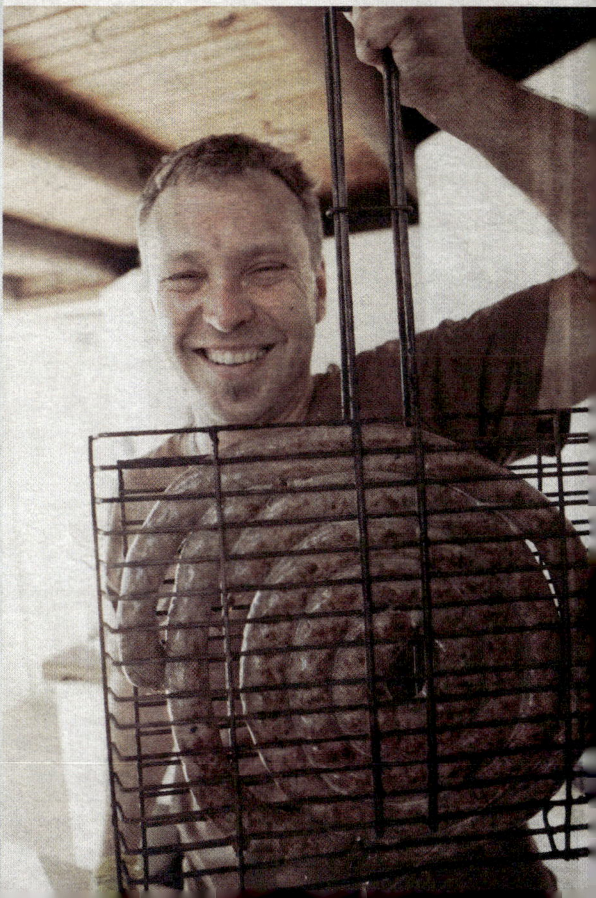

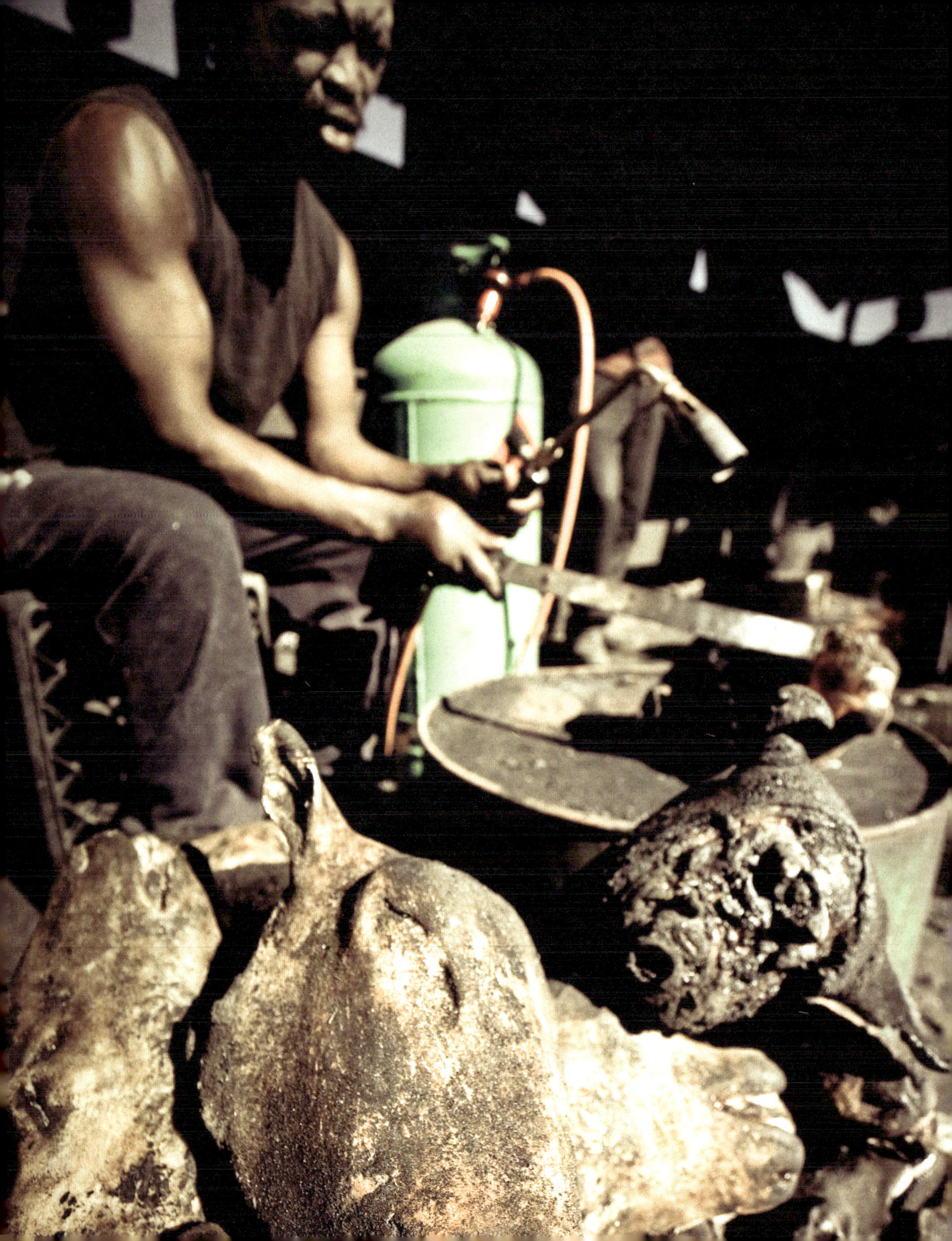

SMILEYS

> Whether you're South African or a tourist, I think that the life, culture and raw energy of a township is something everyone should experience as often as possible. It will probably change your perception of what it means to live in our country and I believe the only way we can shape our future is by understanding our past. On that note, it's funny to think that we used to eat every part of an animal. Nothing got wasted or thrown away. Somehow, in our recent past, we've forgotten that you can eat the tongue, the brain, the tripe and the guts of an animal. The idea of boiling a sheep's head is taboo for most of us.

My friends and I (a couple of *umlungus* – which is Xhosa slang for 'white trash or white person') got down and dirty in Gugs (Gugulethu) on the outskirts of Cape Town. One of the items on our to-do list was to eat smileys. This uniquely African dish costs only a couple of bucks, but beware: it's definitely not for the faint-hearted or for those who are disconnected from their food.

Traditional Method of Preparation

First you're going to take your blowtorch and scorch off any visible hair, skin and other bits. If you don't have a blowtorch just use fire. You'll know it's done when you can see the sheep smiling up at you; in other words, the lips have been burnt off, exposing the teeth.

Chuck it into your drum of boiling water and let it bob around for about thirty minutes. Grab your first willing mate, the saw and the sheep's head. Cut it in half right along the line between its eyes (that's the sheep's head – not your mate's!)

The common misconception is that when you eat a smiley, you eat the brain and all the horrible bits and pieces. Truth is you eat the tongue and all that sweet meat around the cheeks.

You'll need:
- decapitated head of one unlucky sheep
- blowtorch or fire
- one 45 gallon boiling drum
- one rusty saw

★ The only problem when eating a smiley is that you've got to get your head around it . . . no pun intended! If you can't stomach the idea of cooking it yourself, visit a township, buy one ready-made and support your local community.

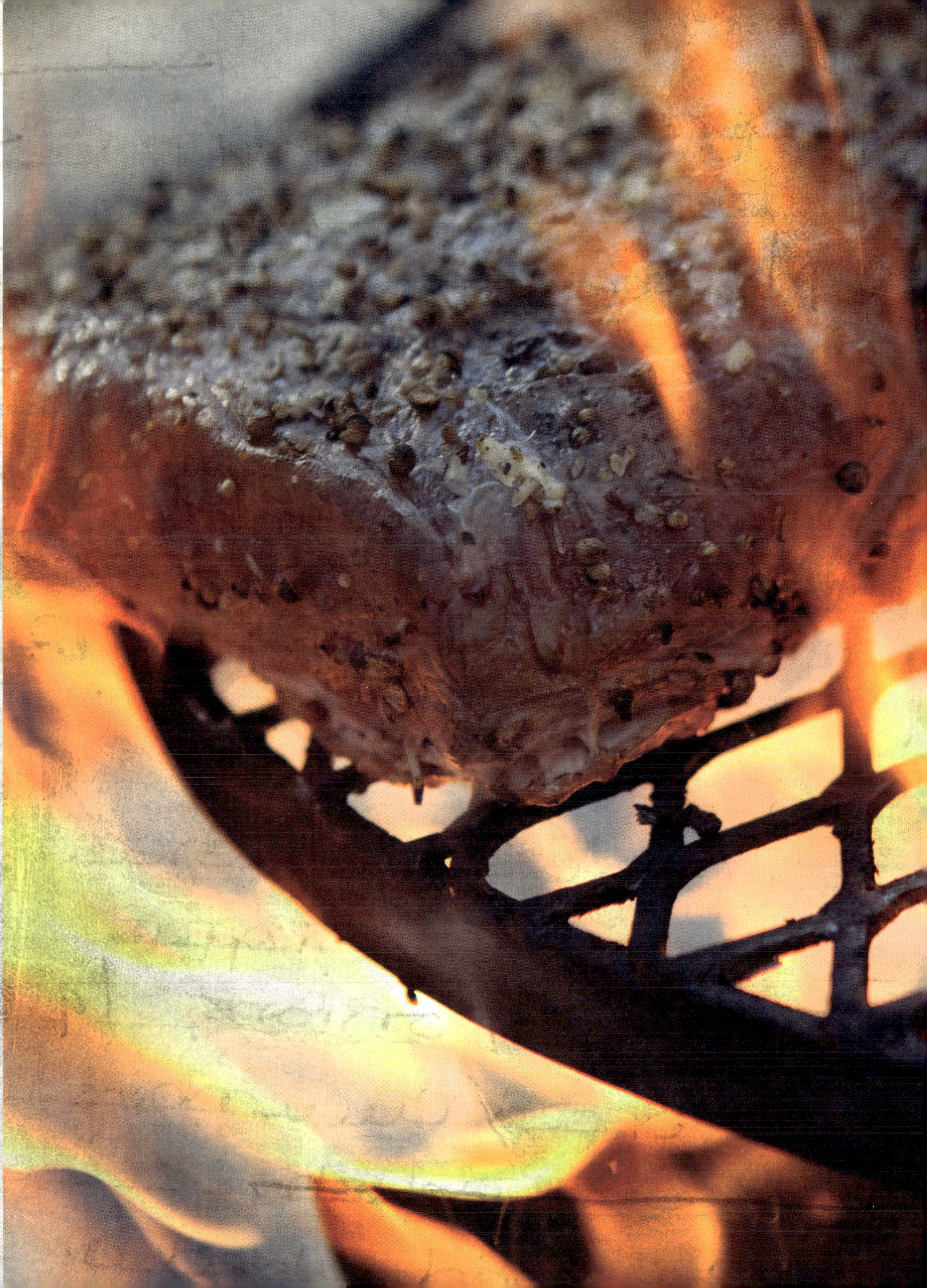

PEPPERCORN OSTRICH FILLET

Towards the end of our first season of *Cooked*, after we'd been on the road for several weeks and covered thousands of kilometres, we were nearly back home in Cape Town. As much as I love a good road trip with friends there are always those left behind whom you miss, and having a bunch of them come up to the Koue Bokkeveld in the Cederberg to join us was like that warm fuzzy feeling of getting letters from home. No wonder they reward *Survivor* contestants with visits from loved ones! We spent a wonderful afternoon walking through orchards pink with apple blossom and frolicking in the ice cold river working up hearty appetites all round. To feed the masses I chose ostrich fillet encrusted with peppercorns and served it with a salad of warm mushrooms and smashed baby potatoes.

> Back when we filmed this episode I was still learning how to cook the perfect fillet but over the years I've perfected it, which is lucky for you. The basic recipe for the peppercorn rub is on page 42 (Smoked Fillet in a Kassie) which you can follow, but in this case triple up the quantity of peppercorns in relation to the other seeds.

To make the rub, take equal quantities of coriander seeds, mustard seeds, Maldon salt, and peeled garlic, plus three times as much peppercorns. Chuck them all into a mortar and pestle and bash it until you've got a nice crumbly rub. Coat the meat generously with the crushed peppercorn mixture, pressing it into the flesh.

Make your fire. When the coals get to the point where they're almost ready to be spread out and braaied on, it's time to flame-grill the fillet. Put the fillet on the grid and drizzle a little sunflower oil over it to get the flames leaping. Cook on all sides, turning the meat every 2 minutes and adding a drizzle of oil every time you turn to ensure that the meat is completely sealed by the flame grilling.

Remove from the fire and let it rest. This allows the meat to suck all its juices back into itself like a sponge. I suggest you make the salad while the meat is resting.

The rub:
› coriander seeds
› mustard seeds
› Maldon salt
› crushed garlic
› lots and lots of peppercorns of every colour

★ The meat will still be very rare. Just before serving, slice it into medallions and cook them to your friends' tastes. Anyone who asks for it well done should be sliced up and put on the braai themselves or, worse, sent to the Spur. Me, I like it blue. Served right off the fire.

MUSHROOM AND SMASHED BABY POTATO SALAD

> This is one of my favourite salads because I get to layer the flavours. What do I mean? Make it and see. Just one note, make sure all your hot ingredients have cooled down before adding them to your salad leaves or they'll go brown and *verlep*.

Start by parboiling the potatoes (skin and all) until they're almost done. Remove from the heat and once they've cooled down enough to handle, squash them one by one with the palm of your hand, until they just break open. Next, heat up a large pan of sunflower oil and carefully add your potatoes – try using a spoon rather than your bare hands! Fry until golden and crispy on the outside but still fluffy inside. Once done, hide them away from your friends, or you'll have nothing left to put in the salad.

Next up

Take all those lovely mushrooms and slice them up. Heat up a non-stick pan, add a generous knob of butter, the mushrooms and all the garlic. Do as Julia Child tells you and 'don't crowd the mushrooms'. Once they're cooking add a smattering of crushed salt for flavour. Fry until all the moisture is released and the mushrooms are nicely browned. Make sure that no one is watching you and add them to the potatoes.

Now, using the same pan, fry your leeks and when they're soft set aside and let them cool down. Chuck your chickpeas into a bowl, drizzle with olive oil, red onion, about 2 cloves of crushed garlic and a sprinkling of black pepper. Mix it around.

Toss the salad leaves in a good splash of sesame seed oil. Put them in a wide-bottomed salad bowl and season with crushed salt and black pepper. Next, layer in the mushrooms and potatoes, leeks, litchis, chickpeas and sprouts and drizzle with a good quality olive oil. Finish the whole lot off with some more cracked pepper.

★ Serve with the peppercorn fillet (page 65).

PS: Helena says this salad tastes even better with a splash of fresh lemon juice … she says the same thing about drinking tequila shots – so who knows!

You'll need:
- about 500 g baby potatoes
- sunflower oil
- a whole whack of mushrooms (dried, porcini, Portobello, white button and giant browns)
- butter
- 2 cloves of garlic – peeled and crushed
- a smattering of crushed salt
- a bunch of leeks – sliced
- 1 cup chickpeas
- olive oil
- red onion – finely chopped
- black pepper
- cos lettuce
- rocket
- sesame oil
- 15 or so fresh litchis (or one tin preserved litchis) peeled, de-pipped and cut in half
- 1 cup mixed sprouts
- lemon (optional)

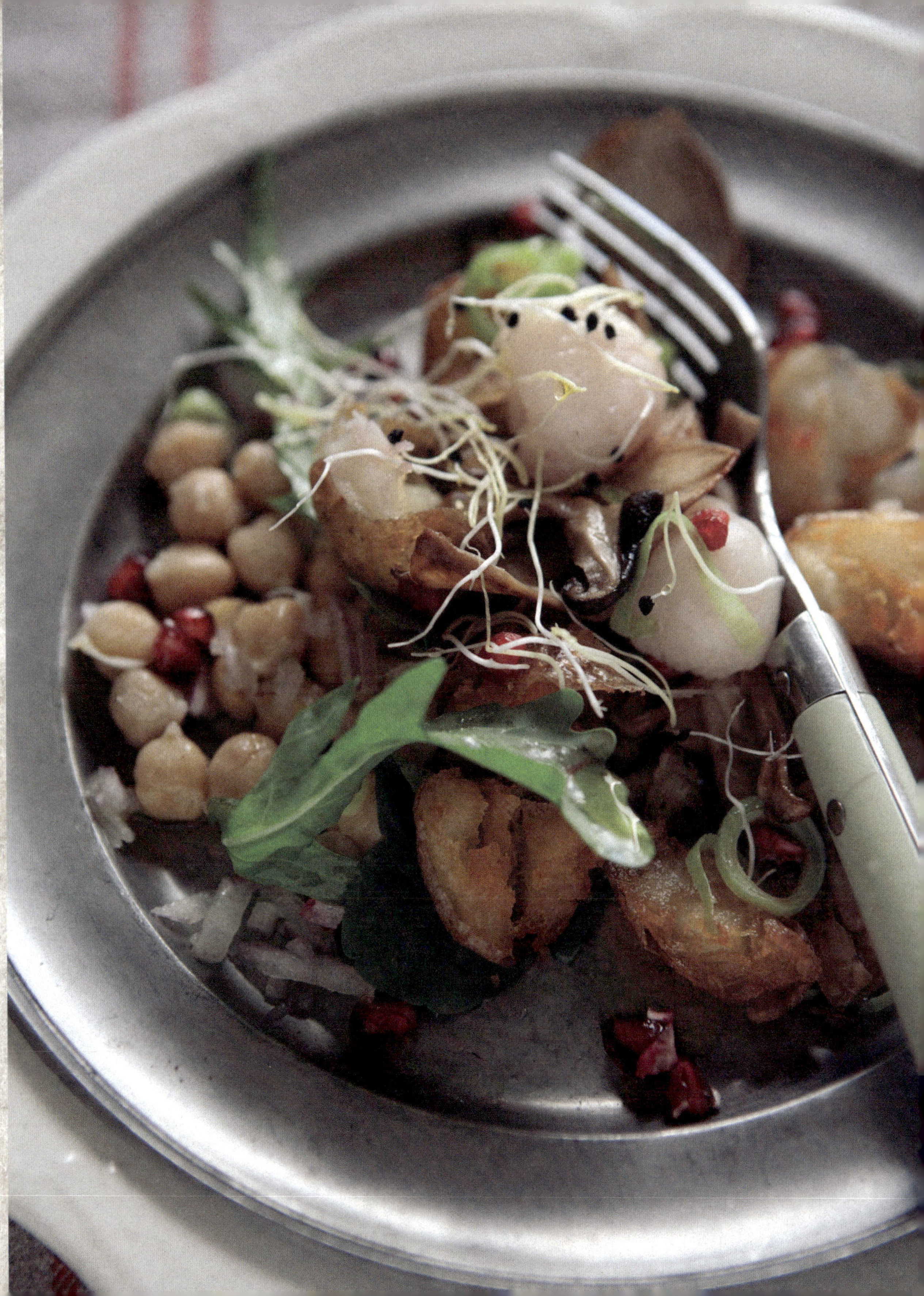

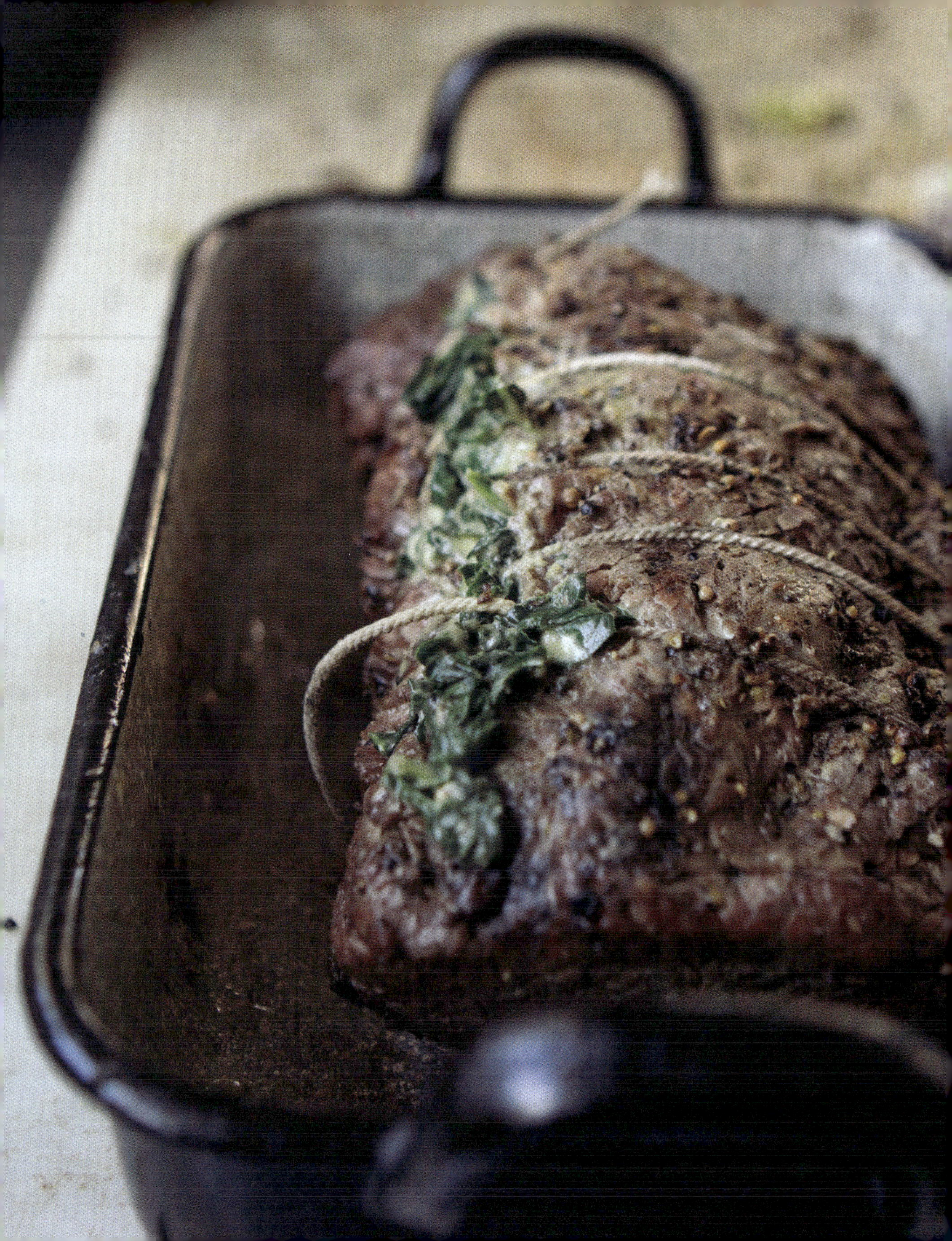

STUFFED FILLET

Fillet is definitely a crowd pleaser at any braai, so imagine how happy your friends will be if you present this stuffed baby to them!

> ★ Just a note on buying beef. Get free-range. I've been in a feedlot, and without wanting to put you off ever eating meat again, I've got to say it was one of the most traumatic experiences of my life. No one should eat grain-fed beef. It's not natural and there's a whole lot of other stuff in it too so, chances are, if it's not veld-fed, you're eating more than just the meat on your plate.

Start by making the rub on page 65, then rub it generously all over the meat. Chuck the meat on a grid over a very hot flaming fire. Drizzle with sunflower oil to really get it flaming and be sure to seal it all over, then take it off the flames and let it rest for 15 minutes or so while you make the stuffing. If you're only making one fillet, choose which flavour you like best.

CREAMY SPINACH STUFFING

Melt a generous knob or two of butter into a pan, add the garlic, and fry for a moment or two. Remove from the pan, add another big knob of butter, add the spinach and cook until it stops releasing juices and begins to dry out. Then add the fried garlic, crème fraiche and salt to taste and let it simmer until the filling is moist, but not runny.

For the Creamy Spinach you'll need:
> butter
> a couple of cloves of garlic – crushed
> loads of fresh spinach with the bitter stem removed
> about 1 cup of crème fraiche
> salt to taste

CARAMELISED ONION AND KALAHARI TRUFFLE STUFFING

Truffles aren't always readily available (Kalahari or otherwise) and they're usually on the pricey side, so if you're on a tight budget, you can use some truffle oil instead. The trick is to get that deep earthy taste, but be aware that the Kalahari truffle isn't as strong as its European counterpart, so you've got to use more.

Heat up a pan and chuck in a knob of butter and then add the onions. Fry until just soft, then add the sliced truffles. Add black pepper and a small pinch of salt to taste and cook until the truffles have released their earthy flavour.

For the Caramelised Onion and Kalahari Truffle you'll need:
> butter
> a whole whack of onions – quartered
> a handful of truffles – sliced
> black pepper and salt to taste

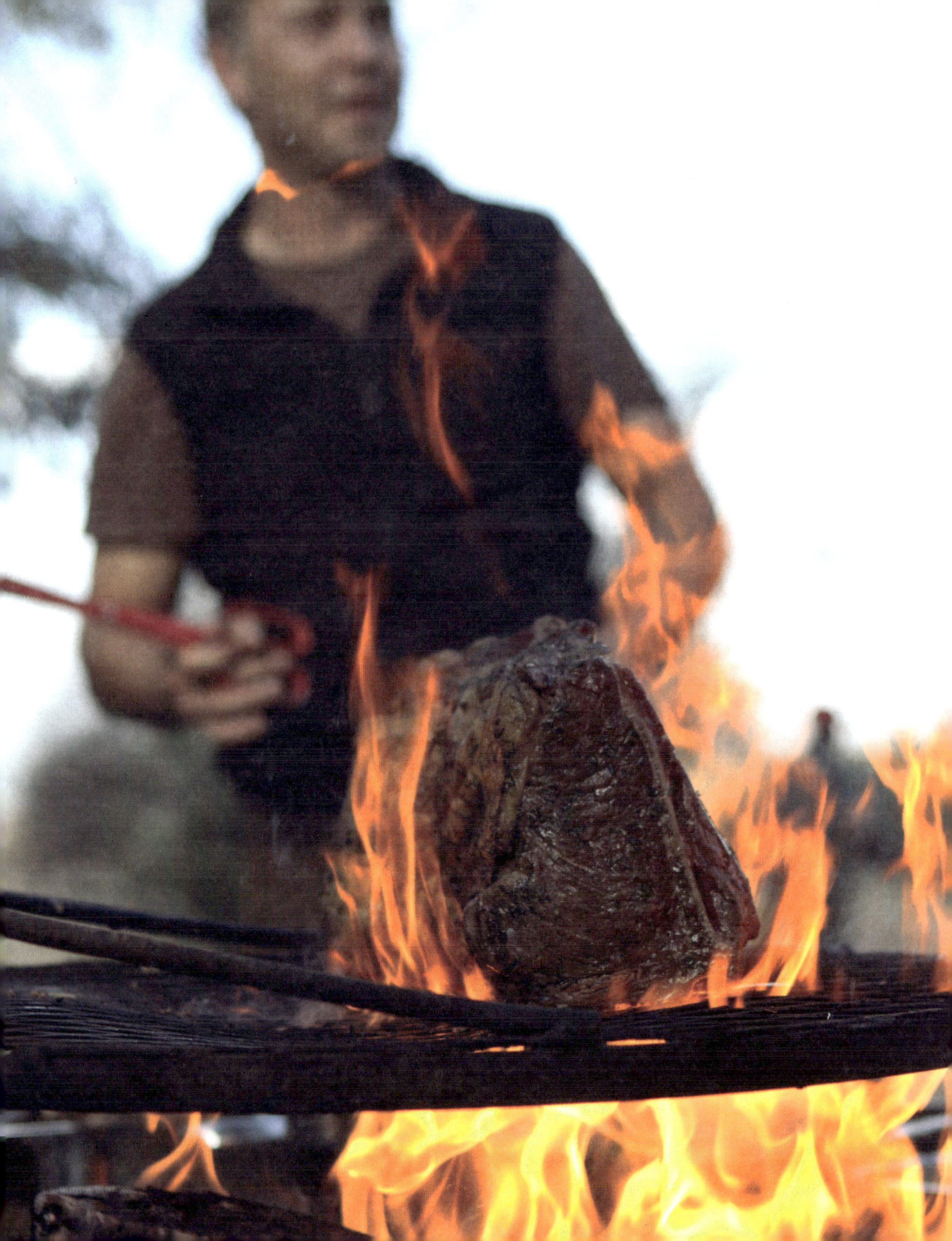

★ PREPPING

Make a cut lengthwise down the side of the fillet. The idea is to create a pocket, so try to get as deep as possible, but stop cutting about 2 cm from each end and 2 cm from the bottom. Using your hands, stuff the pocket with the filling of your choice, being careful not to overdo it otherwise it'll just spill out of the fillet while cooking. Next, tie it up with string at about 3 cm intervals to keep the whole thing together (think of what a nice trussed pork belly or loin looks like).

Bake in a preheated oven at 180°C until it's done to your liking. Not all fillets are the same size so baking time depends on the thickness of the cut of meat. The rule of thumb is to cook for 20 minutes for every 500 g if you like it medium rare, and 15 minutes per 500 g for rare. I'm not going to tell you how long for medium or well done . . . that's no way to treat a great piece of meat! Please don't ever overcook fillet.

Give it time to rest before slicing into rounds and serving it with whatever tickles your fillet fancy.

PS If you have vegetarian friends who will head for the hills if they see a piece of fillet on their plate, don't worry. Give them stuffed mushrooms instead (page 72).

STUFFED MUSHROOM SANDWICHES

Remember the saying, 'Life's too short to stuff a mushroom'? Shirley Conran first coined it in her 1975 book *Superwoman*. Don't confuse it with Superman. It's actually about how to be a working wife and mother and how to save time and money. You get the picture. Sorry to say, Shirley obviously went about stuffing mushrooms the wrong way. Even the busiest of businesswomen will have time to make my stuffed mushrooms (on a braai, nogal!) with time left over to hoover the lounge, wash the dishes and put the kids to bed. (Just kidding!) But, seriously, this is how you stuff a mushroom and live to talk about it the next day.

Start by pan-frying the spinach in a large pan with loads of butter until it is dryish but still moist. In another pan, dry-toast the pine nuts to give them some colour and to bring out the flavour. Toss them into a mortar and pestle and pound until they're crushed, then add to the spinach. Lastly, crumble some blue cheese into the spinach – how much you add depends on how much you love blue cheese. Mix it all together then add some salt and pepper to taste.

Next, scoop a couple of spoonfuls of the stuffing on to half of the mushrooms. Place the other half of the mushrooms on top and tie them together with string soaked in water. Whack them on the braai and cook both sides until the mushroom is moist and has released all its flavour.

Cut in half just before serving.

> ★ And that's it. Stuffed mushrooms on the braai – proof that life's not too short after all.

You'll need:
- loads of baby spinach
- butter
- giant brown mushrooms
  – two per veggie friend
- a handful of blue cheese
  – crumbled
- a small handful of pine nuts
- salt and pepper to taste
- string

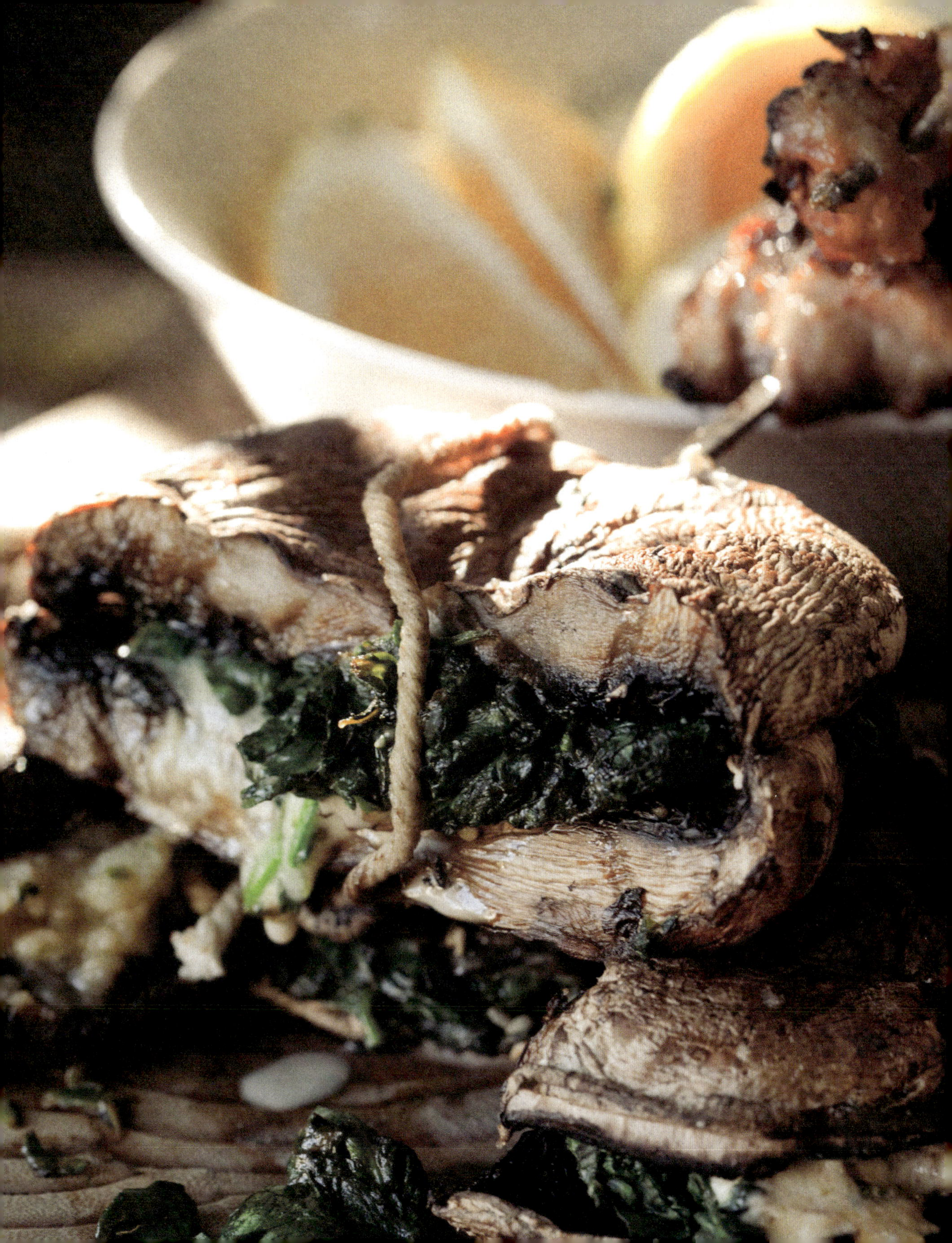

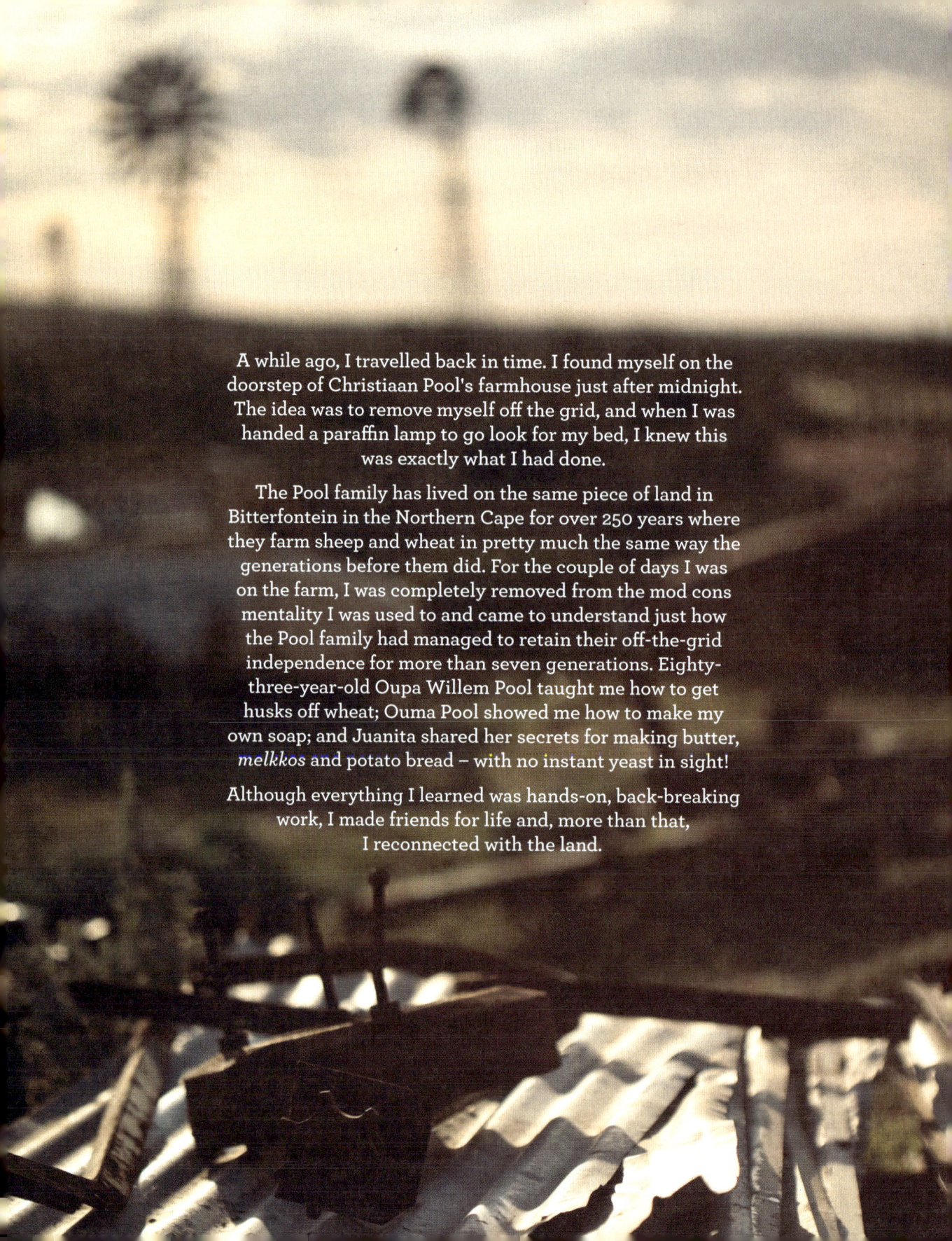

A while ago, I travelled back in time. I found myself on the doorstep of Christiaan Pool's farmhouse just after midnight. The idea was to remove myself off the grid, and when I was handed a paraffin lamp to go look for my bed, I knew this was exactly what I had done.

The Pool family has lived on the same piece of land in Bitterfontein in the Northern Cape for over 250 years where they farm sheep and wheat in pretty much the same way the generations before them did. For the couple of days I was on the farm, I was completely removed from the mod cons mentality I was used to and came to understand just how the Pool family had managed to retain their off-the-grid independence for more than seven generations. Eighty-three-year-old Oupa Willem Pool taught me how to get husks off wheat; Ouma Pool showed me how to make my own soap; and Juanita shared her secrets for making butter, *melkkos* and potato bread – with no instant yeast in sight!

Although everything I learned was hands-on, back-breaking work, I made friends for life and, more than that, I reconnected with the land.

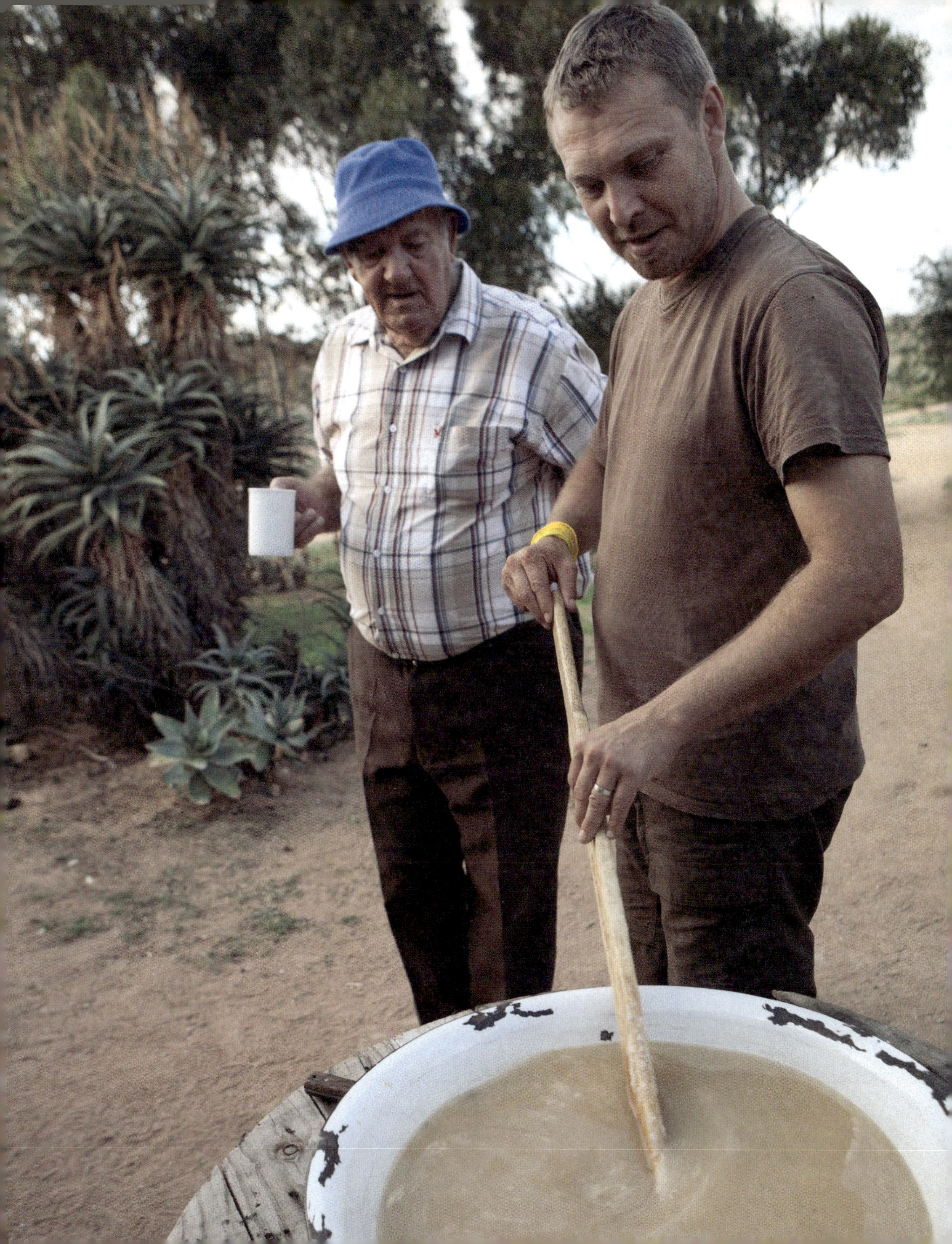

JUANITA'S POTATO BREAD

> ★ Juanita Pool sent me her potato bread recipe, which she no doubt learned to make as a young girl growing up in rural South Africa. This recipe comes from an era when people not only had the time to do these things, but also to teach their children and grandchildren. And now I get to show you. Thanks, Juanita!

Try to get your hands on a 2-litre enamel bucket, then add:
- 4 cups of boiling water
- 1/2 teaspoon bicarbonate of soda
- 2 tablespoons sugar
- 1 medium potato (with or without skin, cut into quarters)

You'll also need:
- bread flour

Making the Sour Dough

Once the mixture in the bucket has cooled down (in other words, you can stick your finger in without jumping through the roof) stir in some flour. Juanita says whole wheat flour works best. You'll know you've added enough when the dough has a loose texture similar to the consistency of pancake batter. Cover the dough with a cloth and let it sit in the warmest spot in your house for roughly 9 hours or overnight. (You'll probably have to chase your cat away first.)

When you next work the dough, it should be foaming at the mouth. Stir in one cup of hot (not boiling) water and a little more flour and cover again. It's a good idea to put the bucket into a plastic bag, in case the sour dough starts creeping over the sides.

Depending on the weather outside, the dough should start to rise (you can peek if you want to), and at a certain point the contents of the bucket might look as if they're about to bubble over. When it's ready, it will have a very distinct sour smell. And when all of this has happened, you know it's ready and it should be enough sour dough for 3 to 5 kg of flour.

Now to make your bread

Sift the flour (3-5 kg) into a bowl, add a pinch of salt and the sour dough mixture and knead, adding splashes of lukewarm water if necessary. Keep kneading until you work up a sweat and the dough has gone silky smooth (or about 15 minutes). Place the dough into fat or butter-greased bread tins and leave it to rise for about 1½ hours, then bake at 180°C for about 1½ hours – you'll notice the bread has loosened off the sides of the tins. Serve with homemade butter (yes, I actually made this!) and a selection of jams. *Pure plaas!*

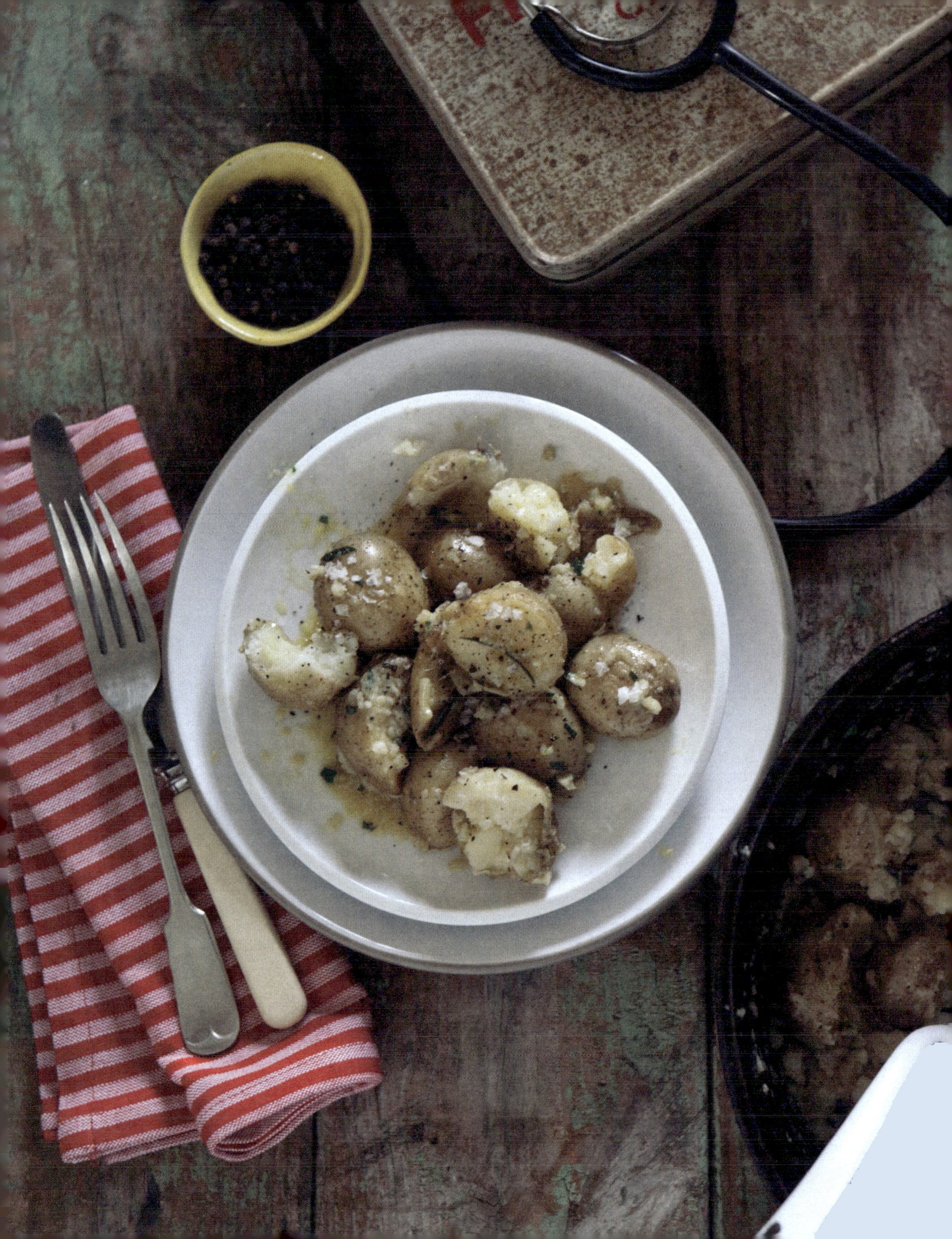

POTATO POTJIE

The Heart Stopper

Man cannot live by meat alone. He needs potatoes too. For a hearty side dish, this is the perfect potjie and it goes especially well with braaied snoek, lamb – flip it, anything and everything!

You'll need:

- 1 killer kg or more of butter
- 2 kg baby potatoes – washed but unpeeled
- a couple of large onions – roughly sliced
- several large cloves of garlic – peeled and crushed
- big handfuls of rosemary, sage and/or parsley – roughly torn or chopped
- salt, pepper and spices to taste

★ First grease your potjie with a whole slab of butter. Don't be shy. Fill it about halfway with whole baby potatoes, washed but with their skins on. On top of that goes a layer of sliced onions and a whole lot of chopped garlic – at least two heaped handfuls. Forget the cholesterol for a while and chuck in several more huge knobs of butter. We don't call this the Heart Stopper for nothing. Jean Pierre, who taught me how to make this at his farm in Ceres, used marge at this point, but not me. You'll never find margarine in my kitchen; it's butter all the way.

★ Fresh herbs are the magic ingredients here, but you can use dried if you have to. Rosemary and potatoes are a match made in heaven so start with that. Rip the spiky little leaves off the stalk, chop them roughly, and add to the potjie. Sage is another herb that plays well with potatoes, and parsley just loves everything. Chuck them all in if you want to.

★ Season well with salt, ground black pepper and a handful of whole black peppercorns. Jean Pierre used BBQ spice and insisted on a hefty shake of Aromat but, like the margarine, I never use those ready-made things that are full of preservatives and artificial flavours.

★ In a normal world potjies are all about layers that are left alone during cooking, but not this one... pop the lid on and place the potjie in the fire, over a medium heat. At this point you get to sit back with a few beers while it does its thing, but remember to give it the odd stir now and then so it doesn't stick and at the same time softly breaks up the potatoes as they cook, giving you a thick, chunky, mashy pot of rich buttery yumminess.

BOTTOMLESS APPLE CRUMBLE

It's the story of my life as a bush cook. All my friends are sitting in the shade, drinking beer and relaxing at the Beach Camp in Paternoster, while I am stuck in the blistering midday heat making an apple crumble for tonight's dessert. Which is why I have only one real rule in the kitchen: if I cook, I don't clean up. So, later, when I am basking in the glory of my delicious cream-coated apple crumble, they will be in the kitchen . . .

Peel the apples, remove the cores and cut them up into slices. In a preheated pan, add a big knob of butter, the sliced apples, a couple of pinches of cinnamon and a generous sprinkling of brown sugar. Fry them for as long as it takes for them to go soft and almost caramelised (about five minutes).

If you're like me and don't like anything to go to waste, freeze the apple skins and add them to smoothies for extra fibre, or just feed them to your worms (if you have a worm farm) or add them to your compost heap.

Take a greased baking tin and scoop in the cooked apple mixture until it is about 1 cm from the top of the tin. Set the tin aside and get ready to get your friends' hands dirty.

★ For the crumble

Chuck the flour and butter into a large mixing bowl. Rub them together with your fingers until you have a crumbly dough, then add the sugar and mix it around loosely – you don't want the dough to compress, but to stay light and crumbly.

Cover your apples with the crumble and whack it in a preheated oven at 180°C for 45 minutes. The apple crumble is ready once it's golden on top and the sugar has caramelised. Serve with whipped cream and tuck in.

If you cock up on the crumble, and it's now become like dough, you can grate it over the apple.

For the filling:
> a mix of 6-10 Golden Delicious and Gala apples
> butter
> ground cinnamon
> brown sugar

For the crumble:
> 150 g butter
> 225 g cake flour
> 150 g brown sugar

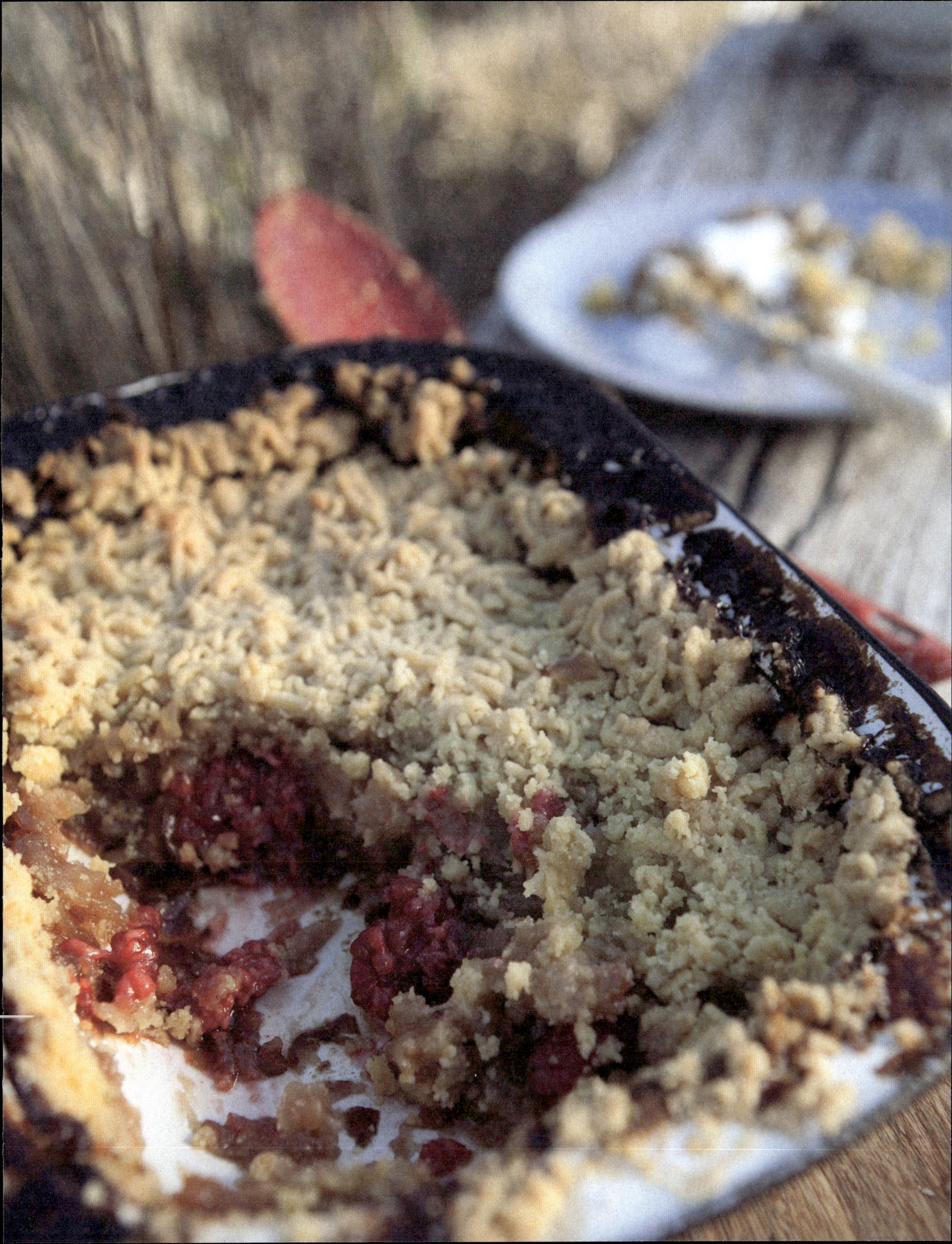

CHAPTER 3

LET'S GOO!

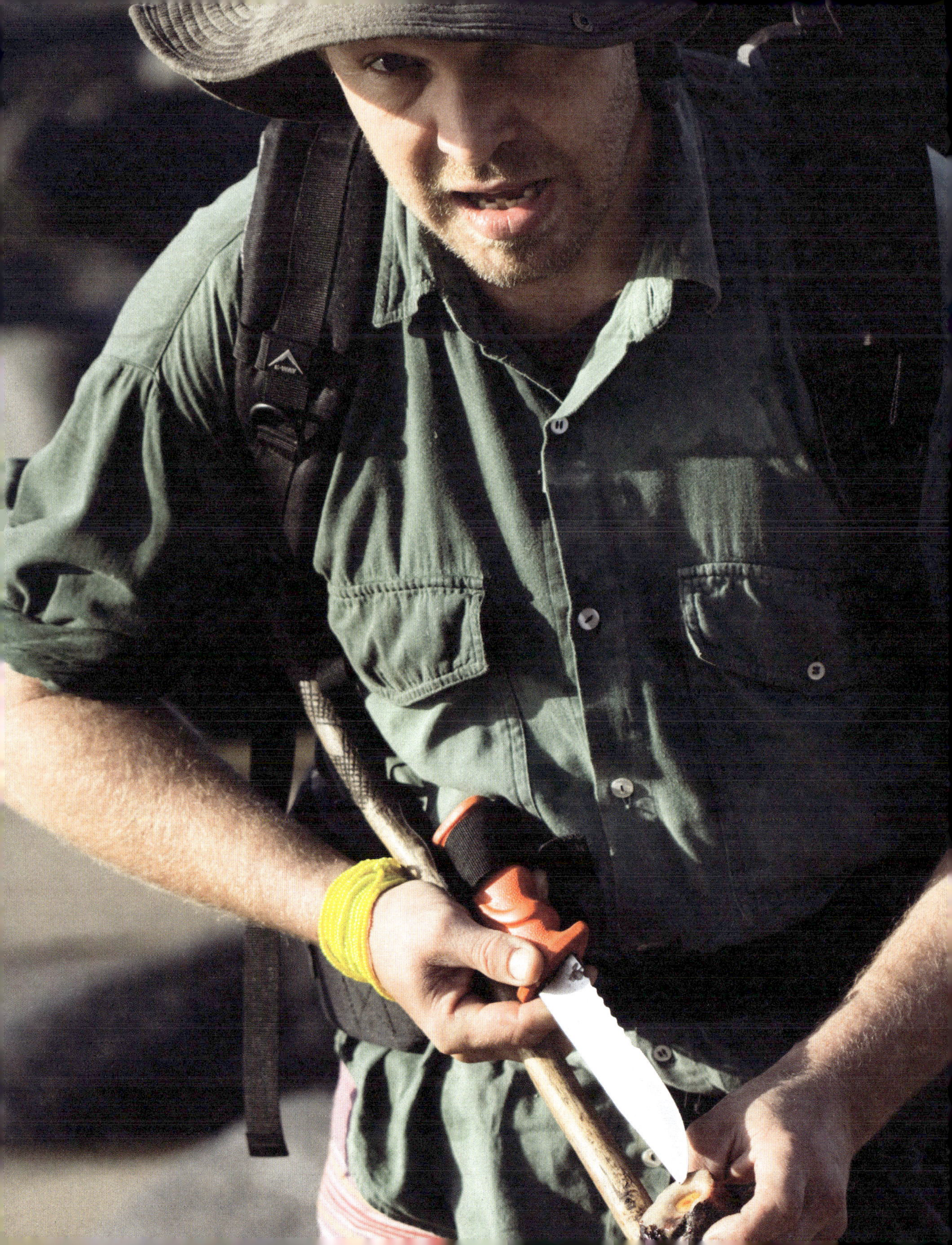

After putting my friends through the 'Hungry Ones' experience on the Wild Coast, I knew I had to feed the scavengers something other than fish and sand before they turned into characters from Lord of the Flies. We had to turn our backs on trying to be Strandlopers and evolve into the modern equivalent. Our initial rules were that we had to live off the beach, foraging, harvesting and cooking our seafood with what was at hand. The new rules were that we could add mod cons including pots, utensils, spices, herbs and, of course, beer.

THAI MUSSELS ON POT BREAD

> And as a reward to my mates for not killing me or each other the previous day, I thought I'd make them a seafood feast. I thought fish, oysters, mussels... maybe a seafood potjie? But nature wasn't in the mood to play and I was a bit poked. No fish in sight (and I tried really hard). All I had were the previous day's mussels. In this scenario, hunger was definitely the best cook – I was craving flavour, and the Thai mussels I made didn't disappoint.

The first thing you're going to do is steam the mussels. Chuck them all into a hot potjie, add a splash of wine and steam until they're open. Get your friends to pull off the beards and take the meat out the shells (you can keep some in the shells if you like). Next, heat up another potjie and chuck in a generous knob of butter. Add the sliced leeks and onions and fry until just soft. Add the ginger, garlic, tomatoes, chillies, mussels and the tin of coconut milk. Sometimes I even add just a little of that salty juice left over from steaming the mussels... but just a little – then you don't need salt. If you don't do this, give it a good pinch of Maldon salt and a generous crack of black pepper then leave it to simmer for a bit.

Just before you're about to eat, chuck in a whole lot of torn coriander and serve directly out of the potjie on top of warm, freshly baked pot bread. And please, please dunk your bread in the potjie pot to mop up the last of the sauce.

SPITTING MUSSELS

★ If you harvest your own mussels and want to get rid of all the sand and grit that you sometimes get with them, soak them in fresh seawater for a couple of hours and they'll spit out the sand. Easy.

You'll need:
- a whole whack of fresh mussels (50 or so)
- a splash of white wine
- butter
- a couple of leeks – sliced
- 2 red onions – chopped
- a big chunk of fresh ginger – grated
- about 5 cloves of garlic – crushed
- about 6 tomatoes – cut into chunks
- loads of green chilli – sliced (seeds and all)
- a tin of coconut milk
- a big handful of fresh coriander

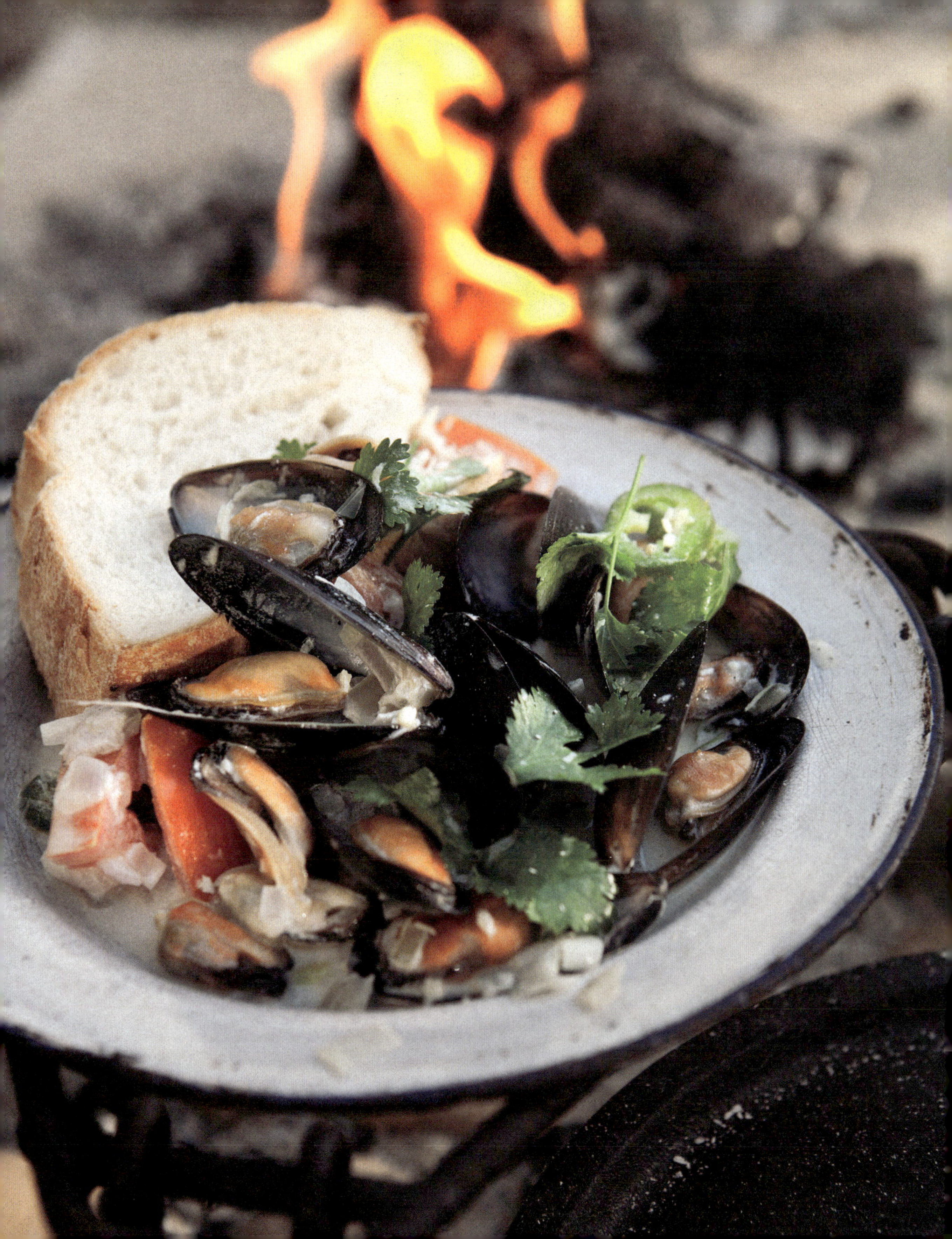

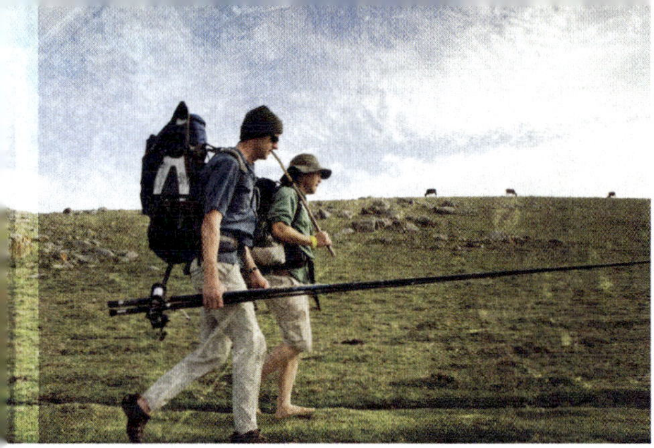
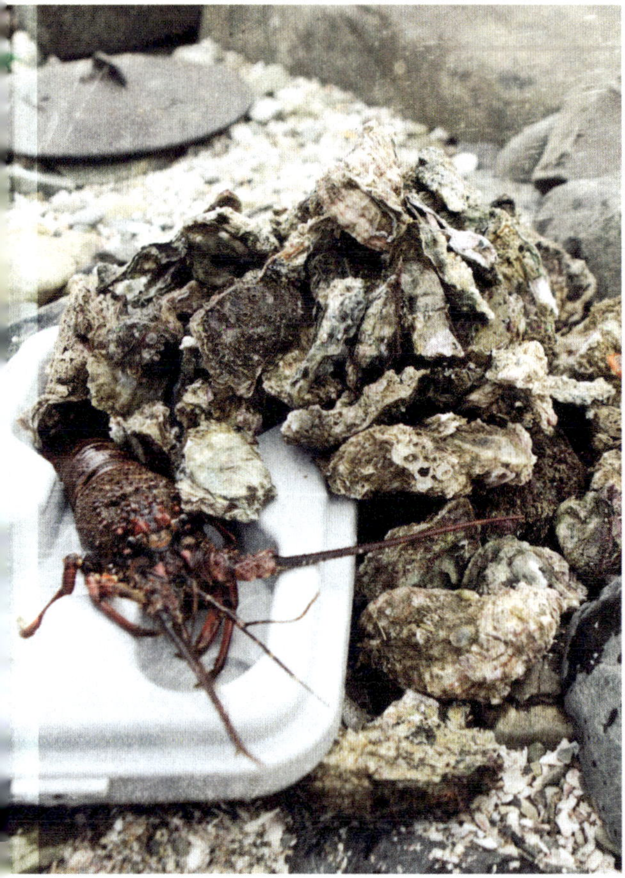
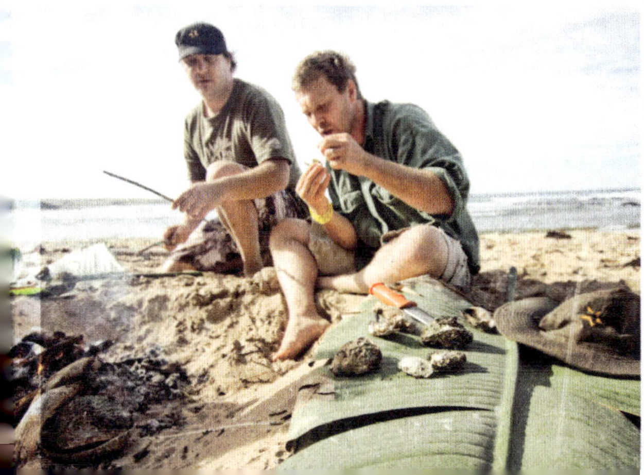
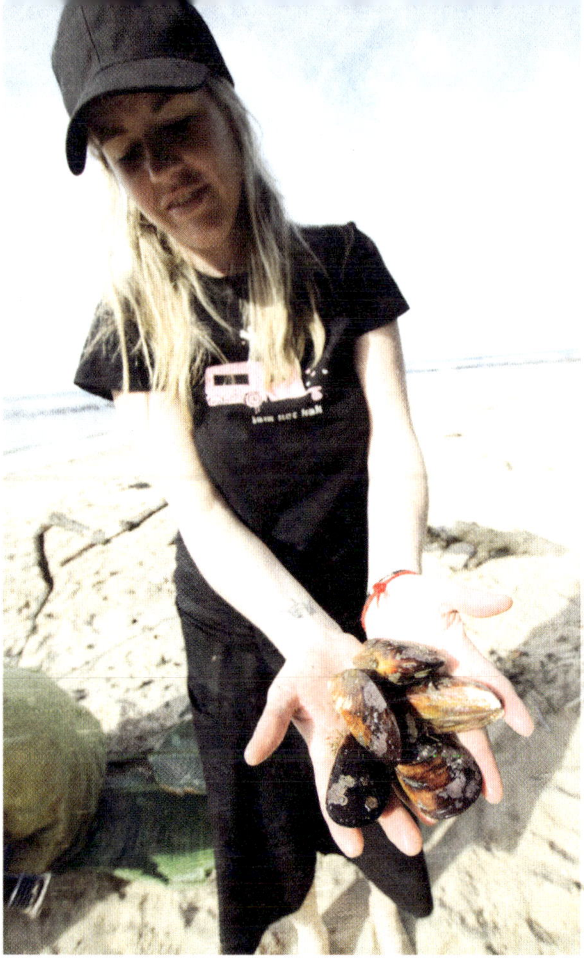
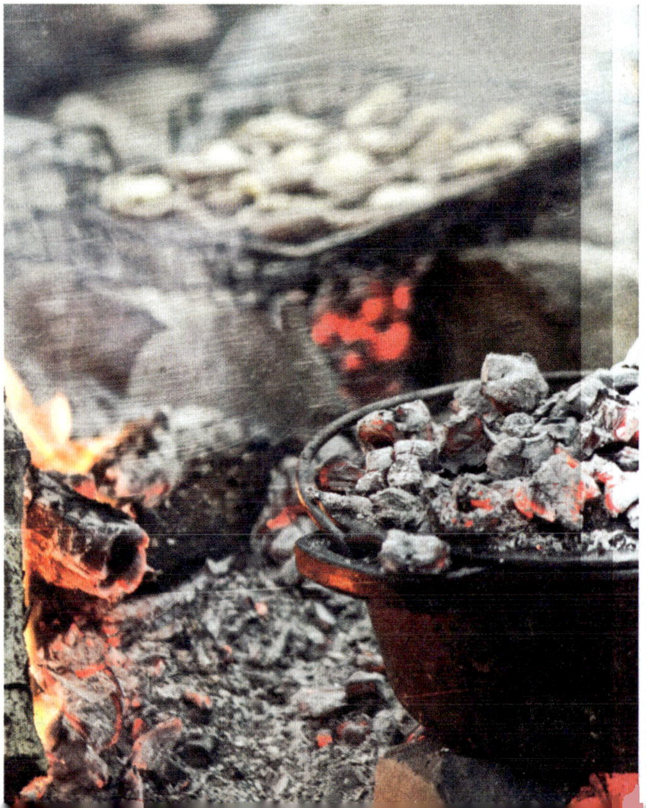
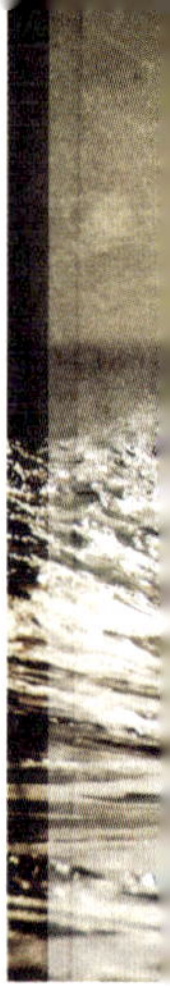
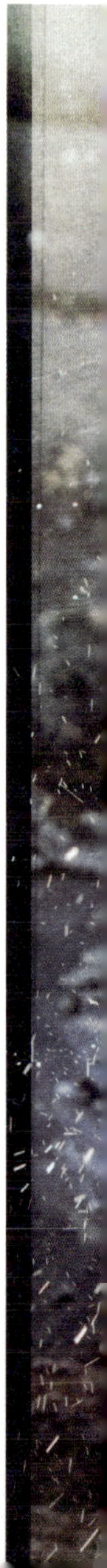

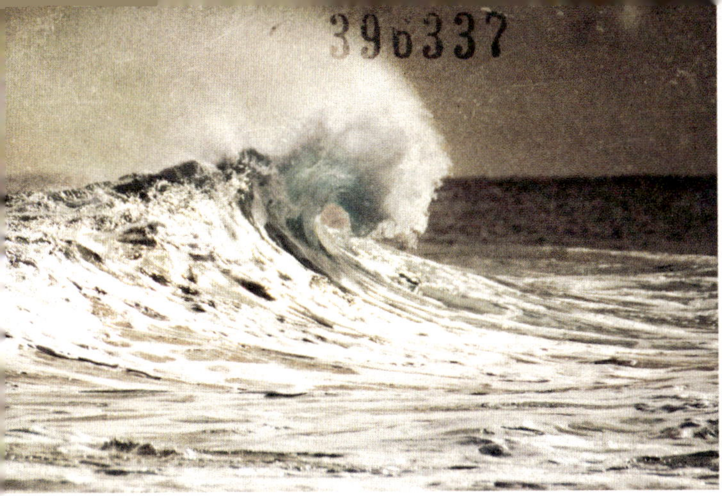

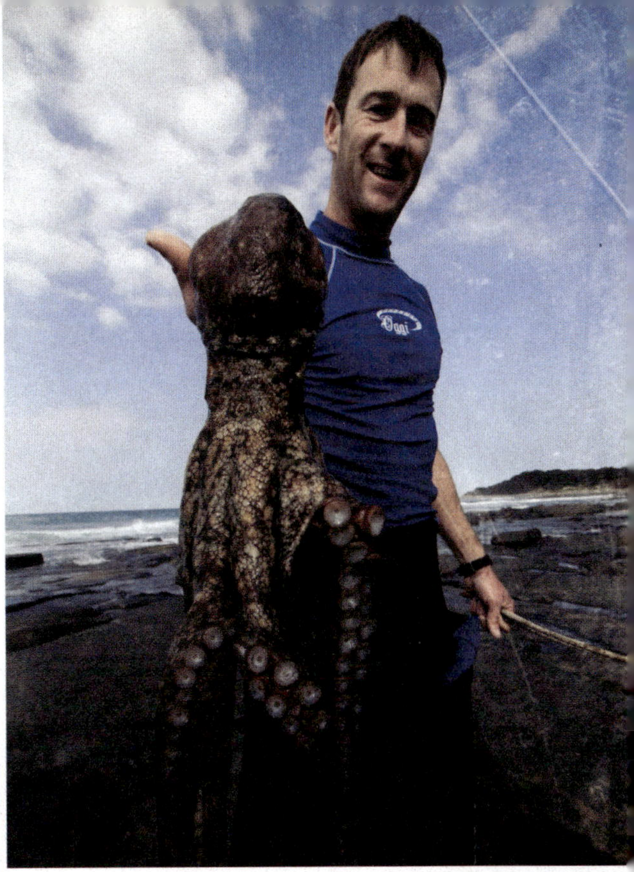

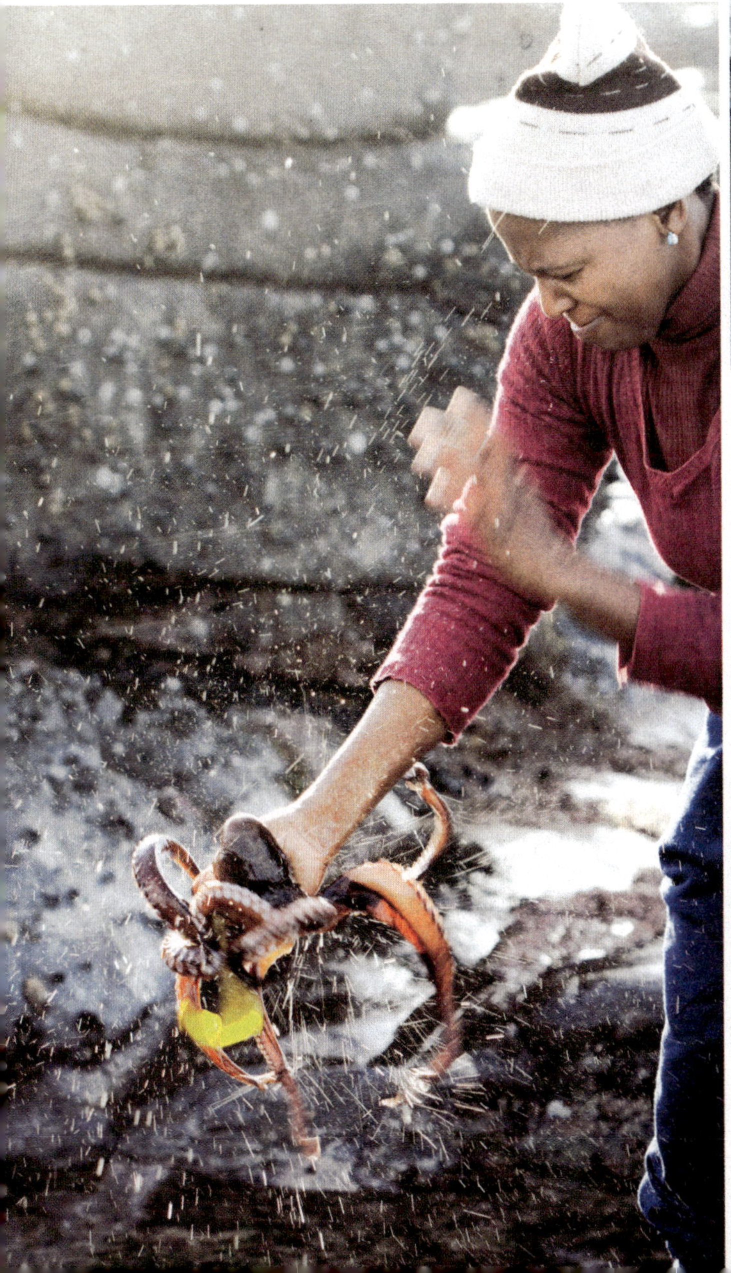

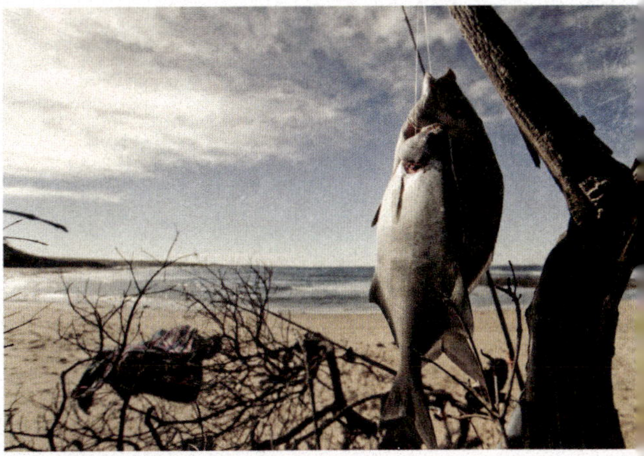

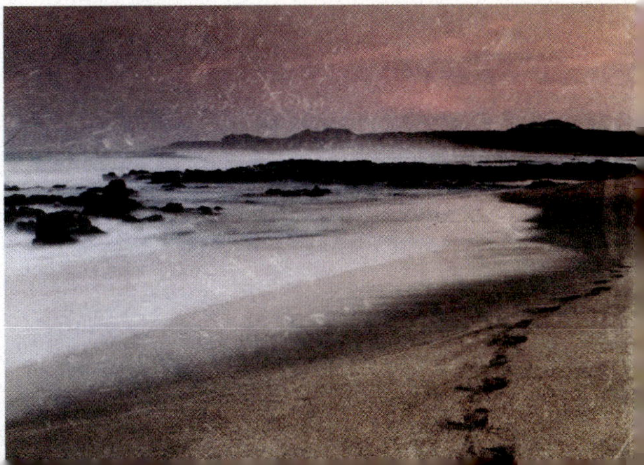

DURBAN

Durban locals live in a world of their own, so it makes sense that they've got their own lingo. I thought I'd share some words and phrases with you. This way you'll know exactly what's potting when a Durbanite tunes you.

HOSE (YOURSELF) LAUGH | **CHUCK/DUCK** TO LEAVE OR GO | **SICK** | EXCELLENT! YOU CHECK? SEE WHAT I MEAN? | **CHILLAX** CHILL OUT

BRAH · SURF BROTHER

SKRIK FRIGHTENED 'YOUR LIGHTIE GAVE ME A BIG SKRIK.'

TUNE TO SAY/TELL 'I TUNE YOU OU, THIS IS HOW YOU'VE GOT TO TALK IN DURBS.'

– OU GUY OR PERSON 'CHECK THAT OU. HE DOESN'T LOOK VERY LUKKER.' –

ALL GOLDS ONE SHOT TEQUILA, ONE SHOT TOMATO JUICE & TABASCO | **NUMBER · SONG** 'THIS IS A LUKKER NUMBER TO JIGGA TO.' | **CUZZIE** COUSIN

HIT A MARCH: TAKE A WALK | **HALF JACK** HALF A BOTTLE OF SPIRITS | **GWAI/GWA** CIGARETTE

SMILING DRUNK | **CATCH A DROP** FALL | **ISIT?** IS IT REALLY? | **LUCKER/LUKKER** LEKKER/NICE

GOING BALLISTIC (THE WAVES WERE SMOKING!) 'THE WAVES WERE GOING BALLISTIC.' | **SLIP-SLOPS** SANDALS

PARK OFF SIT DOWN AND RELAX | **LAAI'TIE/LIGHTIE** | CHILD 'THIS IS MY LAAI'TIE.' 'ISIT?'

DOS SLEEP | **AWEH** HELLO | **NOW-NOW** JUST NOW | **100'S** EXCELLENT | **WOES** | ANGRY/VICIOUS 'THAT CHERRY WE MET NOW-NOW WAS REALLY WOES!'

JIGGA | TO FOOL AROUND

SCHLEP · HARD WORK

– DWAAL WHEN YOU'RE BAMBI-EYED AFTER LITTLE SLEEP 'I'M IN A DWAAL TODAY, BRAH.' –

ROCK UP | ARRIVE 'WHEN YOU ROCK UP, JUST PARK OFF AND CHILLAX WITH SOME OF THAT HALF JACK' | **CRASH** | TO SLEEP SOMEWHERE 'I'M GOING TO CRASH ON YOUR COUCH.'

ACE · TO BE BY YOURSELF 'I'M ON MY ACE TONIGHT, HOPEFULLY I'LL HAVE SOME TIME TO CHILLAX.' | **PULL A JOB** | STEAL SOMETHING 'IF YOU PULL A JOB AND GET CAUGHT, YOU USUALLY HIT A MARCH STRAIGHT TO JAIL.'

BUNNY (CHOW)

When you think of Durban, chances are you're thinking uShaka Marine World, Zulu dancers, rickshaw pullers, the almost unbearable humidity and, of course, the surfers. Let's face it, Durbs is not yet world famous for its culinary brilliance (there are exceptions) but, to be fair, one Food Great does stand out: The Bunny Chow (not to be confused with a vegetarian dish or something made of rabbit meat).

★ **The Bunny** (as indigenous Durbanites call it) is a very simple but *lekker* dish that you should always eat with your hands, the trick being not to let any of the sauce end up on your T-shirt. Locals say that when you ask for a Bunny in Durbs, you shouldn't say, *'I want a Bunny Chow'*, but rather ask for it according to the size and filling: *'Give me a quarter/half/full lamb/beef/chicken/mutton/bean.'*

★ **Eating a Bunny comes with various rules:** if the curry is too hot, you're not allowed to break out in a sweat; never start eating the bunny from the bottom (unless you like a hot mess on your shirt); always eat it in the outdoors (beaches, street corners or a promenade will do); and when you're done eating, scrunch up the paper and aim for the nearest bin (in the manner of a professional NBA player).

★ **Making a Bunny is dead easy.** Just hollow out a quarter loaf of white bread and stuff it full of the curry of your choice. Because it's so filling, Bunnies are hugely popular chow for surfers after they've spent the day on the water. One Bunny is usually followed by a second and a third.

SIX QUARTER LAMBS, PLEASE

Heat up a large pot, add the oil and chuck in the chopped onions and celery. Stir it around and when the onion starts cooking add the garlic, masala, cumin and nutmeg. Next, add the remaining spices and the chillies and fry until all the flavours have been released. Don't stick your head in the pot – your eyes will burn and your nose will start running. Toss the lamb knuckles in seasoned flour. Heat a large pan and sear the lamb until browned. Scoop the lamb into the curry pot and stir until the meat is covered in the spices. Keep the searing pan for later use.

Cover the lamb in water and when it starts simmering add the tomatoes and vinegar. Cook for about 20 minutes then take the searing pan with its *lekker* leftover juices, add a splash of water and bring to the boil. Add to the curry pot with about 2 more cups of water. Simmer for about 5 hours, or until the lamb falls off the bones. Refrigerate overnight and reheat just before scooping it into the bunny. Garnish with fresh coriander.

You'll need:
> a good few splashes of sunflower oil
> 2 large onions – chopped
> 2 sticks of celery – chopped
> a couple of cloves of garlic – roughly chopped
> 3 tablespoons of masala
> a pinch of cumin
> a pinch of nutmeg
> 3 star anise
> 4 large bay leaves
> a good pinch of aniseed
> a couple of pinches of Maldon salt
> cracked black pepper
> 2 cardamom pods
> 2 red chillies – pips removed and chopped (use more if you like it hot)
> 1.5 kg lamb knuckles
> about 2 cups of water
> 6 large tomatoes – blanched, skinned and quartered
> a splash of apple cider vinegar
> fresh coriander

★ *Serve with ice-cold beer.*

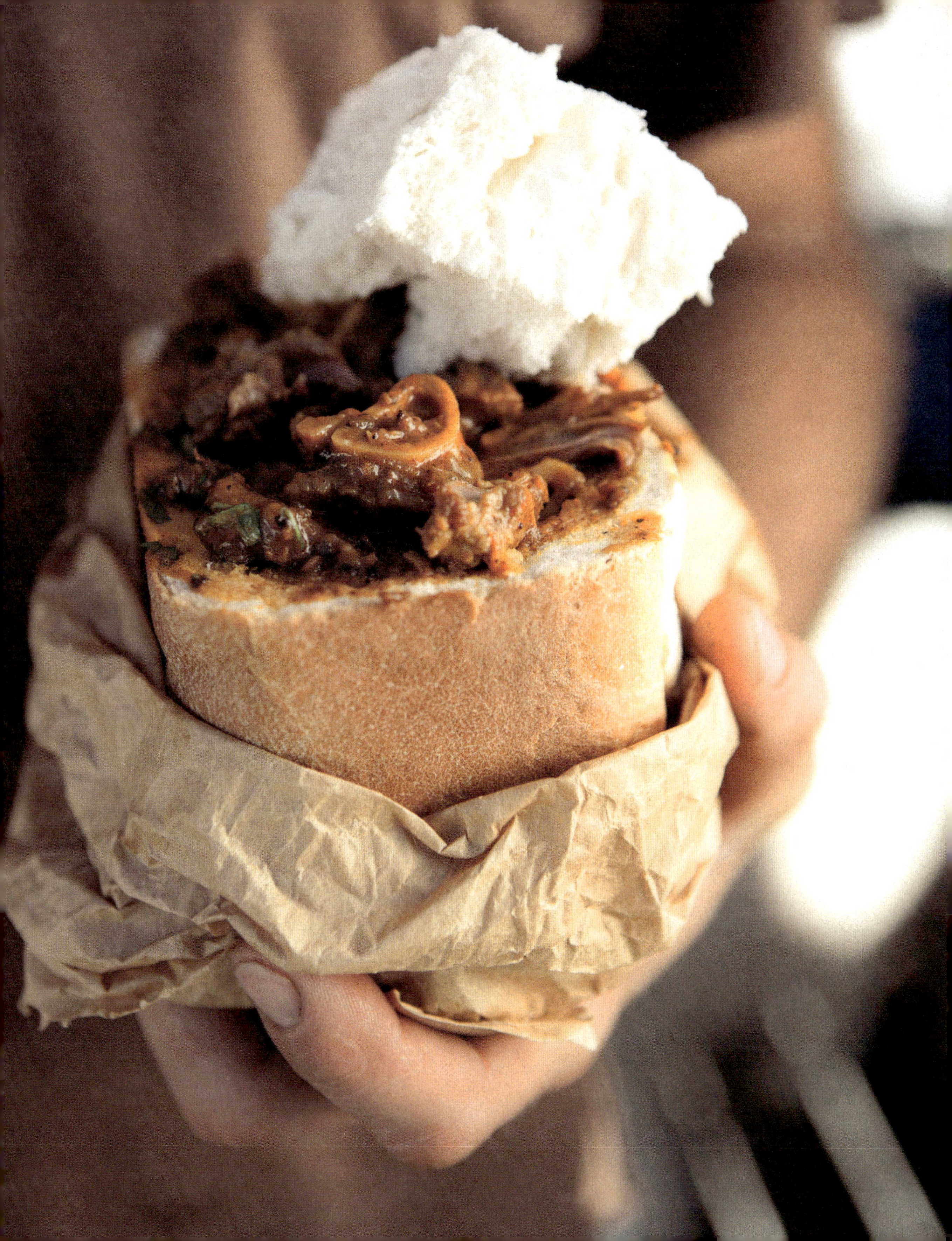

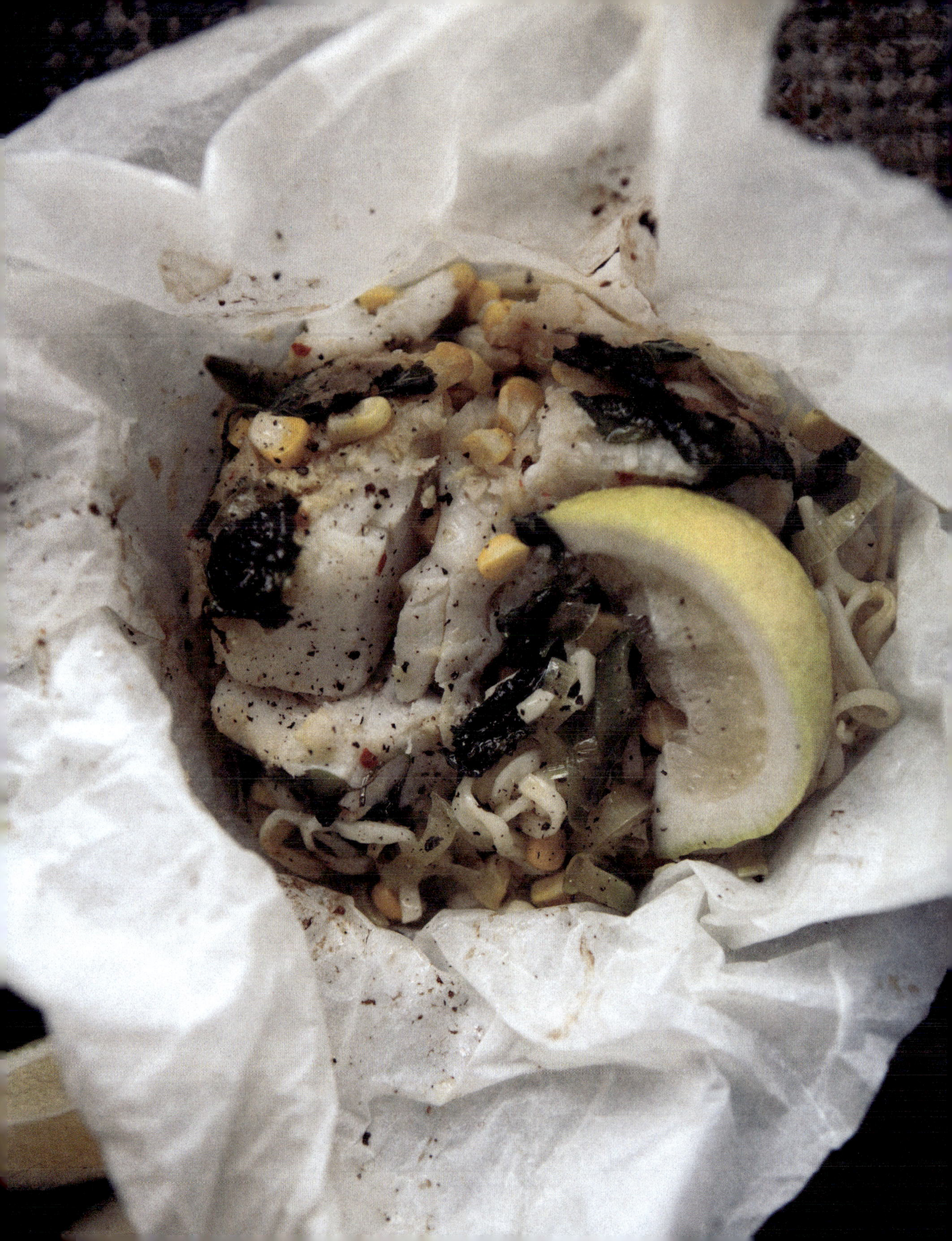

PAPER CHEF
FISH PARCELS

Sometimes I come across the best dishes when I least expect it. On one such occasion, I was sitting in my office (which is right next to the kitchen) and the waft of food came sneaking in, breaking my concentration. Like a bloodhound, I shot up and followed my nose which, surprisingly, took me not to the kitchen, but into the office of my business partner Girdy. There he sat, grinning like a Cheshire cat, opening a paper parcel, layer by layer, eventually to reveal an aromatic explosion of fish on top of pasta. His wife Janet had made it and of course I got my hands on her recipe and gave it a try. Now it's mine and, in turn, yours.

> **EN PAPILLOTE** (*pronounce as if you have a blocked nose: 'aaah poppy yote'*) is French for 'in paper' or 'in parchment'. The first use of cooking en papillote that I could track down dates back to 1818 and then again to 1845, but the story that tickled my fancy was the one where, back in the 1840s, a man named Jules Alciatore allegedly created the first *Pompano En Papillote* in his restaurant in New Orleans to honour a Brazilian hot air balloonist. Apparently the idea was that once the paper envelope started steaming it would blow up, mimicking a hot air balloon. Mine didn't do that, but perhaps I just folded the paper the wrong way . . .

Season the fish fillets with crushed salt and cracked black pepper, and then cover with the marinade. Put it in the fridge for about an hour. When you're happy that the fish have been swimming in the marinade for long enough, take them out of the fridge and get ready to make the parcels.

Put two sheets of baking paper on top of each other then place a handful of the pasta in the centre. Place a couple of cooked leeks on the pasta with the marinated fish on top. Finish off with a small handful of snow peas, mealies off the cob, a squeeze of lemon juice, fresh coriander and mint. Drizzle some of that lekker marinade over everything and twist wrap the parcel to ensure that no steam will escape while it's baking.

Put the parcels directly on to an oven grid and bake for about 15 minutes, which gives you time enough to sit back and enjoy a nice glass of crisp dry white.

★ Janet says you can try the same method with salmon and teriyaki, marinara mixed with tomato and chilli, and sliced up chicken breast. I can't wait to try different ingredients. For me, this is a new way of cooking that I am only just beginning to understand.

★ **Parcel filling:**
- yellowtail or hake fillets (skinned) – use SASSI friendly fish – about the size of a hand
- a handful of cooked fresh pasta
- a couple of sheets of baking paper
- sliced leeks – cooked in a bit of butter
- uncooked snow peas
- fresh mealies – cut off the cob
- a small handful of chopped coriander and fresh mint leaves

★ **For the marinade mix together:**
- about 2 teaspoons of ginger – freshly minced
- 2 cloves of garlic – crushed
- chopped chillies – as many as you can handle
- 4 kaffir lime leaves – shredded
- a generous sprinkle of palm sugar (brown sugar is also fine)
- the rind of 1 lemon – grated
- about a tablespoon of grape seed oil
- a good splash of fish sauce
- sweet chilli sauce to taste

TROUT THREE WAYS

Throwing my line in the water and catching a fish is one of my favourite things in the world. I was lucky enough to grow up fishing in the ocean on the Wild Coast but had never really bothered with trout. For my 25th birthday a couple of my mates gave me a fly fishing rod – thanks, Vince, Graham and Chris! – and took me up to a trout-stocked dam near the Du Toitskloof Pass. There wasn't a catch-and-release policy so whatever we caught, we had to buy. Of course, with my luck I hooked a 5½ kilo monster which cost me an arm and a leg – but, on the upside, it made a lifelong fly fisherman of me. To tell you the truth, though, that trout was possibly one of the worst-tasting fish I have eaten in my life. What I didn't know then was that the flavour of the fish depends entirely on the kind of water it lives in – if it's brown and muddy, it tastes brown and muddy. Up in the highlands of Lesotho I had a revelation: the water is crystal clear and beautiful and the fish tasted beautiful as well.

★ Trout is such a beautiful fish with its delicate rose pink flesh, so you don't want to mess with it too much when cooking it. Just make sure you know where it was caught or you'll have the same mindset I did all those years ago.

THE PURIST

The easiest way of all is to score the fish with a couple of deep cuts, rub it all over with butter, season to taste and whack it in the griddle and braai. No fuss, no other ingredients, and you will be rewarded with all its delicious natural flavours.

★ Remember, never overcook your fish – it's a cardinal sin!

ROLL IT

The second way is to make a tin foil parcel containing the filleted fish with lashings of butter – both inside and outside the fish. Stuff the cavity with some sliced onion and fresh fennel or dill and flat leaf parsley, splash with a good white wine (the same one you are drinking) and sprinkle with salt and pepper to taste.

Seal the tin foil and place the parcel on the coals. Cook it for about 5 minutes, rework the coals and do the other side. It's virtually impossible to overcook the fish this way because all those lekker juices are sealed inside the foil. When it's cooked, open up the parcel and eat directly from it with your fingers, making sure you have plenty of soft fresh bread on hand to mop up all the juiciness.

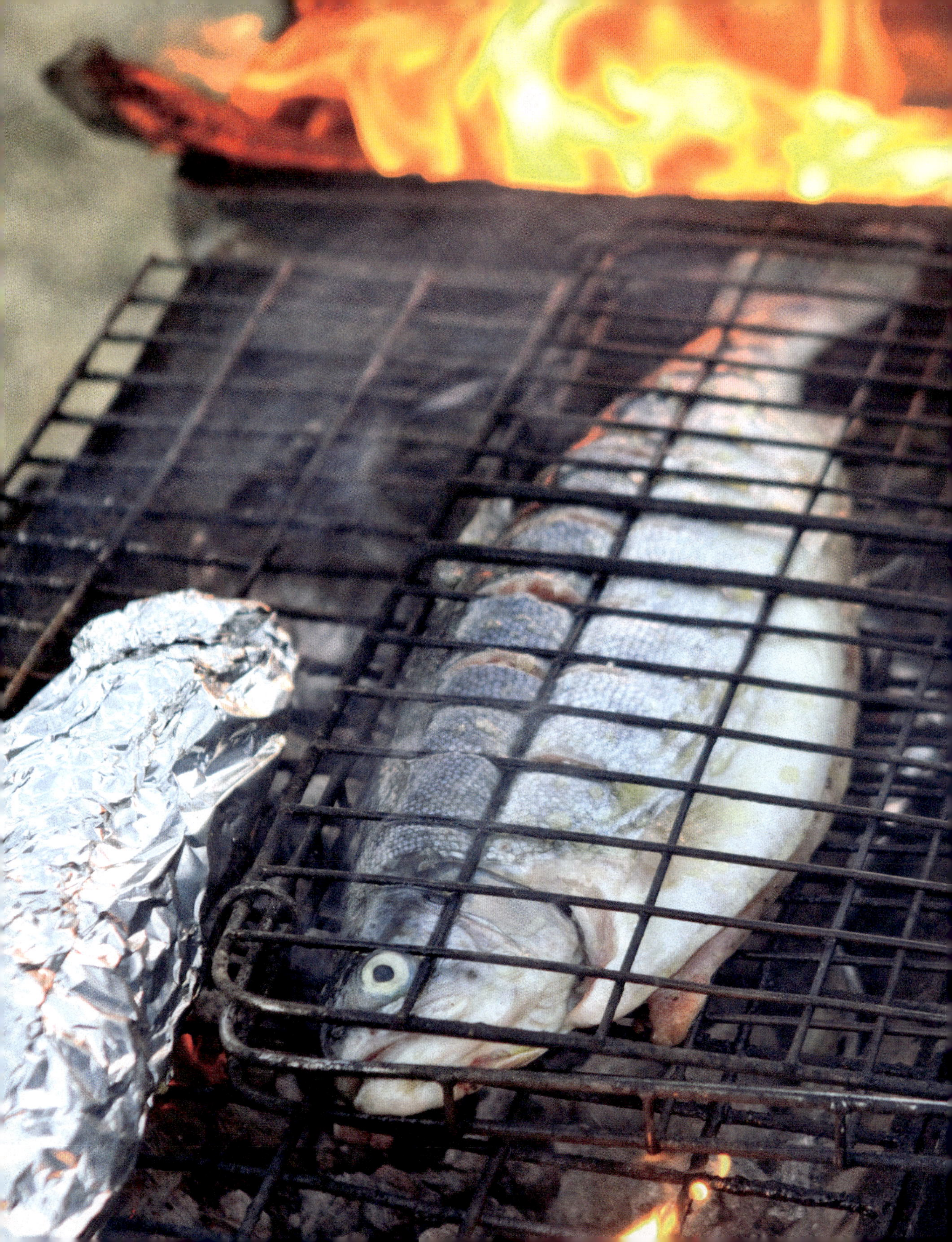

SMOKE IT

★ *To smoke fish, or meat, all you need is a source of heat and a sealable container of some kind, which could be simply a roasting pan covered with tin foil – or you can use the kassie (see page 37).*

Spread a small quantity of wood chips across the bottom of your smoking device. Oak or fruit woods work well with trout, and rooibos tea (instead of wood chips) is my secret weapon. You can get wood chips from most hardware and camping stores, and it will last forever since you use only a small amount each time – about a palmful (I've had the same bag for years).

The important thing to remember when smoking is that the meat or fish must not be wet, but dry and tacky, otherwise all that wonderful smoky flavour goes into the moisture and not the fish. I normally find a handy hook on a wall in a windy place to hang it for half an hour before smoking.

Season the deboned skin-on trout fillets with a little salt and pepper and lay them skin-side down on a wire rack in the smoker. Seal tightly and place over the coals for about 10 or 20 minutes, depending on their size. Serve with a green salad. Yup. That simple.

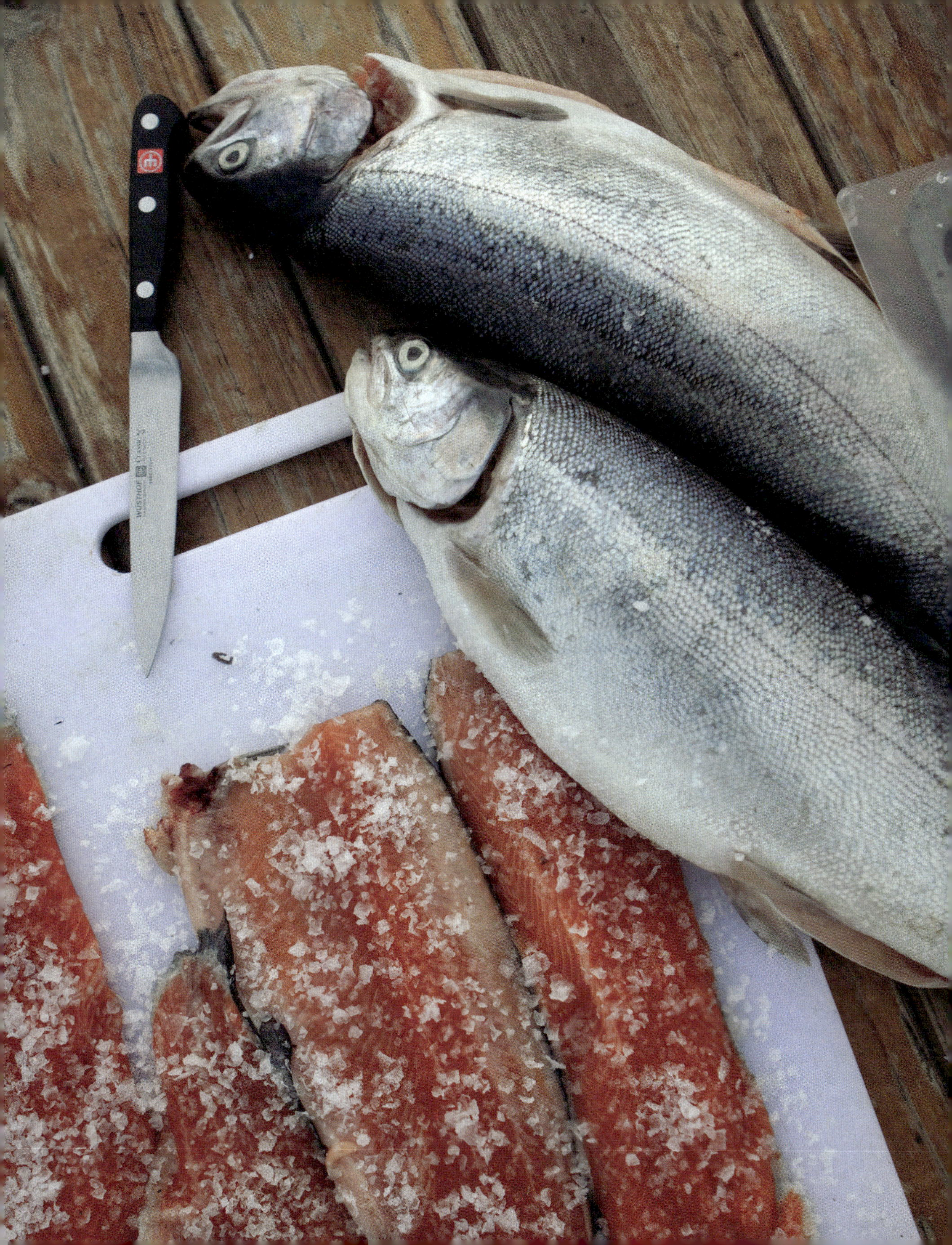

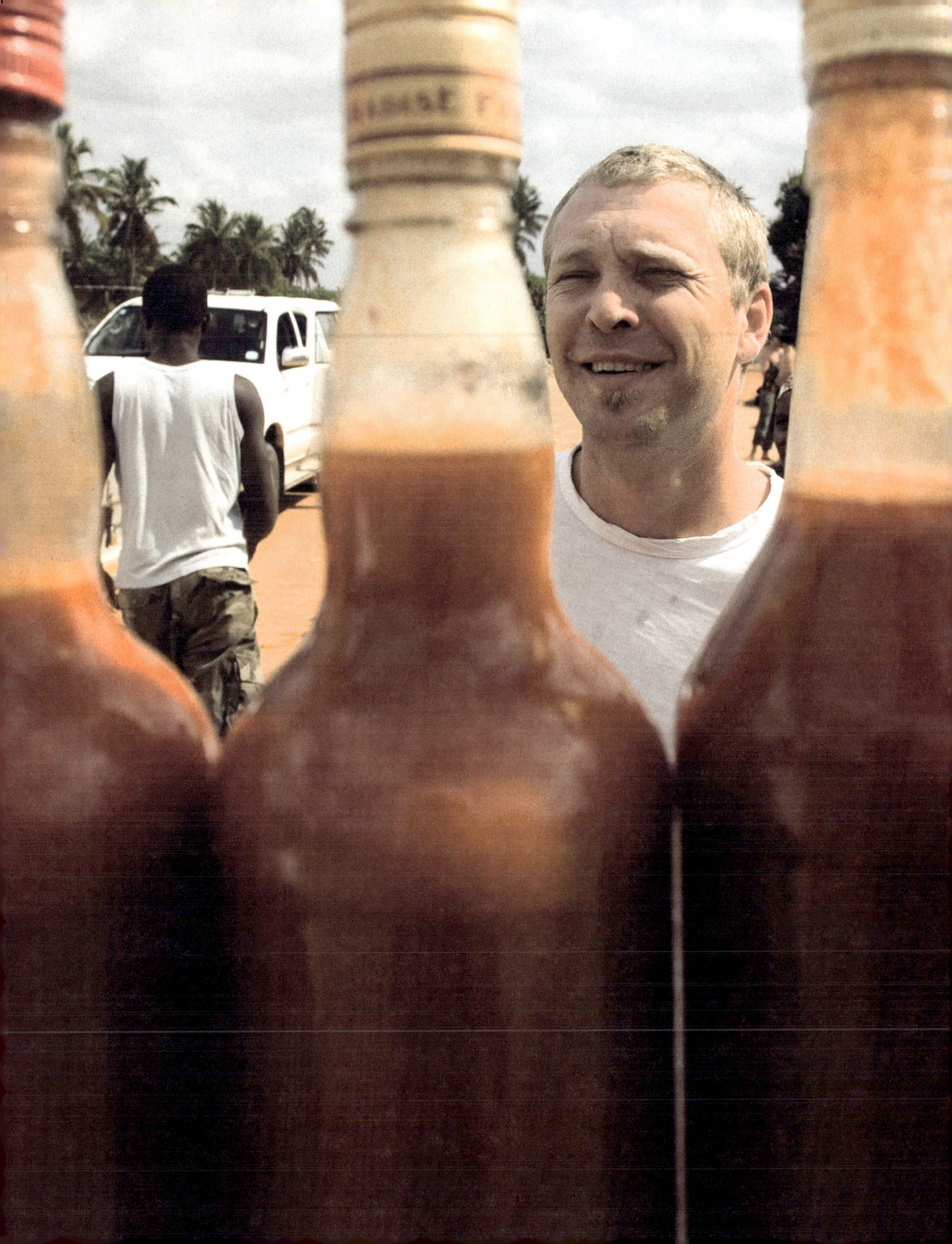

On one of my trips to Mozambique, I had to make an unexpected mission to try and secure lunch. With no supermarkets at my disposal, negotiations took place on the side of the road with locals about whose produce was fresher than fresh. Why? Two of my very good friends – Gareth Beaumont aka the Fish Assassin and Andrew Faber aka Comic Relief – had gone out to see what they could catch. But with them I know it's always good to have a plan B so I headed to the markets to see what was available. I didn't recognise half the stuff there so I knew it was going to be an off-the-cuff cooking experience to work out what I would do. I didn't realise it then but what I was about to make was perfect finger food which has its roots in a Thai dish – I just Africanised it.

CRAB IN PUMPKIN LEAVES

★ Quantities depend on your palate, and the number of hungry friends.

The starting point was a bag full of mangrove crabs. The most difficult part is cleaning them. You have to stick your thumb in under the carapace and pull it off, then remove the guts and lungs. The lungs are called dead man's fingers. When you do it you will see why. Rinse well and put them straight on to the grill over a medium heat until they change from translucent to whitish pink. Don't overcook!

When they're cooked you're going to remove that delicate, sweet, succulent crab meat with your fingers and flake it into a bowl. Get your lazy friends to do this while you get on with the next stage.

Boil a pot of water for the pumpkin leaves. Just about every country in Africa has a version of these staple greens, collectively known as *morogo*. So if you can't get pumpkin leaves, ask around for the local version. Cook them in salted water until soft and pliable. You don't want them to get too *verlep* but, if necessary, you can refresh them in a bowl of iced water. You could also use spinach leaves which taste very similar, but you don't need to boil them.

You'll need:
- fresh crabs, crayfish or any other firm white fish
- pumpkin or spinach leaves
- cashew nuts
- lemons – peeled and sliced into segments
- garlic – peeled and grated
- ginger – ditto
- onions – ditto
- papaya – ditto
- equal quantities of soya sauce and honey

Next, prepare some small bowls of condiments:

Roughly crushed cashew nuts, roughly sliced lemon segments, grated garlic, peeled and grated ginger, peeled and grated papaya and grated onion.

To serve (bit of a fancy word for Moz Finger Food), put a pumpkin leaf on a flat surface, pile on some crab meat and add your choice of condiments. Mix and match and try different combinations. Roll the leaf up tightly and dunk in a dipping sauce of soya and honey. The sweetness of the crab meat bites against the sourness of the lemon, the crunch of the cashews, the sharpness of the garlic and the soya/honey dipping sauce just rounds it off. Try it. It's bloody brilliant.

> **PS** If you can't get crab meat, use crayfish or prawns. Raylene, my erstwhile office wife, once made them for me with rice paper instead of leaves and it was just as good. Just dip the rice paper in water, place it on a drying towel and fill with the goodies.

To finish the story: Gareth and Andrew came back in the dark with no fish. Lucky I went with Plan B.

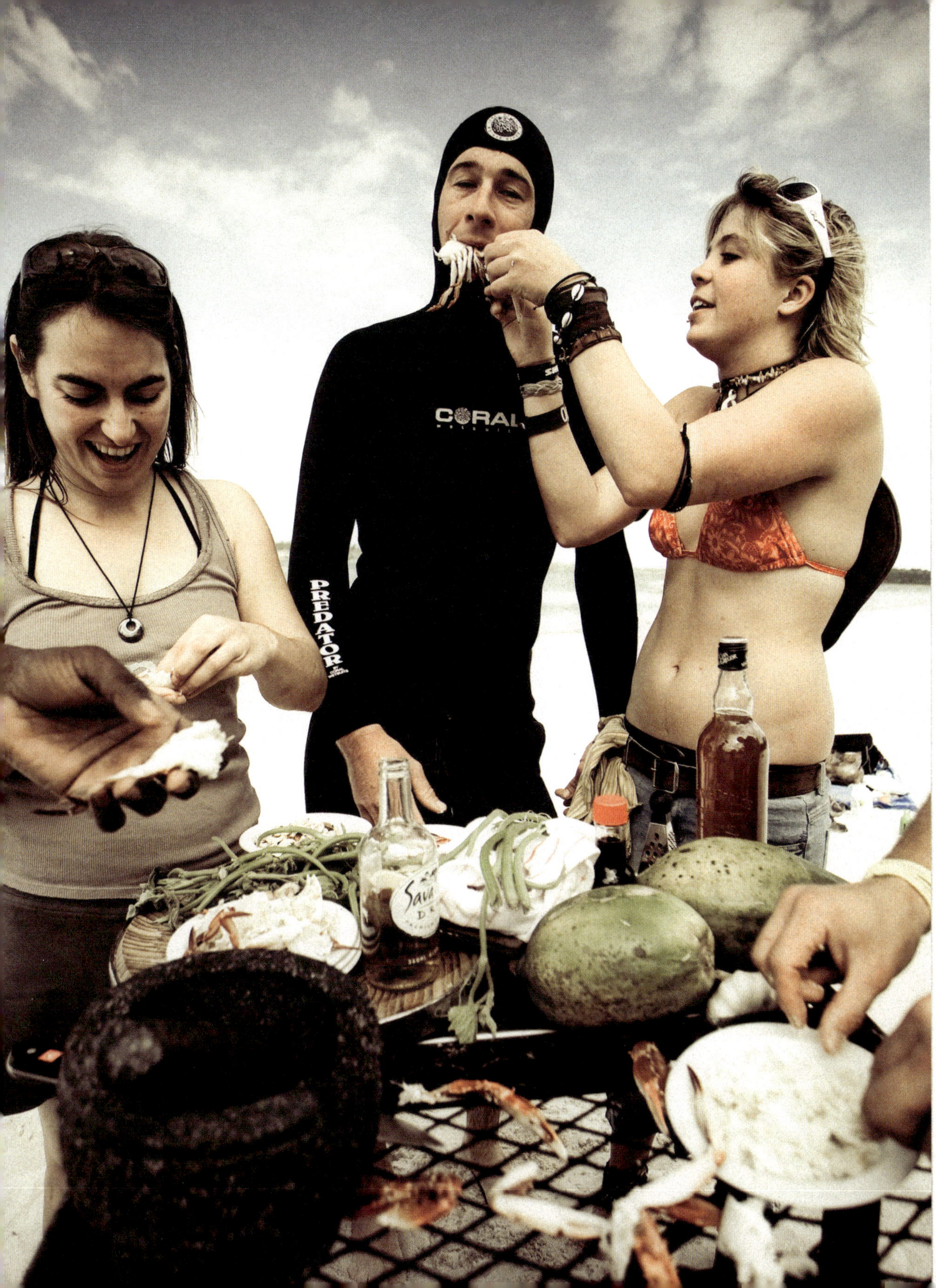
CORAL
PREDATOR

FISH ASSASSIN

COMIC RELIEF

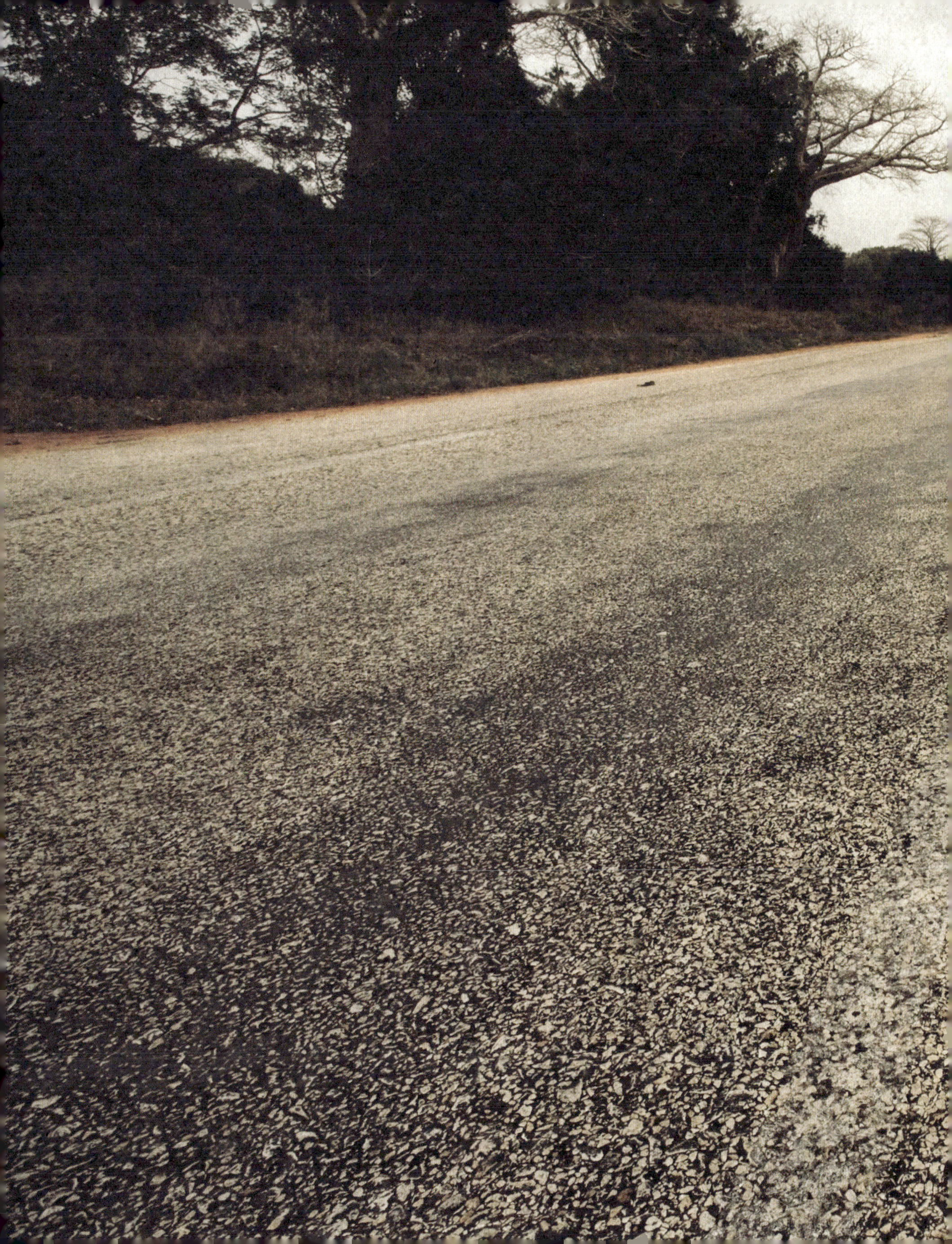

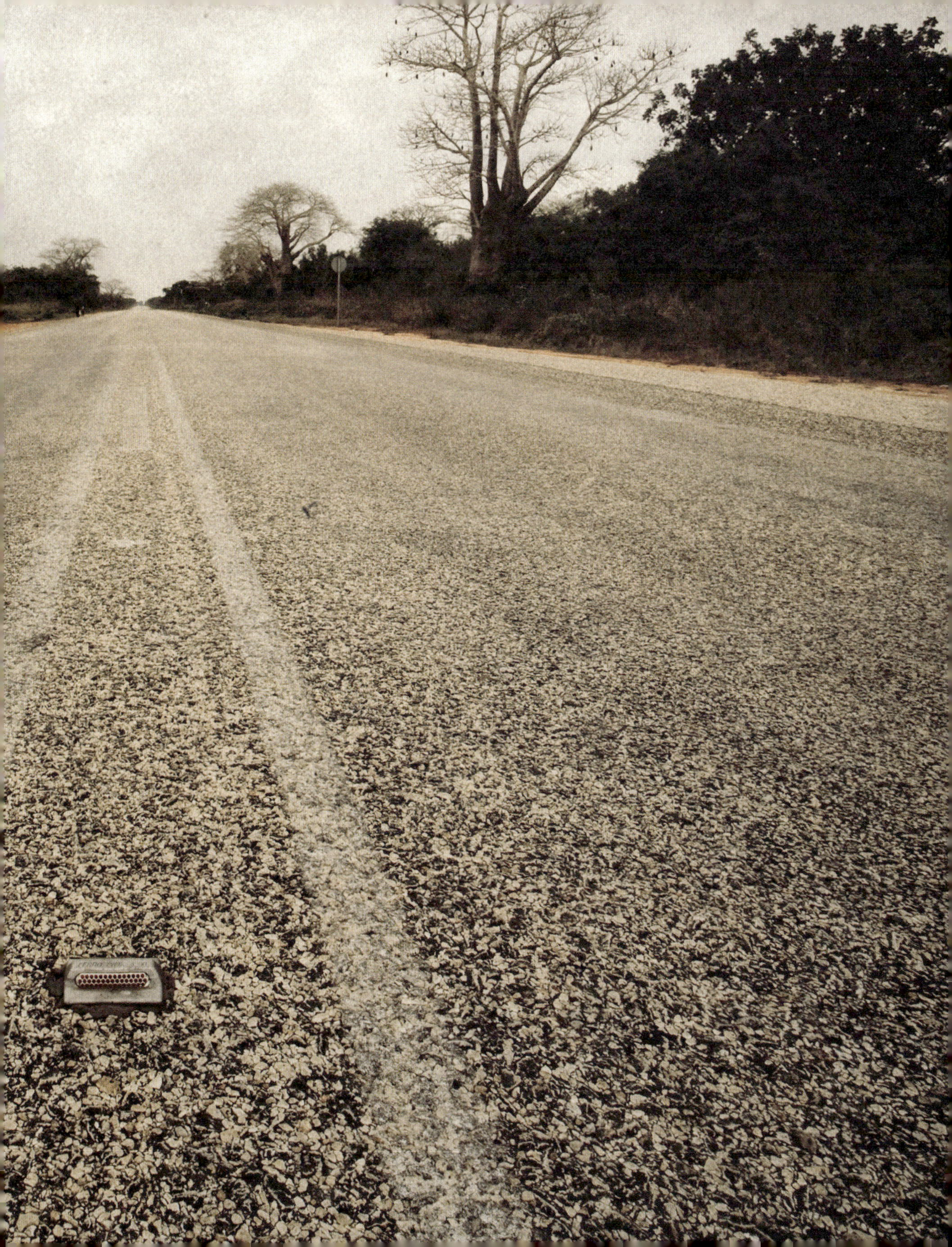

República de Moçambique VISTOS / VISAS

Vist
Pass
Cate
Tipo

Vali
Auto
pelo
em

Assi
Obse

06

RES

PREGO ROLL

Who hasn't had a prego roll from a dodgy takeaway at 4am? Sometimes even a bad one can be good, but the best ones are when the rolls are soft and floury, the thinly sliced fillet steak is perfectly grilled and the peri peri sauce is hot enough to leave that nice tingly burn on your lips for half an hour afterwards. I thought about telling you how to make your own prego roll but after my extensive travels and research I have concluded that this is the perfect recipe and cannot be improved upon.

You will need:
- 1 passport
- 1 car (or a plane ticket)
- a change of underwear and a toothbrush
- a smattering of Portuguese

From Cape Town, South Africa, get yourself to Maputo, Mozambique. If travelling by car, allow three days travel time; by plane – fly to Johannesburg and then allow for lengthy delays for the flight from Joburg to Maputo. Come to think of it, it's probably quicker to drive. From Maputo, catch a crab-walking overloaded bus to Xai Xai, and then onwards to Inhambane, remembering to buy *padkos* for the hair-raising trip. From there, organise a taxi to Tofo – but negotiate before you get in or be prepared to pay tourist rates.

When you get there

Look for Fatima's backpackers and tell her I say hi, or stay at the Bamboozi Lodge and say hi to Paul and Cindy. Get up early the next morning and make your way to the Inhambane market and feel up the fresh produce. Everything from organic tomoatoes, bananas, lettuce, and so on. If you're feeling brave, I dare you to try the hot devil sauce!

With your back to the stalls, turn right, left, then left again. On the right hand side of the road you will find a small restaurant called Ponta Final. Sit down. Order a beer, then order a prego roll. Drink the beer, saving a little to wash down the prego roll. One promise. When you sink your teeth into that juicy perfectly rare fire-stripping inferno, you'll know that it's the best one you will ever eat – simple and delicious.

> ★ Please bear in mind that it's a roll and a piece of perfectly grilled steak with no trimmings other than a side of peri peri sauce that's about 11 on a scale of 1 to 10. It takes a while to be served so sit back, relax with an ice cold beer or two and watch the world go by.

SIMPLE PORTUGUESE WORDS

BOM DIA!
HELLO!/GOOD MORNING!

COMPREENDE?
DO YOU UNDERSTAND?

(NÃO) COMPREENDO
I (DON'T) UNDERSTAND

BOA TARDE!
GOOD AFTERNOON!

BOA NOITE!
GOOD EVENING!
GOOD NIGHT!

O QUE É ISTO?
WHAT IS THAT?

OI/OLÁ! | HI!
TCHAU! | BYE!

ADEUS
GOODBYE

POR FAVOR
PLEASE

VAMOS! LET'S GO!

INFORMAL
COMO VAI?
HOW ARE YOU?

ESTOU COM FOME/SÊDE
I'M HUNGRY/THIRSTY

PODE ME AJUDAR?
CAN YOU HELP ME?

BEM/MUITO BEM
GOOD/VERY GOOD

COMO SE DIZ
....
EM PORTUGUÊS?
HOW DO YOU SAY
....
IN PORTUGUESE?

QUANTO?
HOW MUCH?

MAL/MUITO MAL/
MAIS OU MENOS
BAD/VERY BAD/
MORE OR LESS

COMO?
WHAT?
PARDON ME?

VOCÊ FALA INGLÊS?
DO YOU SPEAK ENGLISH?
INFORMAL
(NÃO) FALO...
I (DON'T) SPEAK...

DE ONDE VOCÊ É?
INFORMAL
WHERE ARE YOU FROM?
EU SOU DE...
I'M FROM...

ONDE ESTÁ...?
WHERE IS...?
ONDE ESTÃO...?
WHERE ARE...?

MUITO
OBRIGADO
THANK YOU
VERY MUCH

BEM-VINDO
— WELCOME —

NÃO HÁ DE QUÊ
YOU'RE WELCOME

COM LICENCE
EXCUSE ME

PERDÃO
PARDON

SIM
YES
NÃO
NO

DESCULPE-ME
I'M SORRY

SENHOR
SENHORA
SENHORITA

QUAL É O SEU NOME?
WHAT IS YOUR NAME?

ME CHAMO...
MY NAME IS...

PRAZER EM CONHECÊ-LO
NICE TO MEET YOU

MISTER
MRS
MISS

CHICKEN IN CRUSTY BREAD

★ PASS (ON) THE SALT

A while back I travelled to Bazaruto Lodge in Mozambique by boat via Vilanculos. It's one of my favourite ways to travel because it feels like you're driving at 120 kpm with your head stuck out the window. Life doesn't get any better than that! I had been cooking fish for 3 weeks on end, so when I got to cook a chicken with a twist I was stoked. And, later, I was mortified. You see, 3 things stand out in my memory of this trip. One, catching my first fish on camera; two, spotting a girl in a teeny weeny yellow polka dot bikini; and three, that damn oversalted chicken. The great thing about this catastrophe was that I realised what great friends I have – they'll eat anything I make, even when eating it was equivalent to licking a saltpan. Here's the right way to make this great dish.

★ Make your basic bread dough (see page 45) and let it rest while you prep your chicken.

★ Make a herb rub by mixing butter, tarragon, a decent squeeze of lemon, some cracked black pepper, a pinch or two of salt and about three cloves of crushed garlic. Separate the skin from the body of the chicken and, using your hands, rub the herb butter underneath the skin. Slice up a lemon and stick it into the cavity of the chicken. If you want to add a little bite, rub some piri-piri sauce on to the skin.

★ When your dough is ready, roll it out into a flat circle a little thicker than a pizza base (about 1 cm). Sprinkle flour on a baking tray and place the pizza-like dough wheel on this. Place your chicken on top of the dough and wrap your chicken in it. Make sure there are no holes in the dough – you want it to be airtight.

★ Slide the chicken into the oven (preheated) at 180°C for 60 to 90 minutes. It's almost impossible to overcook this chicken. The bread seals in all the juices, keeping the chicken moist. My advice is to cook it for a while longer than you would cook a normal chicken roast. After about an hour and a half, the bread should be crispy and brown. Stab a skewer into the chicken (breast side) and leave it for about 30 seconds. If the skewer comes out piping hot, chances are the chicken is ready. If the skewer is cool to the touch, cook a little longer. Serve with roast potatoes and root vegetables.

You'll need:
> basic bread dough
> 1 free-range chicken – innards removed
> butter
> tarragon
> lemons
> black pepper
> pinch of Maldon salt
> crushed garlic
> Portuguese piri-piri sauce (optional)

★ The beauty of this chicken is that it literally falls off the bones and when you crack it open, you also get to eat the bread soaked in all those delicious juices.

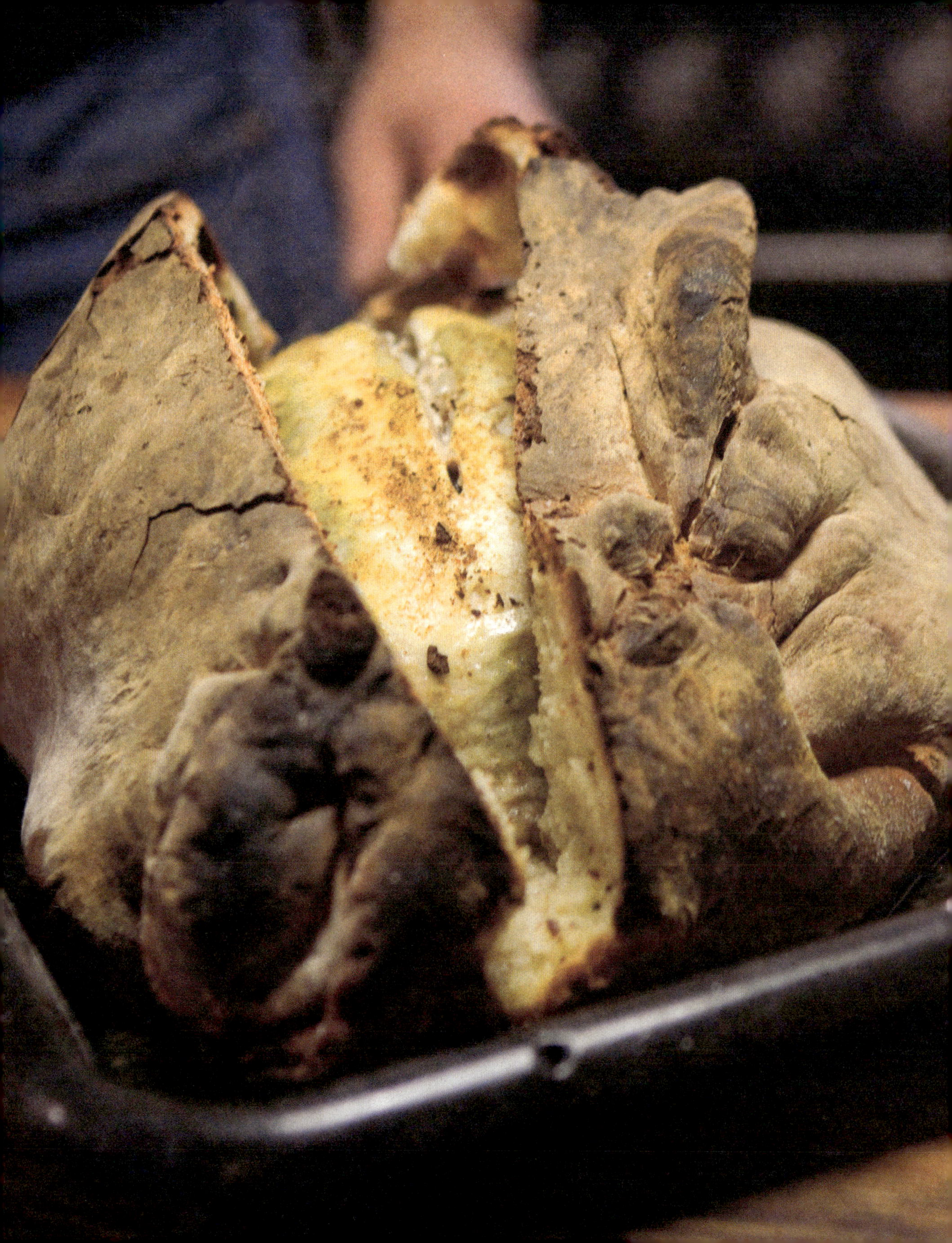

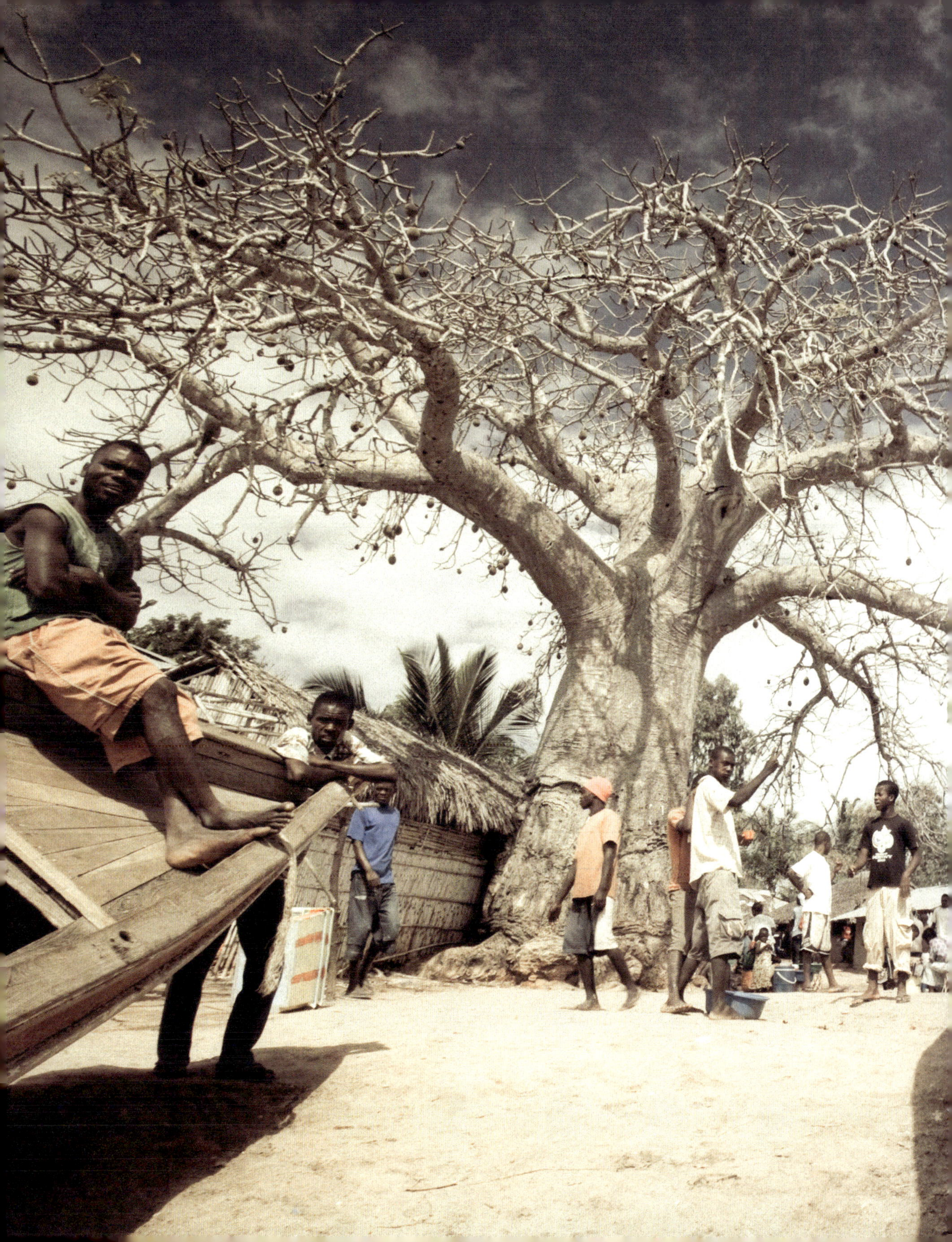

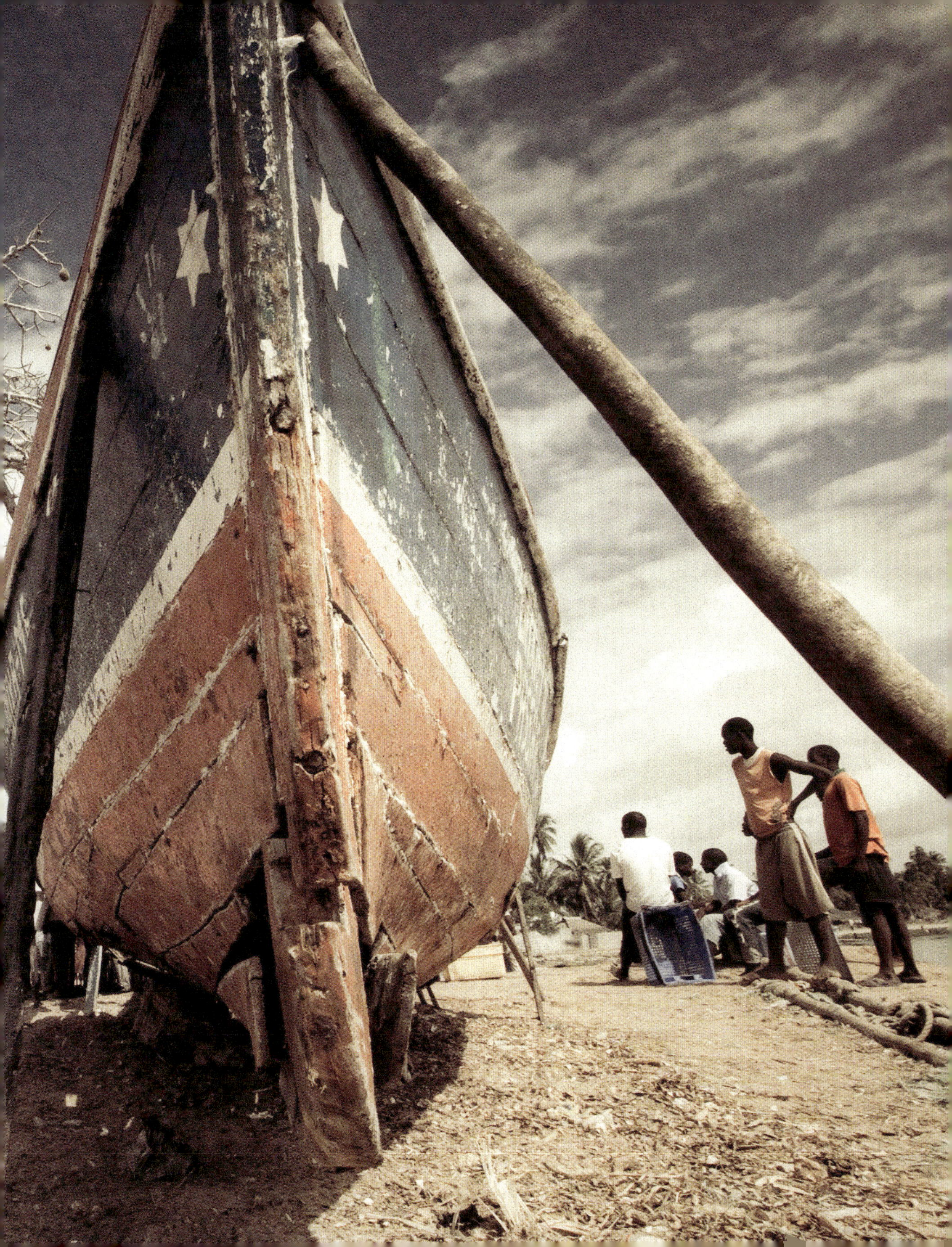

LULA IN ÁGUA NEGRA

I've always said I'm a cook, not a chef, so it was an honour to be asked to teach Bernardo, the head chef at the resort we were staying at in Mozambique, to cook a dish. Lula, or calamari, is available in abundance and wherever I go I try to eat foods that are locally fished, farmed, grown or produced. We can all make a difference if we do the same. And it doesn't matter whether we're in Cape Town, London or Vilanculos, Mozambique.

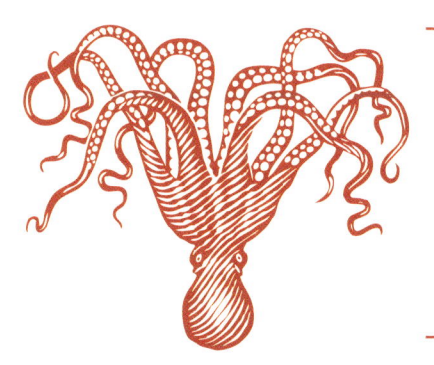

Lula is a great creature and you can use every bit of it once it's been cleaned; you can even save the ink for colouring pasta or rice. Or each other's faces, if you are so inclined. PS: You can also make this dish with octopus.

For this recipe I used the tentacles – not the prettiest part of a creature which is not particularly attractive to begin with (I often call them seafarer condoms) but, hey, it tastes damn good so best you get past its appearance.

Rinse them properly in case they're sandy (the ones I had in Mozambique had sand on them and although I'm up for crunchy, geological crunchy is not to die for). Take deep bread tins – the ones you would use to make a good old government loaf – and add the tentacles, origanum (fresh is best but you can use dried), parsley, some crushed garlic, the zest of a lemon and crushed black pepper.

Now you're going to need a LOT of olive oil, enough to completely submerge the tentacles. Cover with baking paper, press down with another tin, weight it down with bricks, and pop in the oven for about 2 to 3 hours at 175°C or until a taste test has a perfectly tender outcome.

★ SWEET TOMATO SAUCE

While the lula is cooking, make the accompanying sauce because it's going to take about the same amount of time. Slice fat ripe tomatoes in half and place cut side up in a roasting tray. Give them a good seasoning of salt and pepper, drizzle with olive oil and cover with tin foil. They go in the oven at the same time as the calamari, for about an hour or until soft, juicy and sweet. When they're done, pour off all the liquid from the roasting tray into a container and keep it to one side. Push the tomato flesh through a sieve. Place it in a pot with that delicious cooking liquid and reduce by half over a low heat until the sauce is nice and thick. By that time the lula should be perfectly cooked.

Take the lula out of the oil, pour over the sweet tomato sauce, garnish with fresh basil leaves and serve with lemon wedges and thick slices of fresh bread to mop up the sauce. *Lekker*.

You'll need:
- lula tentacles
- fresh origanum
- parsley
- crushed garlic
- zest of 1 lemon
- crushed black pepper
- olive oil
- tomatoes
- fresh basil leaves
- lemon wedges

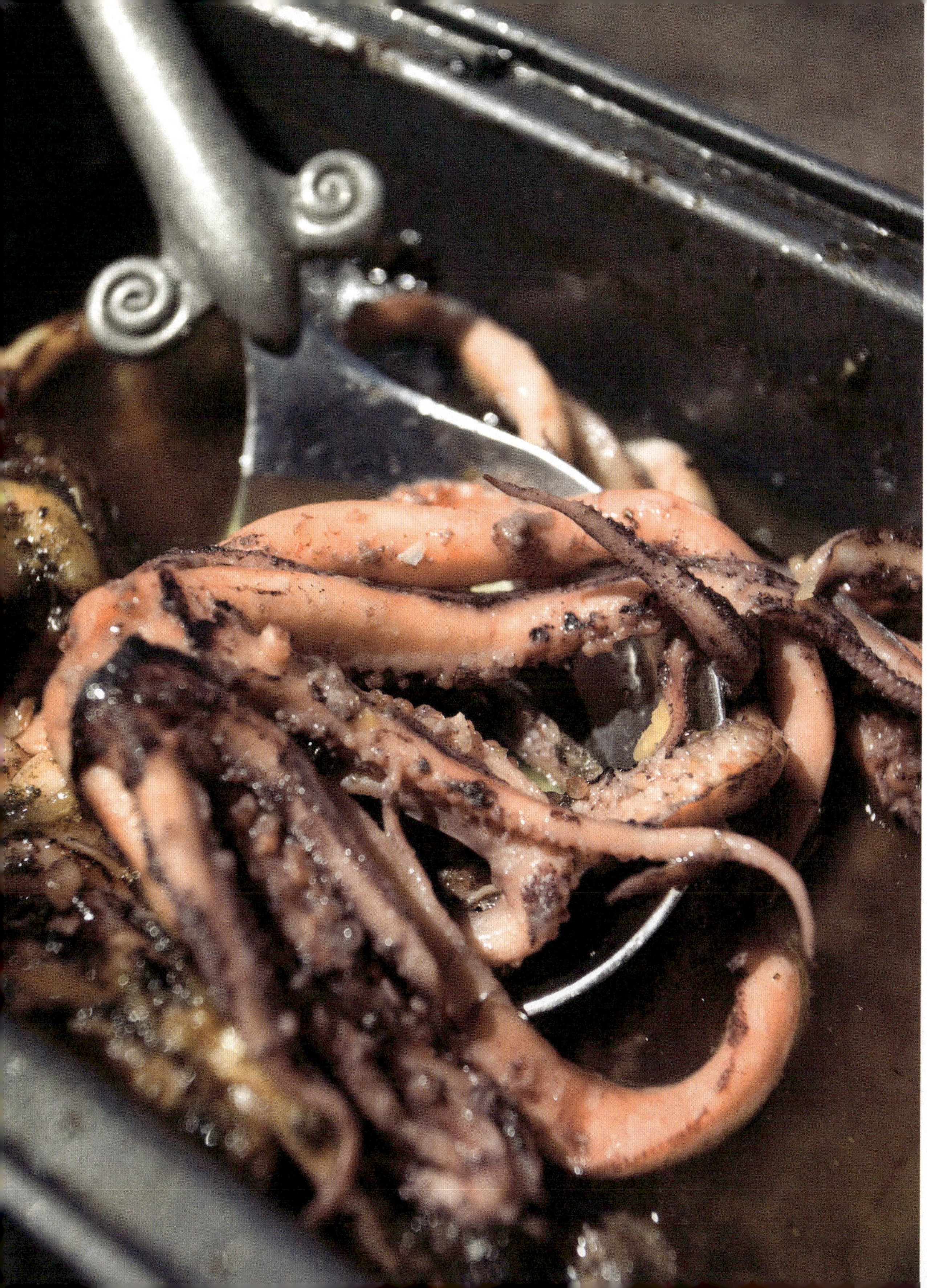

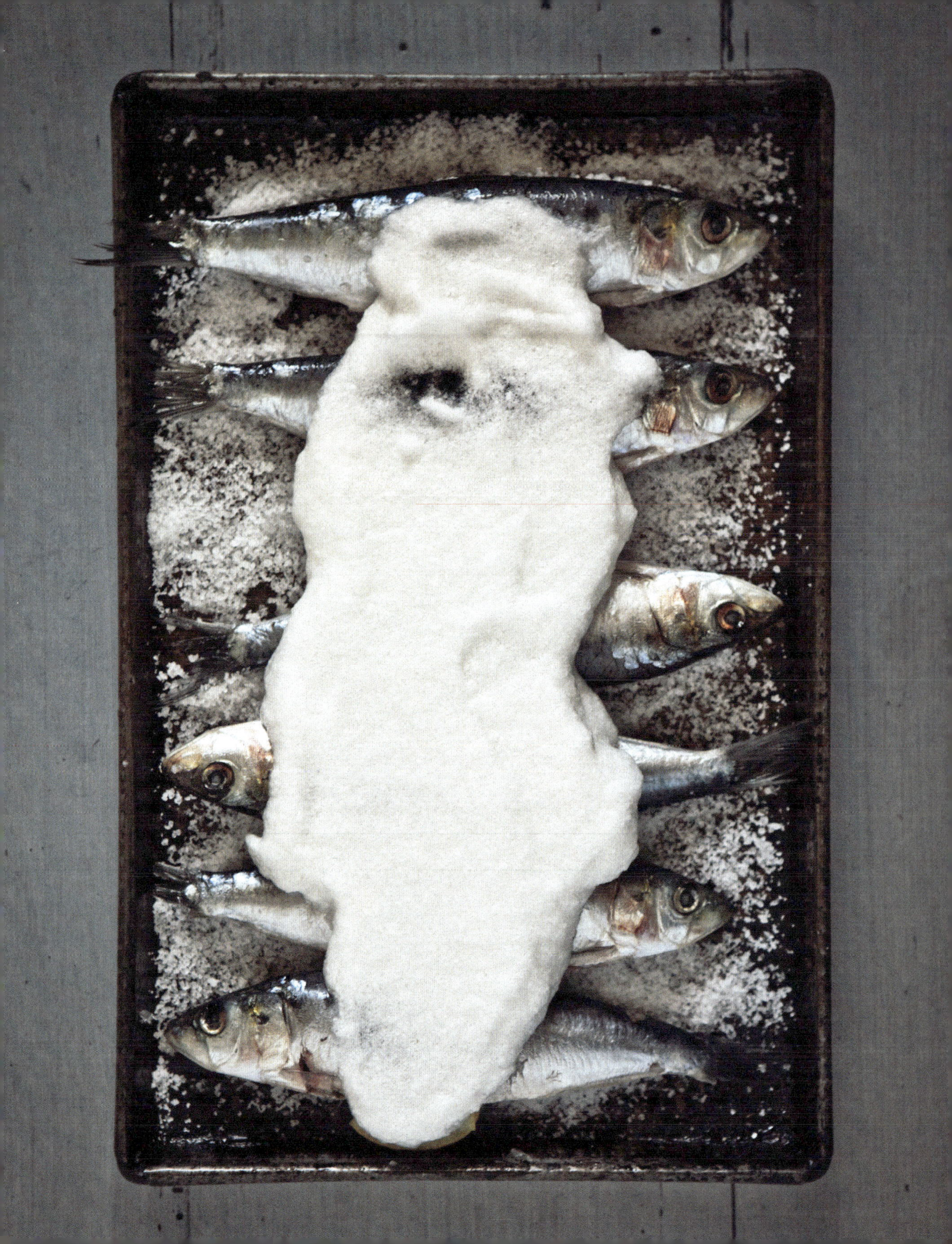

FRESH SARDINES BAKED IN SALT

You would think that a fish baked in a salt crust would leave you with a very dry mouth, but it doesn't. The trick is that the skin on the fish protects the actual flesh and what you're left with is really lekker and tender fish.

The Crust

In a large bowl whisk the egg whites and water until foamy, then add the salt and mix together with your hands. The idea is that the egg should just lubricate the salt. Set aside.

The Fish

Ask the fishmonger to gut the sardines, unless you know how to do it yourself. Rinse the sardines and pat dry with paper towel. Leave the head on (unless you can't face a fish eyeing you) and stuff the cavity with lemon slices.

Sprinkle a layer of salt on the bottom of a baking tray (it should cover the tray completely). Place the sardines on top and cover them with the salt and egg mixture using your hands to smooth it down and make sure it's sealed all round (about 2 cm thick). Put the baking tray in a preheated oven at 180°C and bake until the salt crust turns rock hard and brown (about 25-30 minutes).

For the Crust:
> 2 kg coarse sea salt
> 2 egg whites
> a splash of water

For the Fish:
> sardines – use as many as you like
> lemon – sliced

It may sound strange, but the beauty of cooking fish this way is that the salt-egg mixture becomes like a little self-contained oven. Once cooked, take a heavy object (like a mallet) and break open the salt crust. You'll notice the skin has become really crisp. Peel it away carefully and remove the flesh. The trick here is not to get any of the salt on to the fish, but I'll let you figure out how to do that. Place on a serving dish, drizzle with olive oil, cracked black pepper and a squeeze of lemon.

★ Sardines and tomatoes work well together. Try making the dipping sauce on page 116.

You don't have to stick to sardines. If you want to use a whole fish like yellow tail or mackerel, stuff it with your choice of herbs, lemon and black pepper before covering it in the salt mixture.

FRUITY PANCAKE MOUNTAIN

Building a pancake mountain is a labour of breakfast love (or a decadent midnight feast) but when you have hungry hung-over wolves eyeing you out, it's best you just get on with it.

First up, make a batch of pancake batter. I've never used a blender and prefer making it by hand. Put the flour, sugar and sunflower oil into a mixing bowl, make a well in the centre and then crack the eggs into the well. Next, using a wooden spoon, mix it together until you have a yellow sticky dough. It takes some PT!

Next, you're going to start adding your milk, bit by bit. Every time you add milk, mix it into the dough thoroughly. When it's fully absorbed, add a little more milk. And so on and so forth. When it is just a little thinner than syrup, your batter is ready.

> ★ I always use my old heirloom cast iron crêpe pan – it's the one my late gran gave me when I was seven and I used it to make my first pancake more than 30 years ago. After years of wear and tear it's no longer non-stick. The trick is to salt it, and this works with most worn-out pans. Sprinkle fine salt into the pan until the bottom is completely covered, then put it on a hot stove and leave it until the salt browns. Remove the pan from the heat and wipe the salt off with a paper towel, then grease it with butter and wipe it again.

For the batter, you'll need:
- 4 cups of flour
- 1/2 cup of sugar
- drizzle of sunflower oil
- 4-5 free-range/organic eggs
- milk, about a litre

For the filling:
- bananas
- strawberries
- apples
- brown sugar
- cinnamon
- whipped cream
- organic golden syrup
- lemon juice and whatever else tickles your taste buds

Now you're ready to make pancakes. Put the pan on a medium heat, take about half a ladle of batter, pour it into the pan and, rolling your wrist, spread the batter thinly all over the pan. When it's cooked through, flip and brown the virginal side. Remove and keep to one side. Repeat until all the batter is used – however, keep greasing and wiping the pan in between pancakes.

Slice the strawberries and toss in a teaspoon or two of balsamic vinegar. The balsamic draws out the flavour of the strawberries and makes a really s(ch)weeeet syrup. I do this filling first to let it draw while I make the rest of the fillings.

Slice the apples with a potato peeler, and toss in a couple of drops of lemon juice (to stop them from turning brown). Slice the bananas into nice thin rounds.

The rest is really kids' play. Think of it as building a pancake stack. Place one pancake down, place whatever filling you would like on it, then place another pancake on top of this layer, and repeat – pancake, filling, pancake, filling – until you have no pancakes left. Drizzle the top layer with loads of cream and syrup and eat in big wedges with your favourite tea or coffee. It's just as messy to eat as it is to make!

PS ★ I like to alternate layers of strawberries and cream with layers of apple and cinnamon, layers of bananas and cream and layers of just plain old brown sugar and cinnamon with a twist of lemon juice. Occasionally, I also roll up 5-6 pancakes with fillings, and use them as a layer. The trick is to keep the fruit layers as thin as possible so that you don't end up with a pancake mountain that collapses halfway through the job. The whipped cream also acts as a glue of sorts, so don't be shy.
★ One last tip: works best if you use a pan with a diameter of about 20cm.

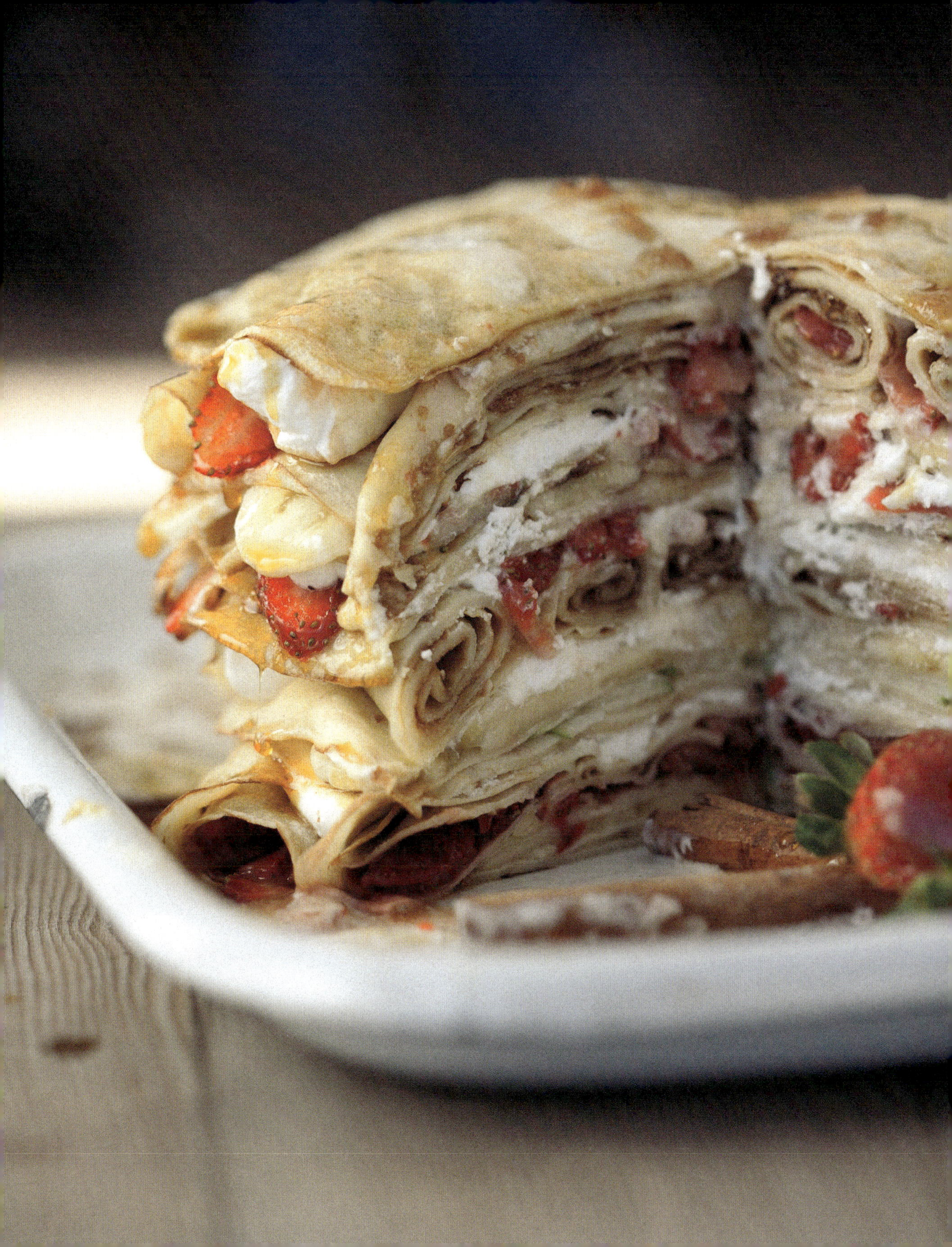

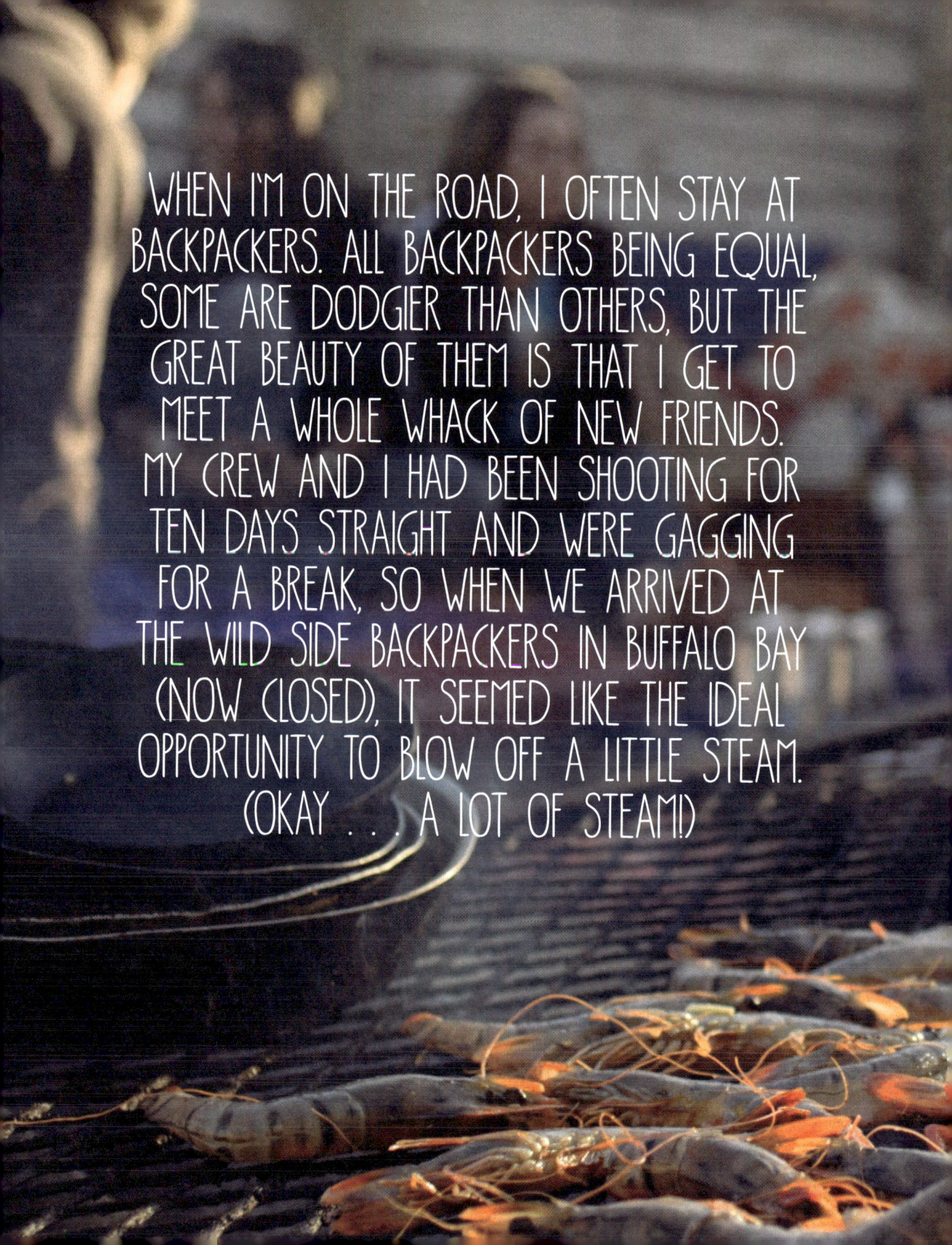

When I'm on the road, I often stay at backpackers. All backpackers being equal, some are dodgier than others, but the great beauty of them is that I get to meet a whole whack of new friends. My crew and I had been shooting for ten days straight and were gagging for a break, so when we arrived at the Wild Side Backpackers in Buffalo Bay (now closed), it seemed like the ideal opportunity to blow off a little steam. (Okay . . . a lot of steam!)

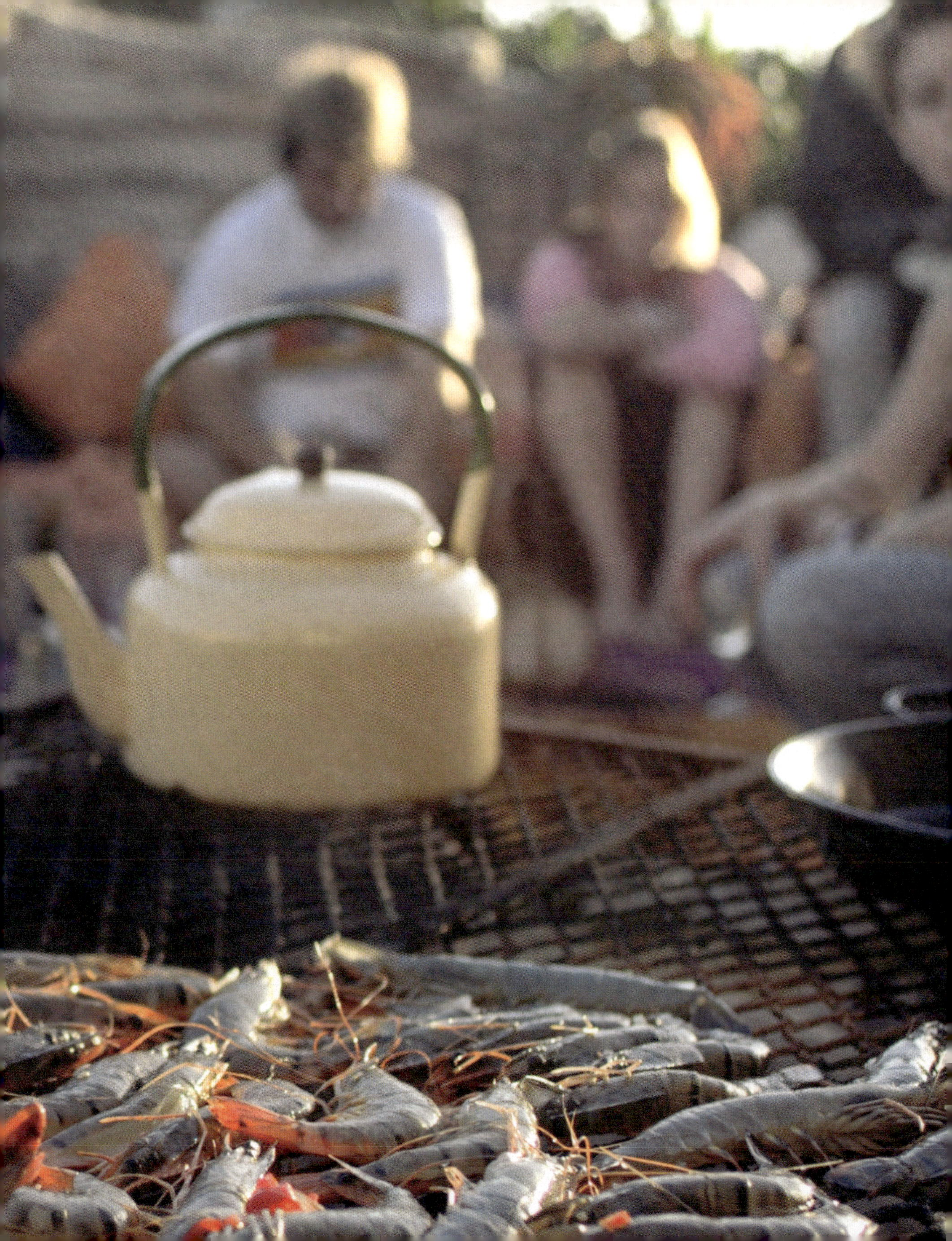

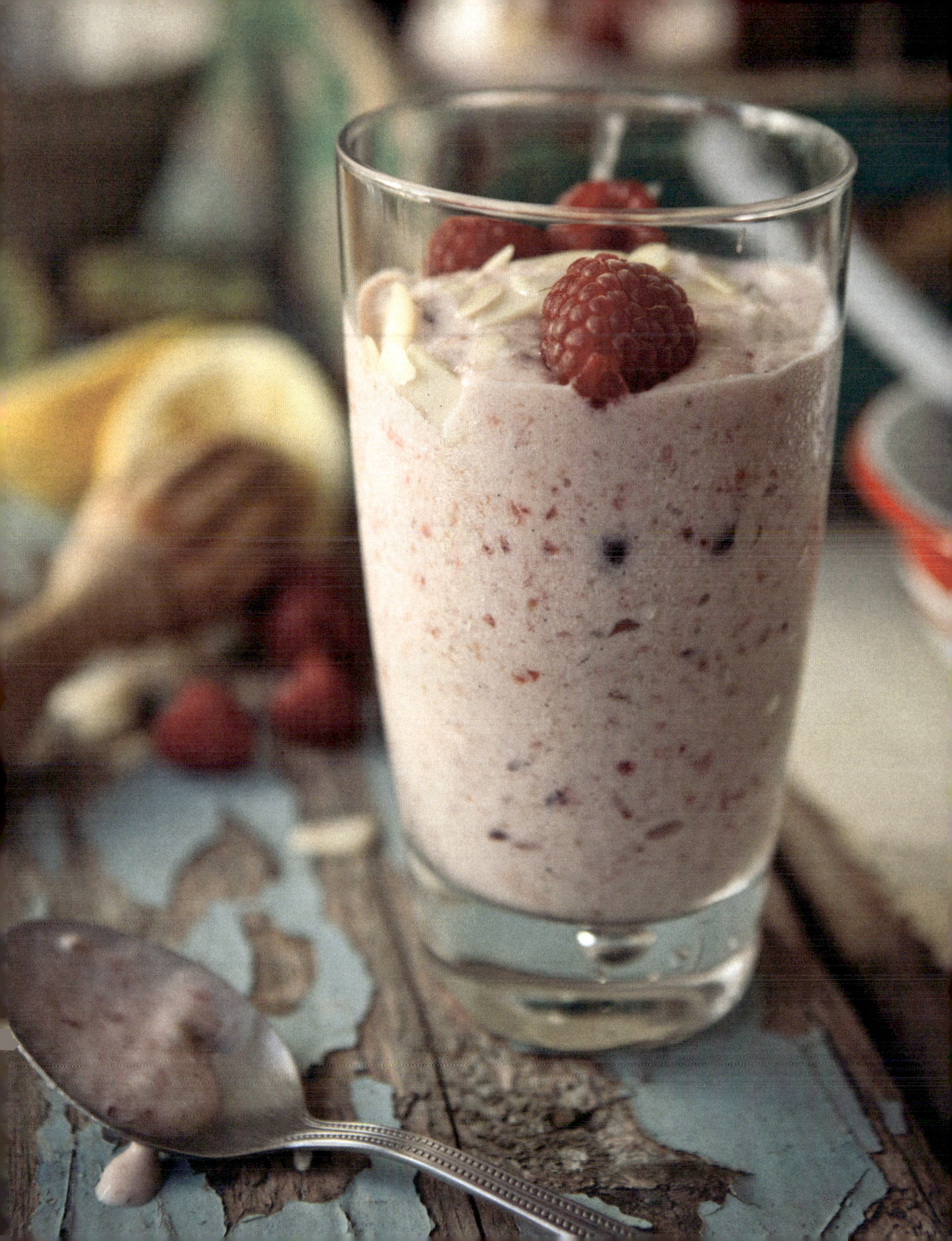

WILD CHILD SMOOTHIES

After a really noisy, somewhat blurry and mostly forgotten-about night, I woke up to a bunch of red-eyed zombies cracking jokes and beers in a desperate attempt to rekindle the fire of the night before. Being a saint (and probably still sozzled) I decided to save us all from any further damage and make the ultimate hangover breakfast. You might be thinking that I jumped in my car and raced to the nearest shop to get my hands on as much greasy junk and red ambulances as I possibly could, but you'd be wrong. What I did was make smoothies with as much fruit and punch to fill all our dietary requirements – a great alternative to junk food, especially after abusing your body on a raucous night out. I promise you, it might not feel so at the time, but a whole lot of fresh stuff will really sort you out.

Once you're able to stand up on your shaky legs without falling over, go scrounge for:

> Greek yoghurt
> fresh juice – the sweeter the better, so don't get something like grapefruit
> blueberries
> gooseberries
> pomegranates
> melon
> bananas
> peanut butter
> honey
> almonds
> vanilla ice cream

Pomegranates are as delicious as they are messy. To remove the seeds easily, roll the fruit around on a flat surface with the palm of your hand before slicing it in half. You'll hear it snap, crackle and pop – a good sign that the seeds are loosening up.

Smoothie Trio

★ BLUEBERRY & POMEGRANATE
★ GOOSEBERRY, BANANA & MELON
★ PEANUT BUTTER, HONEY & VANILLA ICE CREAM SPRINKLED WITH ALMONDS

Grab the ingredients for whichever smoothie you think you can stomach and plonk it into the blender along with a splash of fruit juice and a couple of scoops of yoghurt. If you're having the peanut butter smoothie, add a scoop of ice cream before blending. (Remember to put the lid on.) Blend. Pour. Down!

It takes some time to kick in, so when you've gulped it all down, go *dos* until the room stops spinning. When you wake up, you should feel a lot better. If you don't, it's probably time for the hair of the dog.

--- **THE HAIR OF THE DOG THAT BIT YOU** ---

Here's a scary (scientific) fact: Part of the reason you're feeling hungover is because you're suffering from alcohol poisoning withdrawal, so the best way to cure yourself, is by topping up. Pour a generous splash of vodka into a glass. Top with tomato juice. Add a good dash of Tabasco, salt and pepper. Chuck in a celery stalk, a squeeze of lemon and stir. Drink.

★ CHAPT

PARK

ER 04 ★

OFF

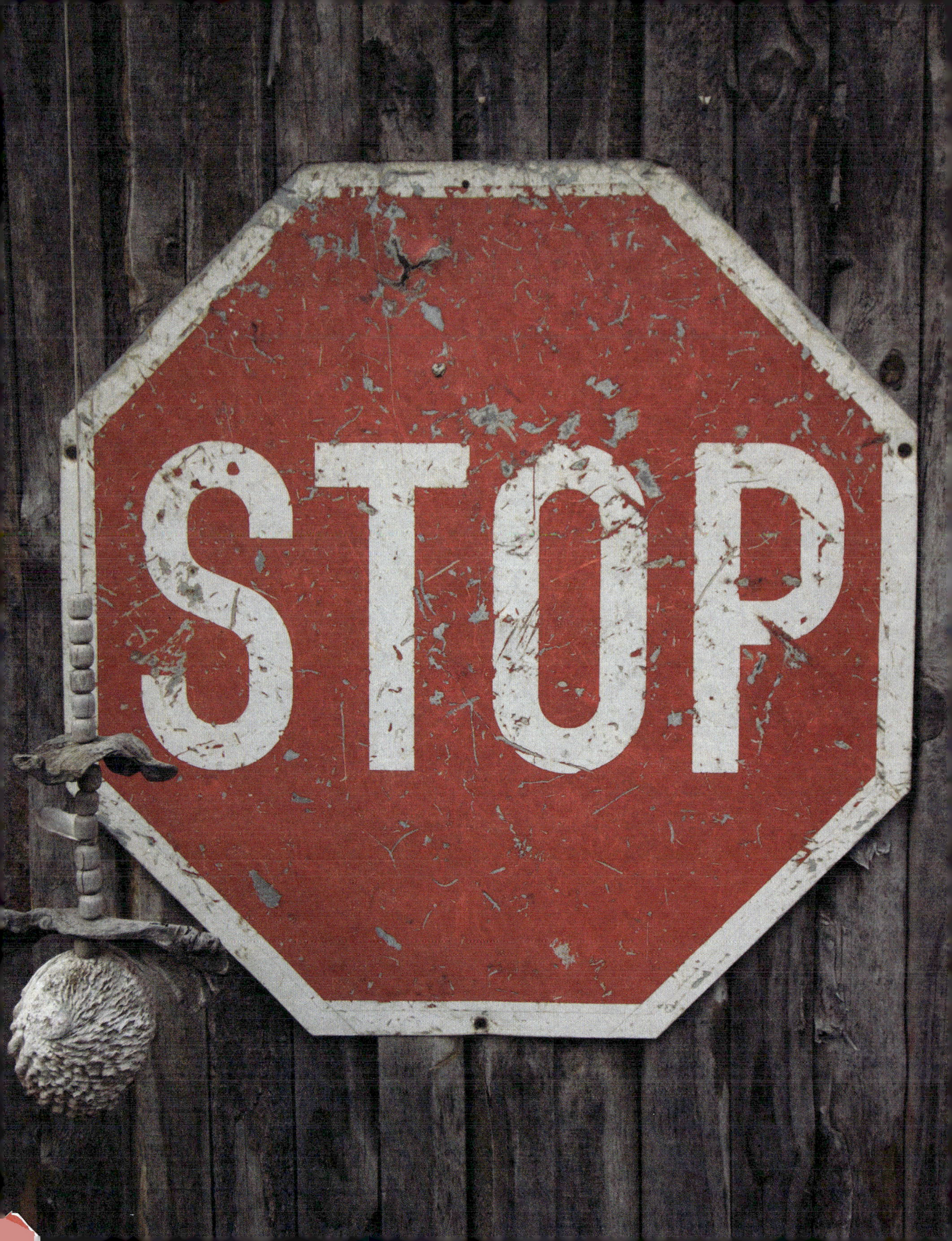
STOP

& smell the coffee

ONE PAN BREAKFAST

★ For those of you who are fans of the tin cup breakfast, this is the super-duper version. Good for 6-10 friends (depending on how hungry they are), it's simply breakfast in a pan.

Heat up the pan and drop in a big drizzle or two of piri-piri oil. Toss in your potatoes and stir around until they're brown on the edges and almost cooked.

Now, crack your eggs into a bowl, whisk them up and add your cooked potatoes.

Using the same pan, chuck in your red onion and garlic. Fry for a couple of minutes (until they're caramelised) then toss them into the egg mixture. Next, fry up the mushrooms until they're nice and brown and have stopped leaking. Chuck them into the egg mixture, give it all a good stir so that all those *lekker* flavours get mixed up. Finally add your spring onion, baby tomatoes and chopped basil, and give it one last stir.

Over the years I've learned that the best way to cook this breakfast is actually to bake it, because it browns up the top while the bottom gets cooked. Grease the pan heavily with oil, pour in your egg mixture, stick it in the oven and let it bake for about 15-30 minutes on a medium heat until it is golden on top. Take it out of the oven and do the wobble test. Give the pan a gentle shake. If the centre wobbles, it needs more time in the oven. It should be set all the way through, but not dry. Slice into wedges and tuck in. If it sticks, just eat it straight from the pan.

There are no rules when it comes to making the perfect one-pan breakfast. Use whatever fillings suit your taste, so feel free to add some chorizo or crispy free-range bacon.

You'll need:
> cast iron pan with iron handle
> a generous lashing of piri-piri oil
> 10 baby potatoes – cut into thin slivers
> 12 free-range/organic eggs
> 1 red onion – peeled and chopped
> a couple of cloves of garlic – crushed
> 2 handfuls of Portobello mushrooms – sliced
> a bunch of spring onions – chopped
> 2-3 handfuls of baby tomatoes – whole
> fresh basil
> salt and pepper to taste

PS This tastes really good when it's cold, so if you're looking for a *lekker padkos* alternative, let it cool down, pack it up with some chutney and munch on it while the world whizzes past you.

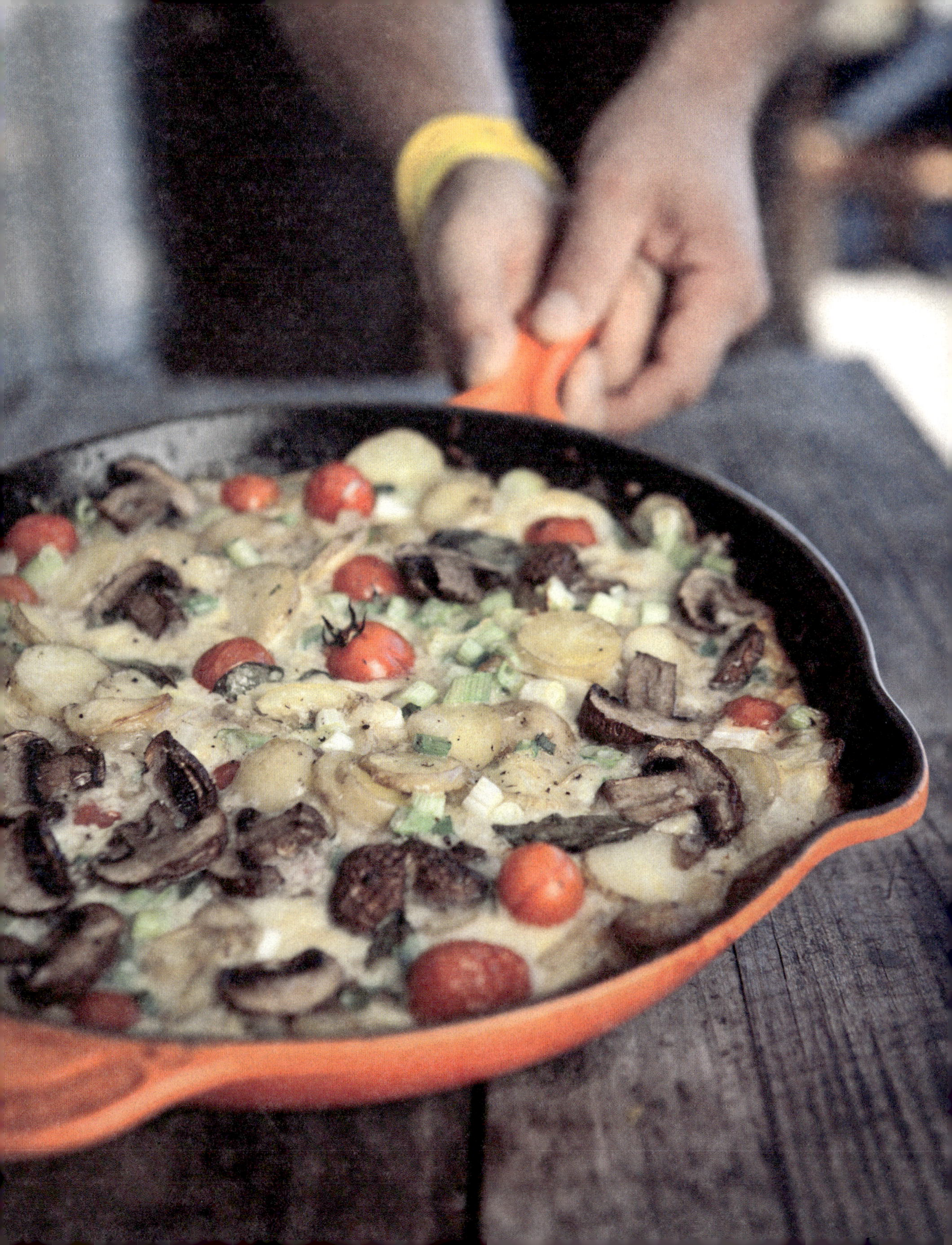

HOMEMADE PIE ON THE BRAAI

When I was first told about the braai pie by Quint, one of my oldest mates, I was a bit sceptical. How could puff pastry be put on the grid, braaied and still turn out to be edible? He promised me it worked. So I gave it a bash and I can now wholeheartedly recommend you do too.

---— First you need to make your fillings ———

SPINACH AND FETA PIES

Preheat a pan and add a couple of knobs of butter. Add your spinach, onion, garlic, salt and pepper and stir around till the onion is soft and the spinach cooked. Spinach and butter are best friends – you can almost never add too much butter. Remove from the heat, let it cool down, and then crumble some feta over the spinach.

You'll need:
> butter
> a whole bunch of spinach – rinsed and with pith removed
> 1 onion – chopped
> 1 clove of garlic – crushed
> a little feta
> salt and black pepper to taste

You'll need:
> a handful of mushrooms – sliced
> half a leek – sliced
> 2 or 3 spring onions – chopped
> a clove of garlic – crushed
> a small handful of cooked leftover chicken
> a palm full of fresh garden peas
> your favourite beer
> a splash of cream

CHICKEN, PEA AND BEER PIES

Pan-fry the mushrooms, leeks, onions and garlic and let them sweat off any excess juice. Take your leftover chicken, tear it up roughly into strips and add it to the pan. Chuck in the peas and then a splash of beer. Be stingy – think of it as though you're giving a six-year-old kid a little taster. (Keep the rest for yourself.) Add a splash of cream and let the sauce cook down. You want the filling to be juicy but not overly moist, otherwise when you braai the pie it'll disintegrate into a soggy bomb.

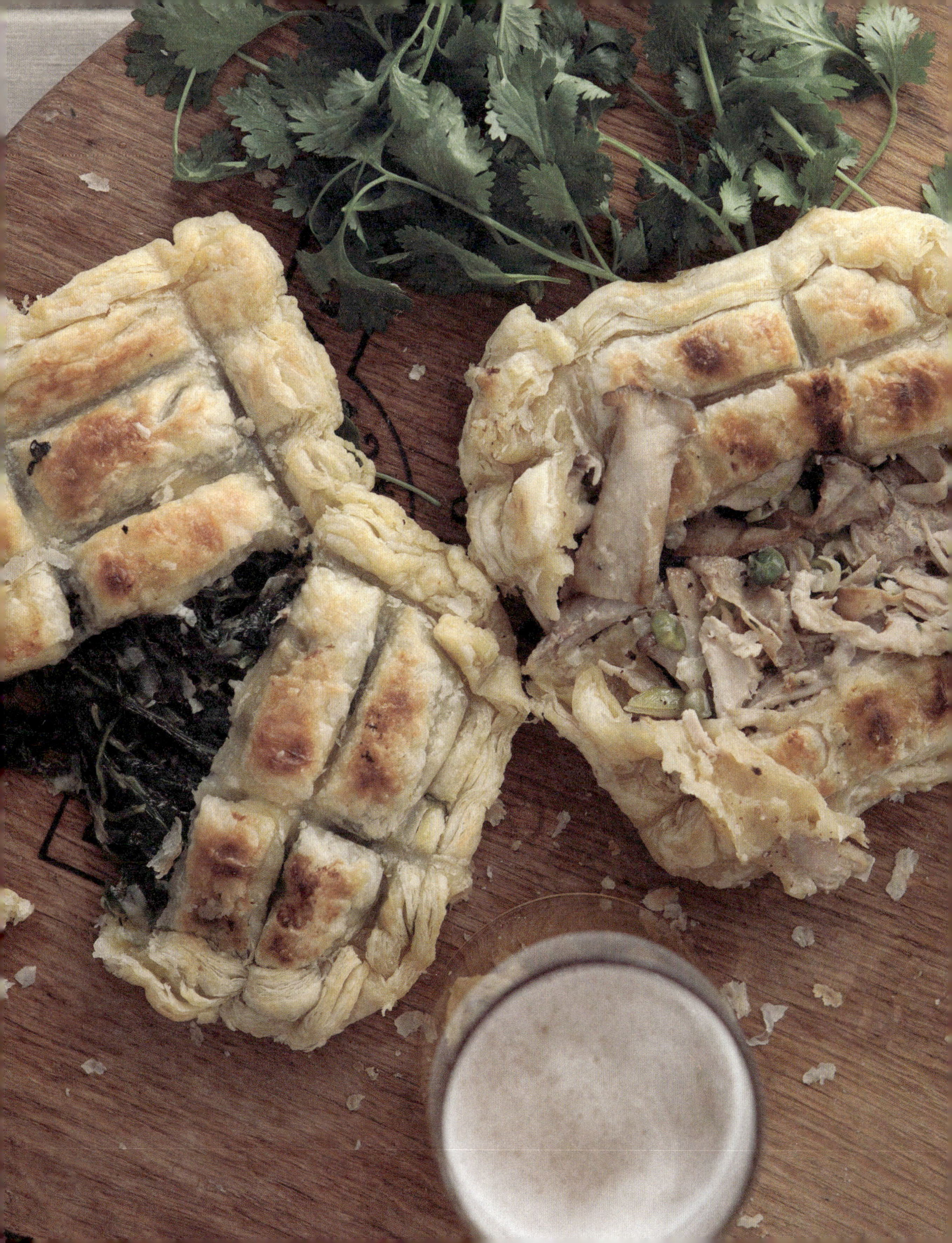

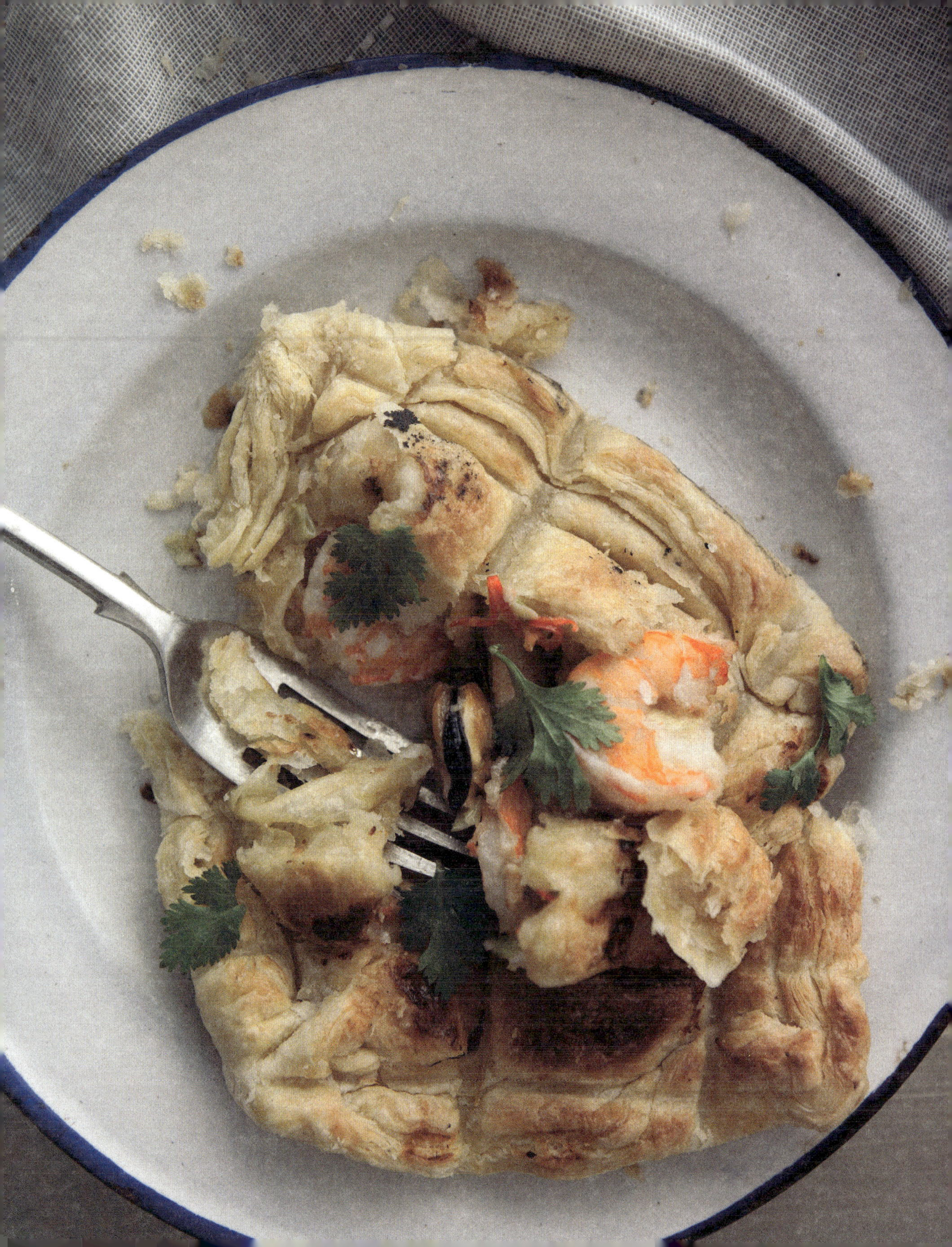

MUSSEL AND PRAWN PIES

Dump the mussels in a pot, add a splash of white wine, put the lid on and steam until they open up. Take them out of the shells, remove the beard (if you haven't already done so) and set aside. Clean your prawns, remove the shells and seal them off in a pan with a knob of butter and the garlic. Add the mussels to the saucepan with a splash of cream and a little drizzle of the salty water you steamed the mussels in. Add the coriander. Mix the whole lot up, chuck in the spring onions and let it simmer until the sauce has cooked off a little. As with the chicken, pea and beer pies above, the mixture must not be too moist.

You'll need:
- a handful of mussels
- a splash of white wine
- 8 prawns, cleaned, deveined and shelled
- a knob of butter
- a clove of garlic – crushed
- a splash of cream
- coriander – fresh and chopped
- 2 or 3 spring onions – cut in half and sliced into thin strips

The Pastry

If you don't have the energy to make your own pastry, just buy some rolls of puff pastry from the store. Sometimes it's okay to take a shortcut. One sheet of pastry will make three pies. Whatever you do, try and keep the puff pastry as cold as possible. Roll it out and cut it into six even-sized squares. Scoop a biggish spoonful of whichever filling you've made on to the centre of one square. Cover with another square and push the sides together using your fingers or the tines of a fork, ensuring that it's completely sealed up. Repeat with the remaining squares of pastry.

Brush the pastry with a little egg white, and using the tip of a knife, cut three small incisions on top of each pie – this will stop the pies from exploding when they're on the grid. Put your pies in the fridge so that they harden up a little before you braai them.

Light A Fire

Once the fire is ready with nice medium coals, place your pies inside one of those braai grids that close up (the same one you use for boerie). There's no need to grease the grid – there's loads of butter in puff pastry, which will prevent it from sticking. Take a couple of bricks and stack them on either side of the fire (about four each side). Place the grid on top of the bricks and turn the pies often to avoid burning them.

If the pies start spitting at you, best you jump out of the way until they've calmed down and if they break open it probably means you weren't turning them often enough or your mixture was too soggy. (If at first you don't succeed, you should try, try, and try again.)

When the puff pastry is nice and golden brown, your pies are ready to eat. Serve the chicken pie with beer, the mussel and prawn pie with a glass of good white wine, and the spinach and feta pie with whatever tickles your fancy.

> ★ The taste of puff pastry cooked over coals is unbelievable and I can't think of a better way to get that smoky flavour to infuse in a pie. Delicious. Umami and all that stuff.

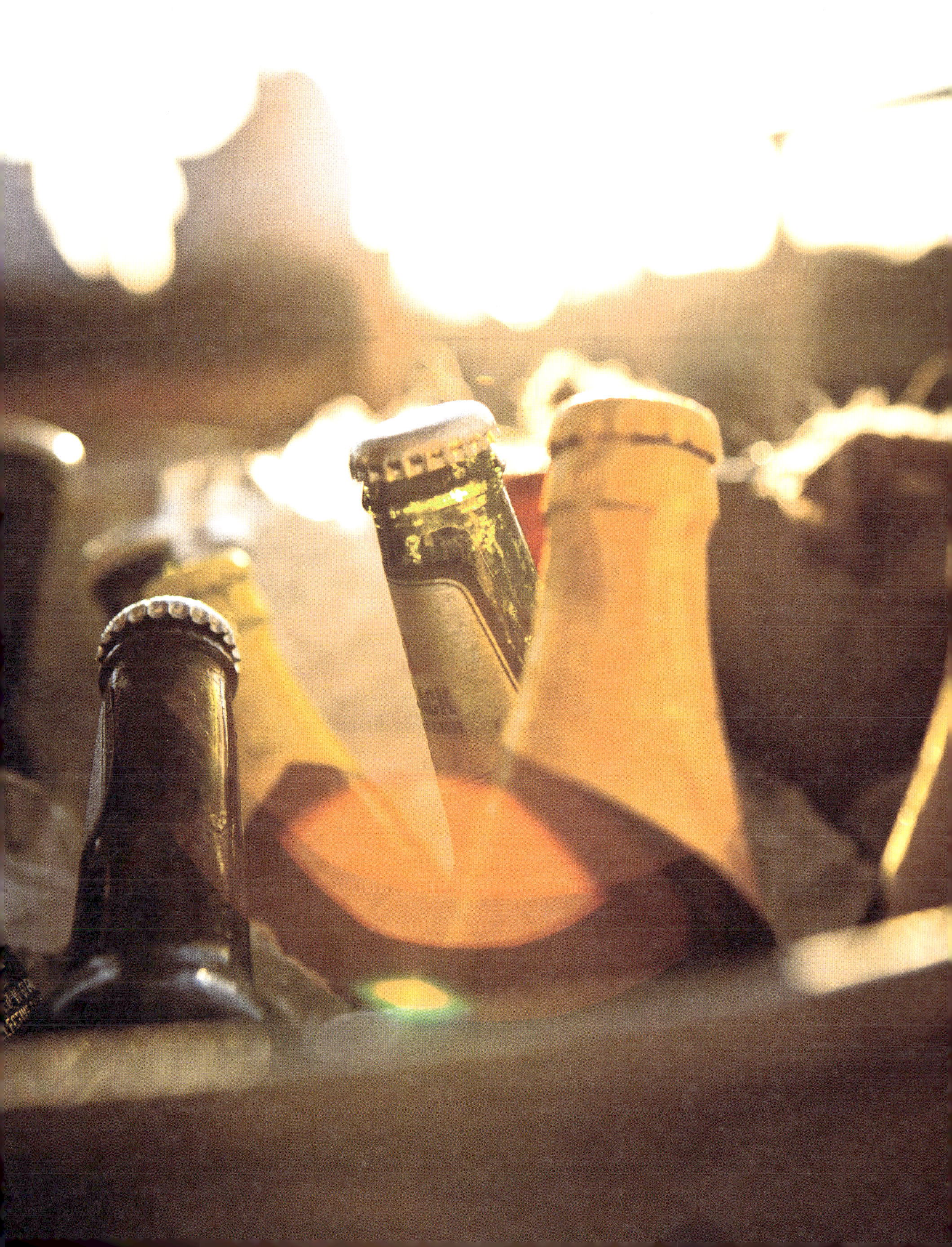

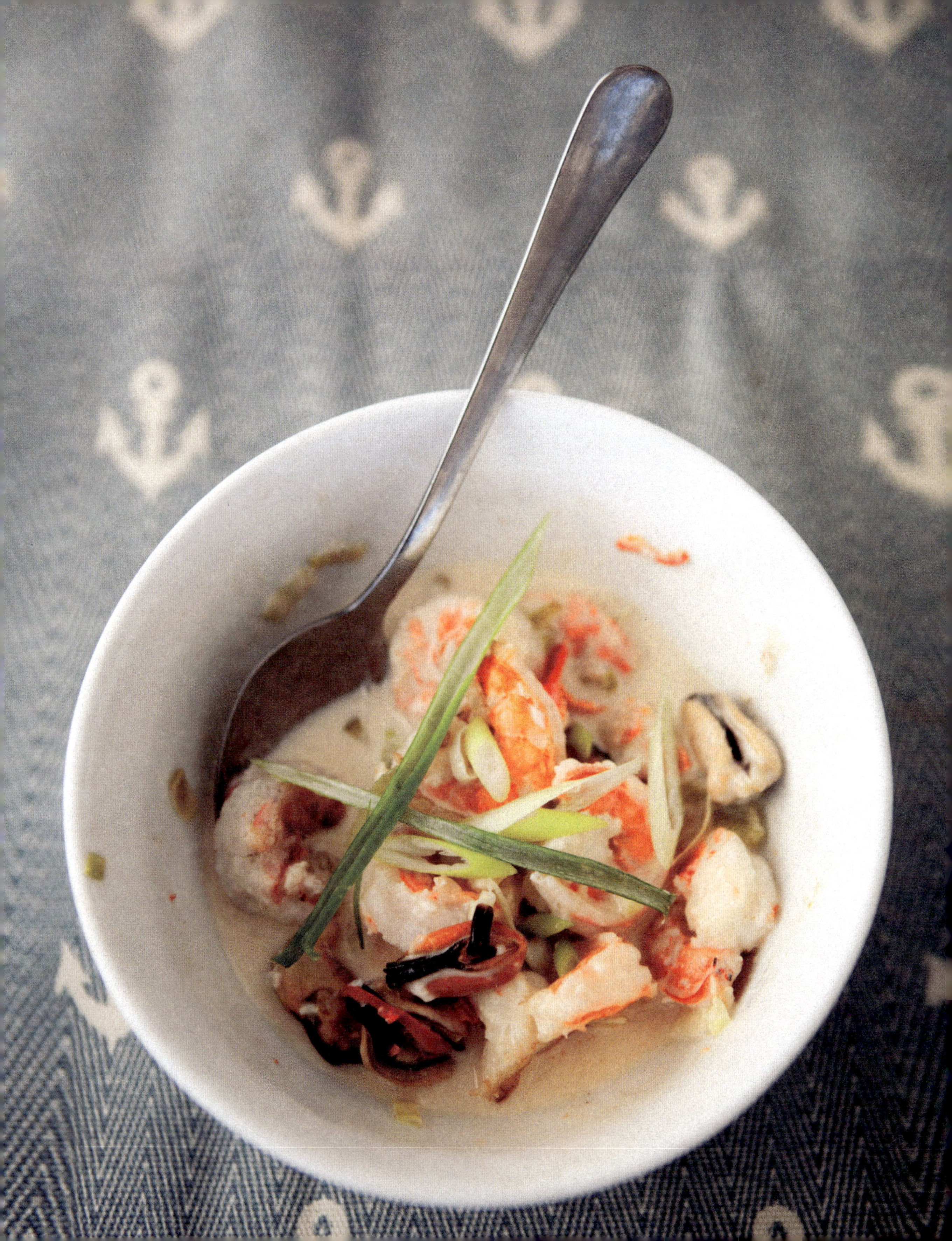

REALLY SCRUMPTIOUS BURGERS

There are millions of burger joints in the world, most of them serving up prepackaged rubbish, where most of the time you don't know what you're eating. Slapping some meat in a bun when you know what you're eating elevates burgers to a gourmet experience.

> ★ Don't use meat that is too lean. The whole point of the crunchy breadcrumbs is that they suck that fat up during cooking – and that's the trick to a juicy patty!

For the patties you'll need:
- 1/2 kg leanish ground mince (beef, ostrich, lamb, veld fed – not grain fed)
- a couple of slices of toasted bread – crumbed
- 1 free-range egg
- garlic, herbs, salt and pepper to taste

Put the mince in a bowl. Add the breadcrumbs to the mince along with all the other ingredients. Mix very well with your hands and then shape into patties. How big or how small you make them depends on your appetite and the size of your rolls. If you're doing this at home, pop the mixture into the fridge to firm up and marinate for a while before grilling.

Now it's time to make your sauces. Mine always start with a basic white sauce (the French call it a *roux*), and I make it the way granny taught me. Melt a big knob of butter over medium heat, remove from heat then add enough corn flour so that you end up with a thick, yellow, creamy paste. Put back over a gentle heat, adding milk a little at a time and stirring constantly until you have the desired consistency. Allow enough time for the starch in the flour to cook off, then add whatever you like – garlic, Madagascan peppercorns, mushrooms. My trick is to pan-fry it first and then add it to the white sauce with all its juices – it's to die for!

Sometimes I like to make tzatziki and use that instead of a roux-based sauce.

You'll need: cucumbers, plain yoghurt, garlic, mint, parsley, dill, salt

Peel the cucumber and then slice it in half (lengthways). Now, using a spoon scoop the seeds out. Grate the remaining cucumber roughly and chuck into a colander over the sink or a bowl. Cover lightly with salt and leave to drain for half an hour. You'll be amazed how much liquid comes out. Rinse and then squeeze the cucumber dry. (Pat it with a clean tea towel if necessary.) Place in a bowl and chuck in lashings of yoghurt, finely chopped garlic, mint, parsley and dill. Mix it around and that's it. Tzatziki in a flash!

Grill the burgers over a medium heat. I like mine medium rare (more medium when I'm doing lamb). The smokiness imparted by the fire will make it really umami (say yummy).

All that's left to do is assemble: fresh poppy seed buns, a juicy patty, a dollop of sauce, some sliced tomato and butter lettuce and whatever else tickles your fancy. When you eat something that is made from scratch with love it will always taste better and when you see your friends tucking in happily you know you're on the right path. *Lekker*.

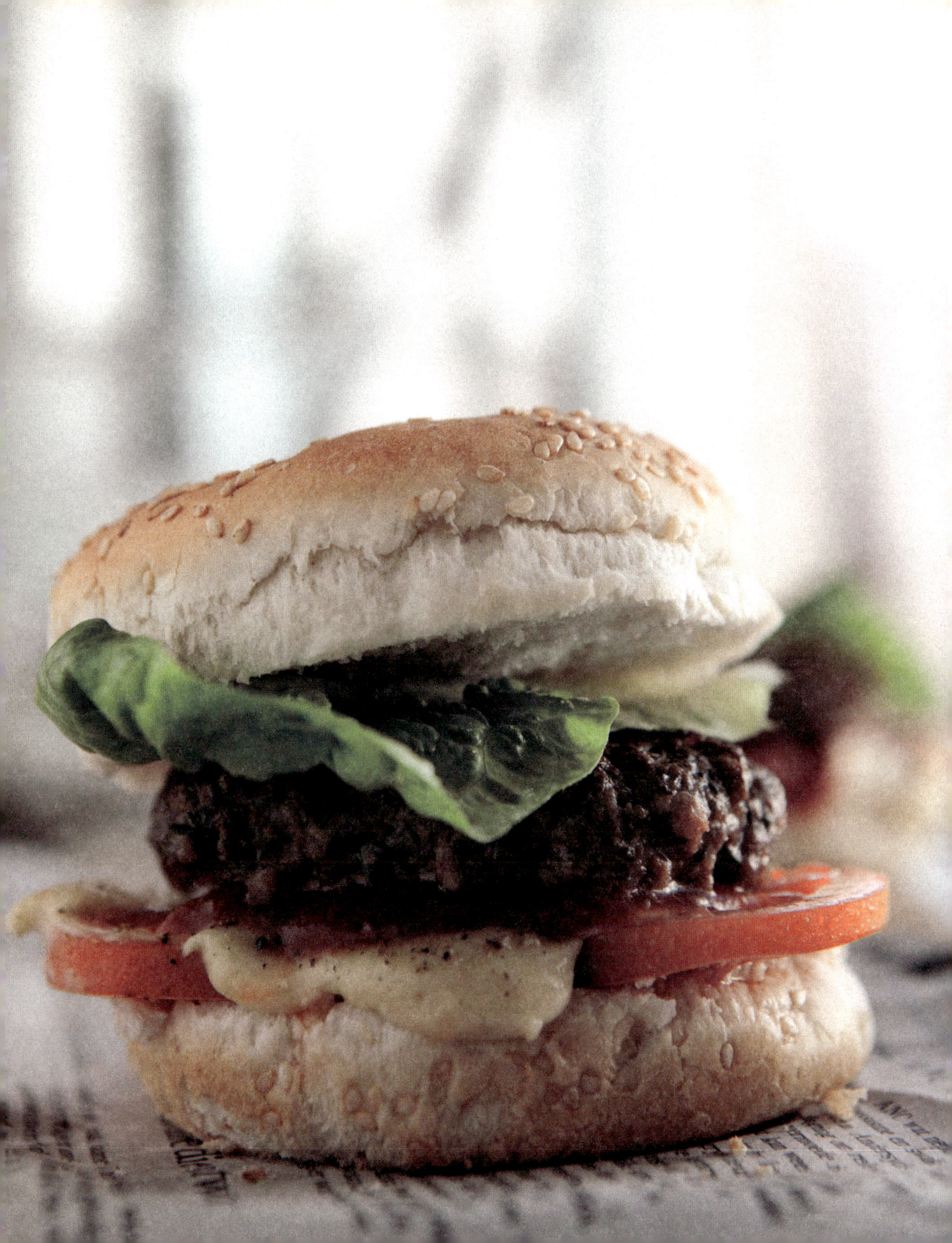

YIN & YANG GAZPACHO

This original Spanish or Portuguese dish (depending on who you're talking to) has carved itself a niche all over the world. As a result, there are many variations – but this is my take on the soup salad, which I first made for a bunch of my heat-stroked friends in Kolmanskuppe, an abandoned ghost town just outside Lüderitz, Namibia. Over the years I think I've improved it and made it my own and it's now become a cold soup that's perfect for those summer days when it's so hot you can you feel your brain melting into a pulp. It brings even my most wilted friends back to life. So back to my original story ... I wanted something fresh and cool, instead of hot and *verlep*. Yin and Yang Gazpacho fitted the ticket.

Just like there are many ways to skin a cat, there are many ways to skin a tomato. This is how I do it: Cut an X through the skin on the top of your tomato. Let it sit in a pot of boiling water for as long as you can hold your breath (or about 30 seconds), then take it out and refresh it in a bowl of iced water. Give it some time to come back to life. After a couple of ticks your tomato can be skinned easily.

★ History of Gazpacho // Gazpacho is an old traditional Spanish peasant dish. Today it's more popularly known as cold tomato soup salad, but it actually started way back in the pre-Columbus days as a simple bread soup made with stale bread, olive oil, garlic, water and vinegar. The introduction of tomatoes and peppers came courtesy of Columbus after he crossed the Atlantic and brought them back to Europe – which is why it is the bread, not the tomatoes, that makes it a Gazpacho. Either way, it's a great dish to cool you down after a long hot day when you're not too hungry but know you have to eat before you have another beer.

SO LET'S GET YINNING AND YANGING

Chop all the vegetables into big chunks for easy blending. Take a third of all the ingredients – except the tomatoes, red pepper and yoghurt – and blend them with the cucumber, green pepper, fresh mint and lemon. This is going to be the Yin side of your soup. Bear in mind you want a soup, not a juice, so don't overdo it.

Now take the remainder of the ingredients, including all the tomatoes and the red pepper (but not the yoghurt) and make two batches of Yang – one smoother and the other a bit chunkier. Mix both together.

Keep your Yin and Yang in separate bowls and give it some chill time in the fridge. Overnight is best to let the flavours mingle.

TO SERVE

This part is a bit tricky, so get a friend to help you. You're each going to take a ladle and, with one on either side, simultaneously pour one third green and two thirds red soup into your serving bowls. Once it's in the bowls add a generous dollop of yoghurt bang in the middle. The idea is that when you're eating it, you scoop up some Yin, some Yang, and a smidgen of the yoghurt – that way, you get to taste all the individual flavours.

If you're too hot and can't be bothered to give it a yin/yang look and taste, blend everything together from the start and chill it. If it's a real scorcher of a day, chuck in some ice blocks just before serving.

A good Gazpacho is really easy to make. They say the secret is to stick to quantities. Me – I often think that cooking is as much about the moon and the stars and good old gut feel, so don't be shy to add something to it. Fresh herbs are always a great addition – just think of fresh sweet basil added at the last moment.

> ★ A little pointer: If the soup is too runny, add a bit more bread to thicken it up. Too thick, add a little water – you get the idea.

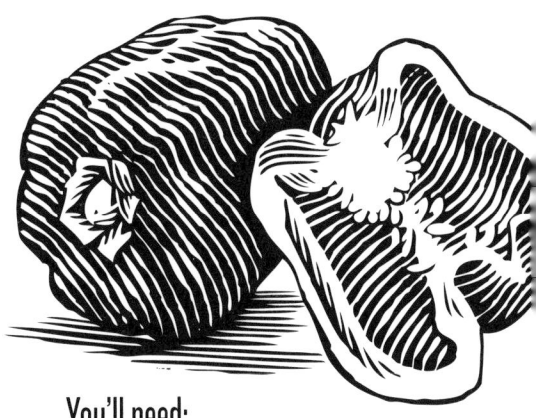

You'll need:
- just under 1 kg tomatoes – skinned (and some would say de-seeded – up to you)
- 2 medium-sized peppers – 1 red, 1 green
- 1 cucumber – peeled
- 3 cloves of garlic – crushed
- salt – it should be 2 heaped teaspoons, but I'm a bit reluctant to add so much. Rather use less and taste and add as you go along.
- olive oil
- 5 tablespoons balsamic vinegar
- about 1/3 of a loaf of stale ciabatta – toasted and turned into chunky crumbs
- a handful of fresh mint
- a squeeze of lemon

To garnish:
- a tub of Greek yoghurt

PARK OFF

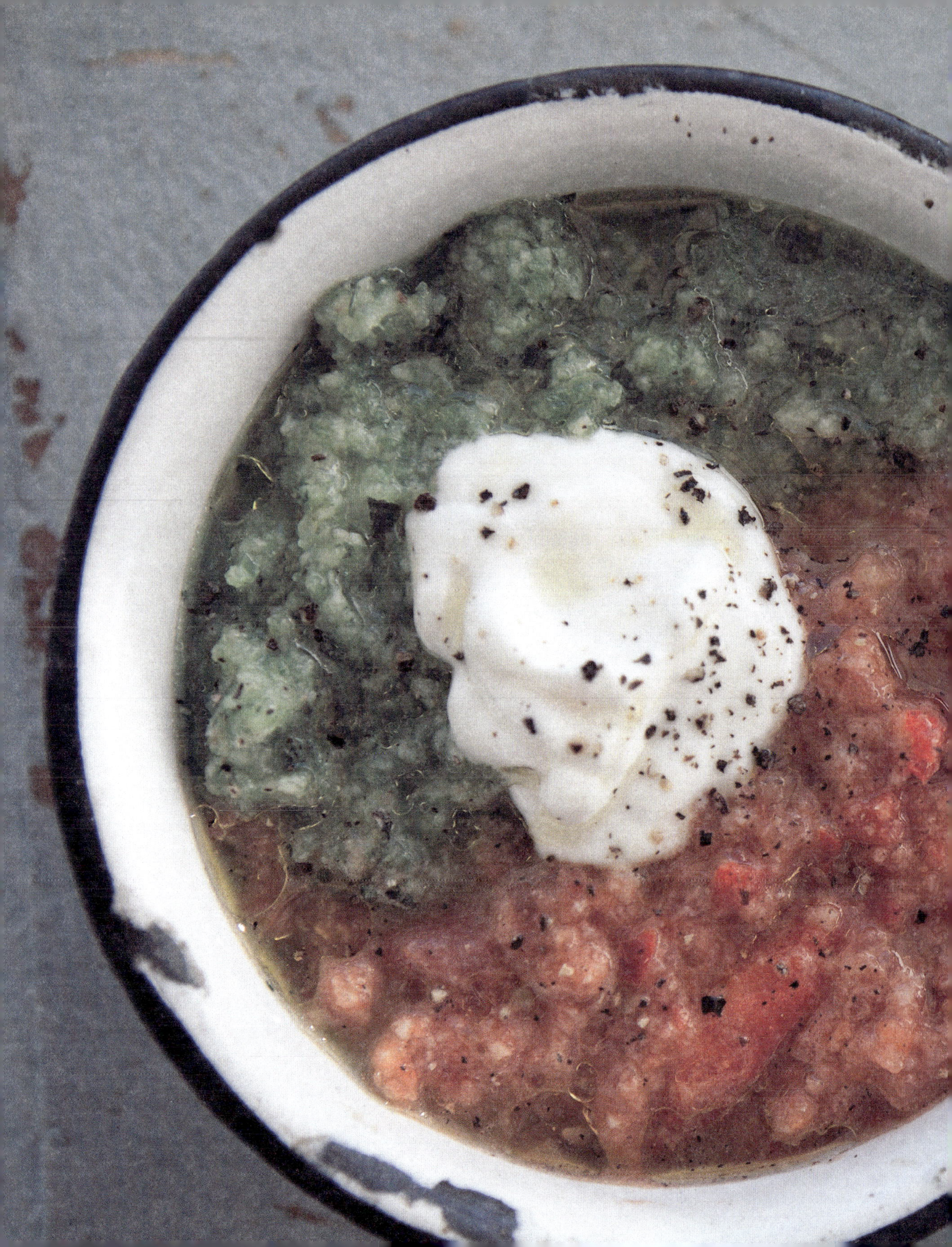

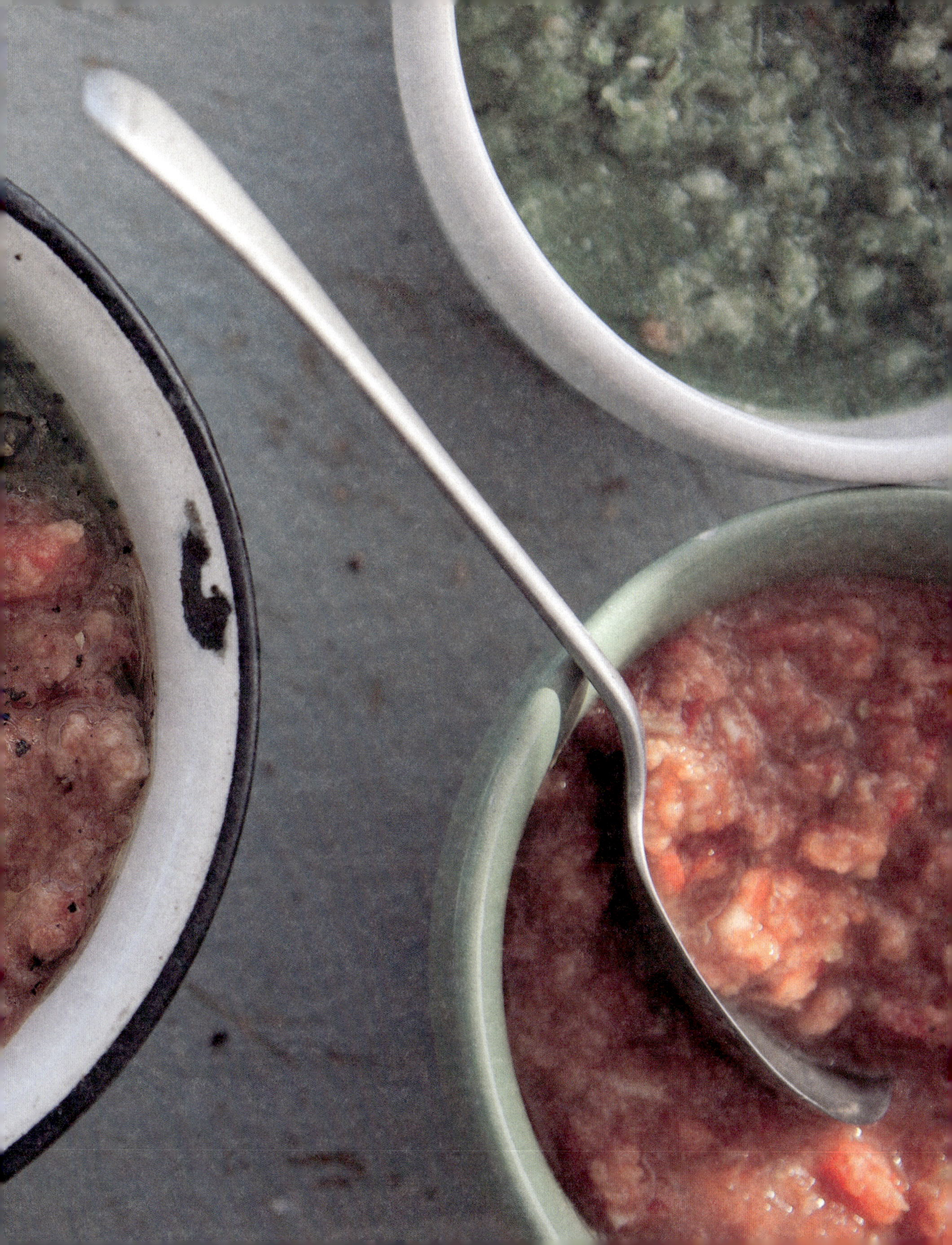

VICIOUS WA!

There's something about slurping soup and dunking chunks of bread into it while watching movies, but maybe that's just because I grew up doing exactly that with my family. On wintery Sundays, my mom made soup and we all crammed together on the couch to watch 35 mm movies on an old school projector (this was in the days before video machines – maybe I'm giving away my age . . .).

This is a thick and wintery soup that's a great 'filler-upper' for those Sunday nights at home with your family. It's based on the French soup vichyssoise, but my rendition of it includes the bite of chillies and it will definitely warm up your bones.

Peel the potatoes, slice them into thin rounds and place them in a large pot. Wash the leeks thoroughly, slice them and add to the potatoes, along with the chopped onion. Cover with stock and when it starts boiling reduce the heat and simmer for 1 to 1½ hours. Remove from the heat and, using a hand blender, blend until smooth. Add salt and pepper to taste and then pour in the cream and stir it in with a wooden spoon.

Dish up into soup bowls, sprinkle with chives and a whole whack of chopped chillies.

> ★ The 'vicious' part depends on how many chillies you chuck in and the 'wa' part is the bite you'll get with every spoonful.

You'll need:
- about 6 large potatoes
- a couple of bunches of leeks
- 1 onion – chopped
- enough organic chicken stock to cover the vegetables
- salt and pepper to taste
- a cup of cream
- chives
- 3 chillies – chopped with seeds removed

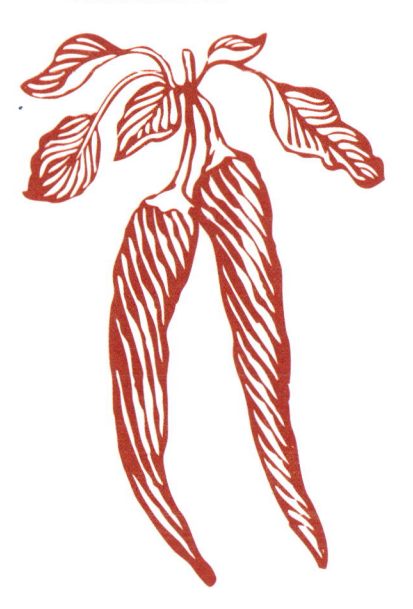

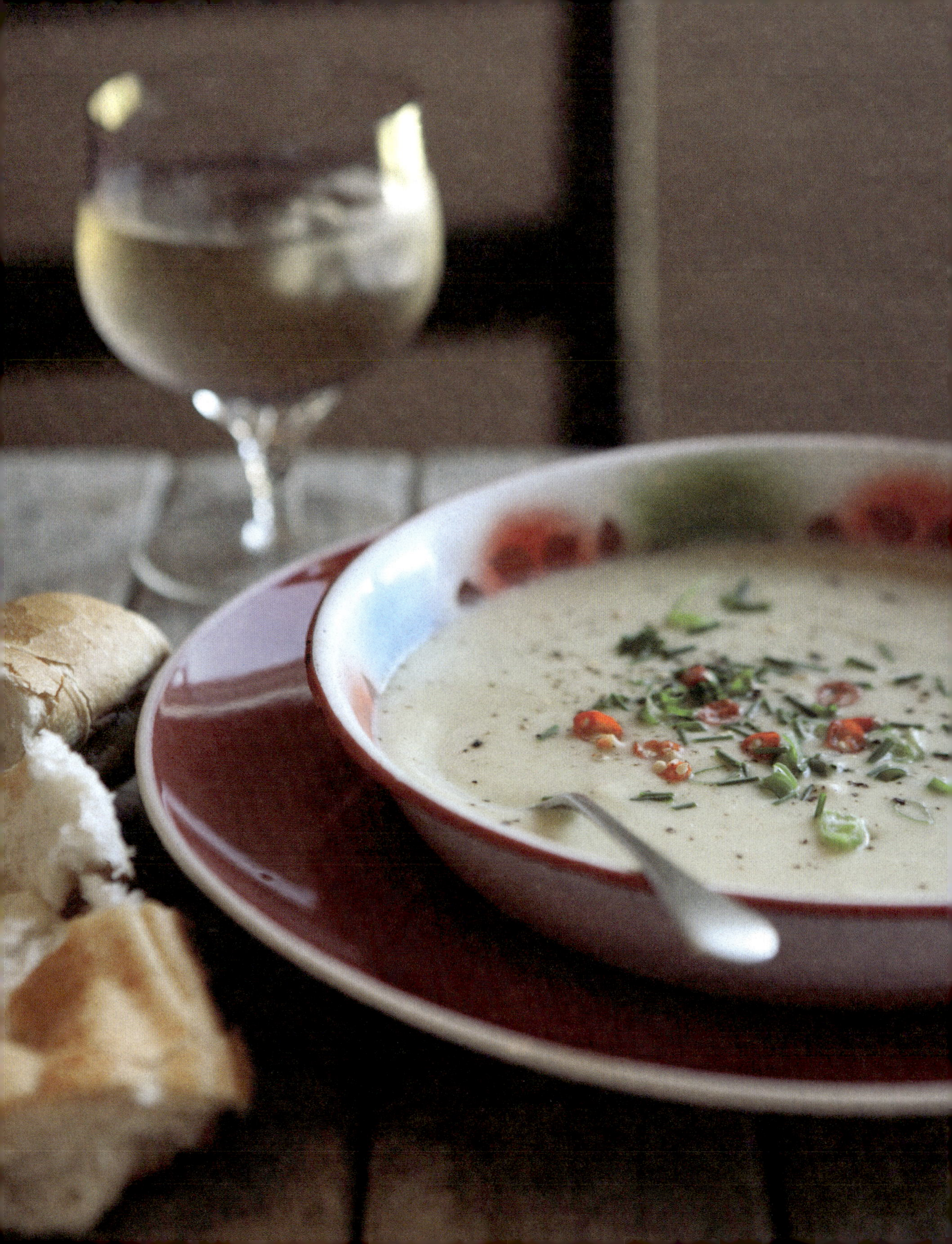

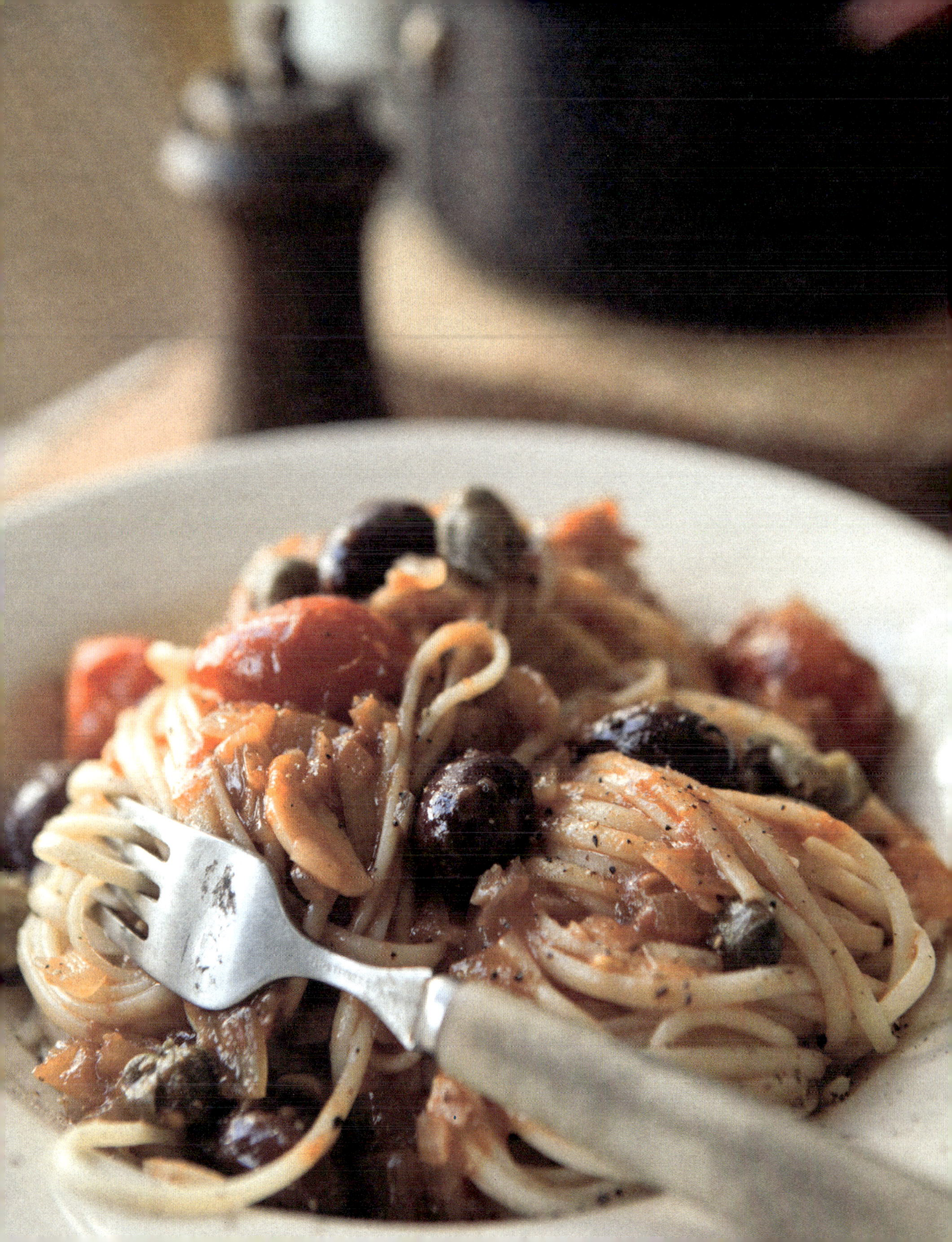

PASTA PUTTANESCA

Apparently this pasta dish dates back to the 1960s, and is rooted in classic Italian cuisine. *Puttana* is Italian for 'whore' and there are many stories about the origin of the *Puttanesca* pasta sauce. One story is that it was made by prostitutes in Naples as a dinner to 'keep them going' all night. Another has it that prostitutes made the dish to lure new clientele. And then of course there's the tale that Italian housewives made it for their husbands as a quick dinner so that they could get on with more important things. You can choose whichever legend you like best. Now, as you can imagine, with so many stories about Puttanesca around every street corner, there are bound to be loads of different versions of this Italian classic. One thing, however, remains the same and that's the basis of the sauce. It's got to be salty, spicy and fragrant.

> ★ A great thing about this dish (other than its name) is that it's really cheap to make. So save this recipe for that end-of-the-month moment when all you have left are some bits and pieces in your pantry.
>
> This is my take on prostitutes' pasta. It's rustic, it will fill you up and it's packed with flavour.

First, heat up a non-stick pan, drizzle with olive oil and chuck in the garlic – be careful not to burn it. Your kitchen will start smelling delicious (which makes me think maybe those prostitutes had a point). Next up, add the onions and while they're frying, fill a big pot with boiling water and a pinch of salt. Once it's bubbling steadily, add the pasta (you can choose whichever pasta you like, but if you're a traditionalist use spaghetti).

Add the anchovies to the garlic/onion pan (you can either keep them whole or rip them up), the tomatoes, chilli, olives, capers, salt and pepper. Mix it all around and then let it simmer for as long as it takes to cook the pasta. Drain the cooked pasta and, in the still-hot pot, toss in some olive oil, top with the puttanesca, whack loads of chopped parsley on top and Bob's your uncle (although if your mother's a prostitute, he might be your dad . . .).

You'll need:
> olive oil (I like to use the local Vesuvio)
> a couple of cloves of garlic – crushed
> 1 onion – finely chopped
> a handful of anchovy fillets
> 1 tin good quality baby tomatoes
> one or two chopped red chillies, depending on how hot you like your Puttanesca
> a handful of olives – pits removed and sliced up
> a whole whack of capers
> Maldon salt and cracked black pepper
> fresh parsley – chopped
> pasta of your choice

STUFFED STICK BREADS

This is something I remember making when I was a Cub (believe it or not, I was once one). The way we did it back then was first to make a fire with just three matches – no wonder I only ever got a badge for perfect attendance! Making Stick Breads is a fun, interactive thing to do when you're having a braai, and everyone can – and should – get involved, especially when you have a bunch of children around (which has nothing to do with age).

> ★ Get hold of as many long sticks as you have friends but make sure you don't use any kind of wood that oozes resin. It's going to make the stick breads taste nasty and might make you sick. So unless you want to poison your friends don't use pine or the like.

Make a basic bread dough using the recipe on page 45. When the dough is ready, knock it back down before tearing off monkey fist sized pieces. Flatten the dough and then shape it into long cord-like snake shapes with your fingers. No rolling pins here!

Now grease the end of your stick with sunflower oil. Next, create a spiral of dough around the piece of wood by making a loop of dough around the top of the stick and pinching the dough together, then spiral the dough around the rest of the stick and pinch the last bit together.

Let the kids cook them over medium coals on the fire until nice and crispy and brown, then slide/twist them off the sticks.

You'll need:
› several longish sticks
› basic bread dough
› fillings of your choice

NOW FOR THE INTERESTING PART

Take a clear plastic bag and fill it with your filling of choice (anything from whipped cream infused with chocolate shavings to tzatziki). Cut a corner off the plastic bag (slightly smaller than the hole left by the stick) and pipe the filling into the hole in the bread until it oozes out the other end. What you've created is similar to those jam doughnuts you used to gobble up as a kid. Eat the filled bread stick immediately.

There are a million different fillings you could make – for example, my friend Bianca likes marmalade (I think she smokes her socks), but there are no rules. Try savoury mince, or cream cheese and jam ... you get the idea. To make your lives easier, below are some of my favourite fillings. I like to add some basil pesto or a salsa verde to cream cheese, give it a rough swirl, then pipe it in. Go ahead ... be a child in the bush kitchen and remind yourself what it's like to be 6 or 7 years old by making a fire with three matches and cooking stick breads.

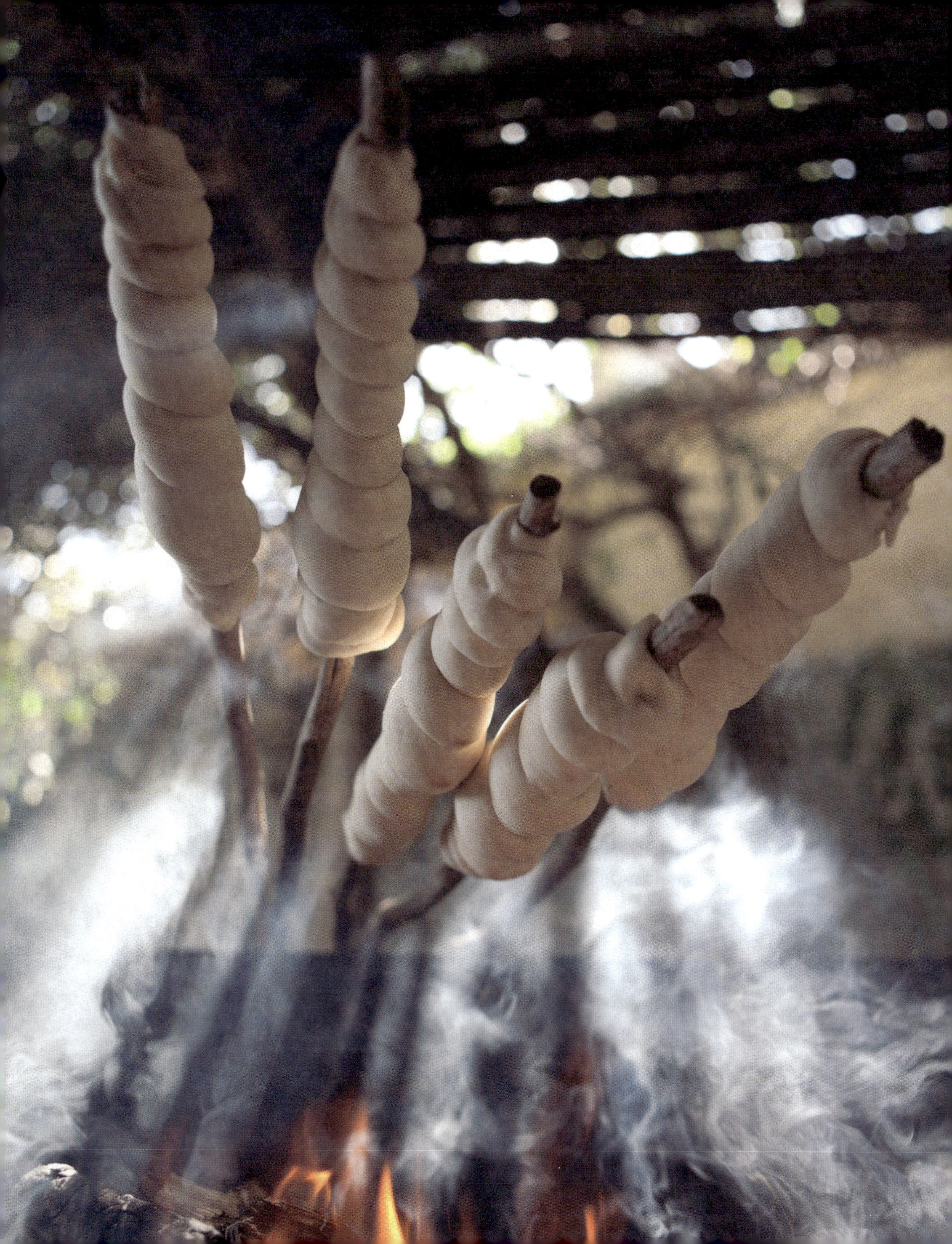

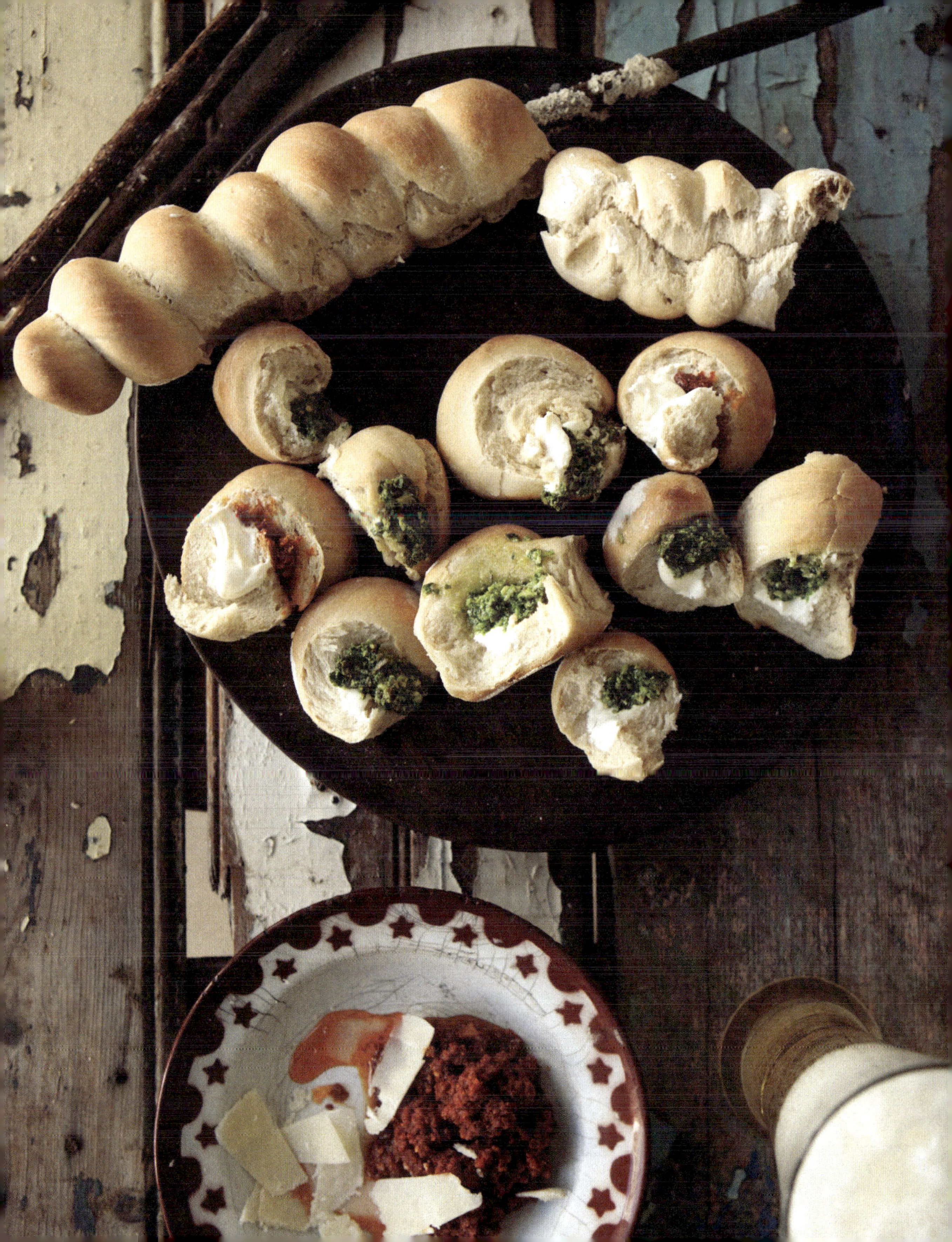

BASIC BASIL PESTO

Mung the basil and the nuts in your trusty mortar and pestle, then add the garlic and mung some more. Once these things have got to know each other, add the olive oil in a steady stream, and keep pounding. Unless you're extremely dexterous, you're going to need to enlist the help of a friend for this part. The cheese goes in second last, then the seasoning. Don't worry too much about it being perfectly smooth; you're not making baby food.

Use this as your basic recipe but try using other herbs instead of basil – like coriander or parsley – and rocket, spinach, roasted peppers, sundried tomatoes or olives. You get the idea.

You'll need:
- 2 man-size handfuls of fresh basil leaves
- a good handful of pine nuts
  – these are expensive but you can substitute chopped walnuts
- 2 or 3 fat cloves of garlic
  (do not under any circumstances be tempted to use that ready chopped stuff you get in supermarkets – it's mostly turnip)
- 1/2 cup of extra virgin olive oil
  (I like to use Vesuvio)
- 1/2 cup of grated Parmesan cheese
  (or any other similarly strong-flavoured cheese like Gruyère. Use the best quality you can afford, it will make all the difference to the taste)
- salt and pepper to taste

SALSA VERDE OR GREEN SAUCE

Put the whole lot into the blender and blitz until smooth. Adjust the quantities of the ingredients you use according to personal taste and make plenty because you're going to want to slather it all over everything. Use it on fish, meat, over pastas, scrambled eggs, frittatas, as a dip, or mix it with cream cheese for your stick bread filling.

You'll need:
- a few peeled cloves of garlic
- a couple of handfuls of Italian flat leaf parsley
- a handful of fresh oregano leaves
- a handful of fresh basil leaves
- wild fennel leaves
- good extra virgin olive oil

FRITTERS

You probably remember fritters as those pumpkin ones your grandmother used to make as a side dish with anything meaty for Sunday lunch. And I'm not saying those weren't delicious, but they're more like pancakes. These fritters are savoury and you get to taste all the individual ingredients, which means you can eat them on their own (and preferably while they're still hot) without having to go to the trouble of roasting a lamb and fighting to get your family around one table on a Sunday. Traditionally, fritters were served on Shrove Tuesday, but there's no need for a religious experience to be a fritter freak.

For the batter:
- 1/4 cup corn flour
- 2 egg whites
- 1 teaspoon baking powder

Take a mixing bowl, add the corn flour and baking powder, then make a well in the centre and pour in the egg whites. Using a wooden spoon, mix it up until it's lump-free. It's that easy. The idea is not to drown the ingredients in the batter, but rather to lubricate them, just so everything sticks together during frying. I tested various combinations, and the ones below came out best.

Once you've decided which combination to make, mix it with the batter, then preheat a pan, add a splash of sunflower oil and then add spoonfuls of fritter mix. Fry until golden on both sides. Serve with flavoured sour cream.

PS: Cold fritter mix is easier to work with. Leave it in the fridge until all the ingredients have cooled down. It helps it settle when you fry your fritters.

PPS: If you've got a bowl of batter waiting to be used, make sure you stir it every now and then otherwise it will stick to the bottom of the bowl.

PPPS: Don't make the fritters any thicker than about 1 cm, otherwise they might not cook right through to the centre.

PPPPS: I like to use fritters as veggie burgers – really! Give it a bash.

★ Sweet Potato and Chorizo
- 1 cooked and peeled sweet potato
- a small handful of coriander – chopped
- a couple of spring onions – sliced
- grated ginger
- 1 clove of garlic – crushed
- 1 chorizo – chopped
- 1 red chilli – chopped
- a good squeeze of lime

★ Pear and Blue Cheese
- 1 pear – grated (skin and all)
- a small handful of crumbled blue cheese
- lots of chopped chives

★ Zucchini and Beetroot
- 1 or 2 cooked beetroots – peeled and grated (how many you use will depend on their size)
- 2 zucchinis – grated
- a whole whack of grated parmesan (probably a handful)
- a pinch of nutmeg
- black pepper
- Maldon salt

★ Corn
- uncooked corn cut off the cob (one should be fine)
- paprika to taste
- a small handful of chopped parsley

★ Raylene's Zucchini and Parmesan
- 2 zucchinis – grated
- loads of grated parmesan
- a pinch of nutmeg
- salt and pepper

All these recipes make between 6-8 fritters. If you have loads of hungry mouths to feed, just double or triple the quantities.

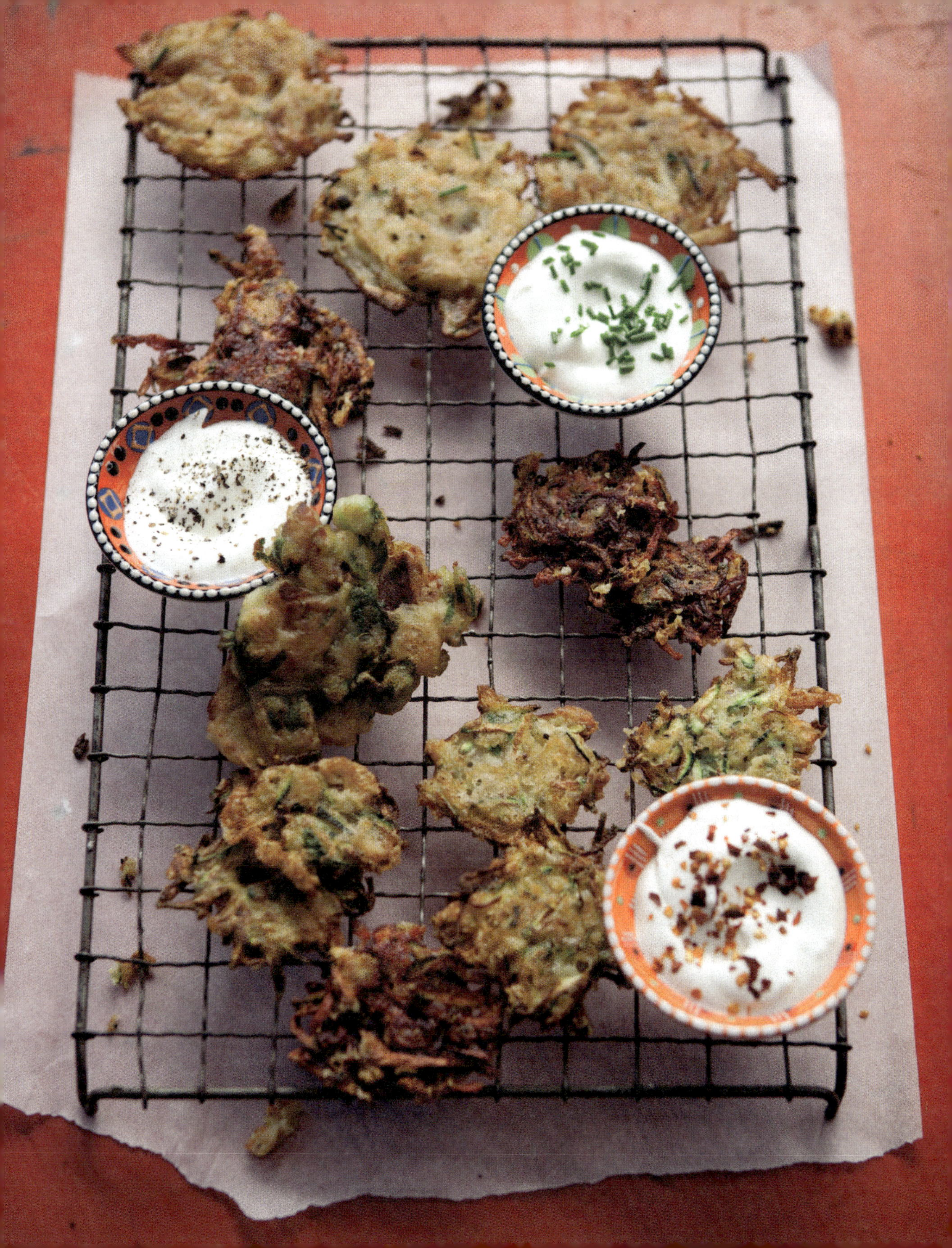

KEBABS

Kebabs – or *sosaties* as most of us in South Africa call them – are not just a fantastic braai dish, they are also a really *lekker* way to use up a whole fridge or cooler-box full of ingredients – you get to mix and match flavours any way you like.

A COUPLE OF RULES OF THUMB

★ If you're using wooden or bamboo skewers, soak them in water first to prevent them from burning away.
★ If you're using ingredients that melt (like cheese), refrigerate them first (preferably in the freezer), so that they don't melt and fall into the fire.
★ Marinate, Marinate, Marinate. The longer you leave all the goodies together, the more the flavours will infuse.
★ Lastly, there are no rules when it comes to ingredients. This is the best thing about a kebab – they're designer dishes that soak up the umami of being on the fire.

CHICKEN SATAY

Chuck the chicken into a large mixing bowl and add lashings of sesame oil, a drizzle of peanut oil and enough peanut butter and honey to coat the chicken. Then grab your trusty mortar and pestle and pound up the coriander and a small handful of pecan and pine nuts until the coriander's bruised and all the flavours have been released.

Add to the chicken and mix the whole lot together – get someone who's willing to get their hands dirty. Leave it in a cool place (if you've got a fridge that'll do nicely) and let it marinate for as long as possible. When the coals are ready, let everyone skewer their own sosaties and grill them to their satisfaction.

You'll need:
> chicken thigh fillets – skin off and cubed (thighs are the moistest, tenderest and most flavoursome part of the chicken and are brilliant on the braai)
> sesame oil
> peanut oil
> chunky peanut butter
> honey
> coriander
> pecan and pine nuts
> salt to taste

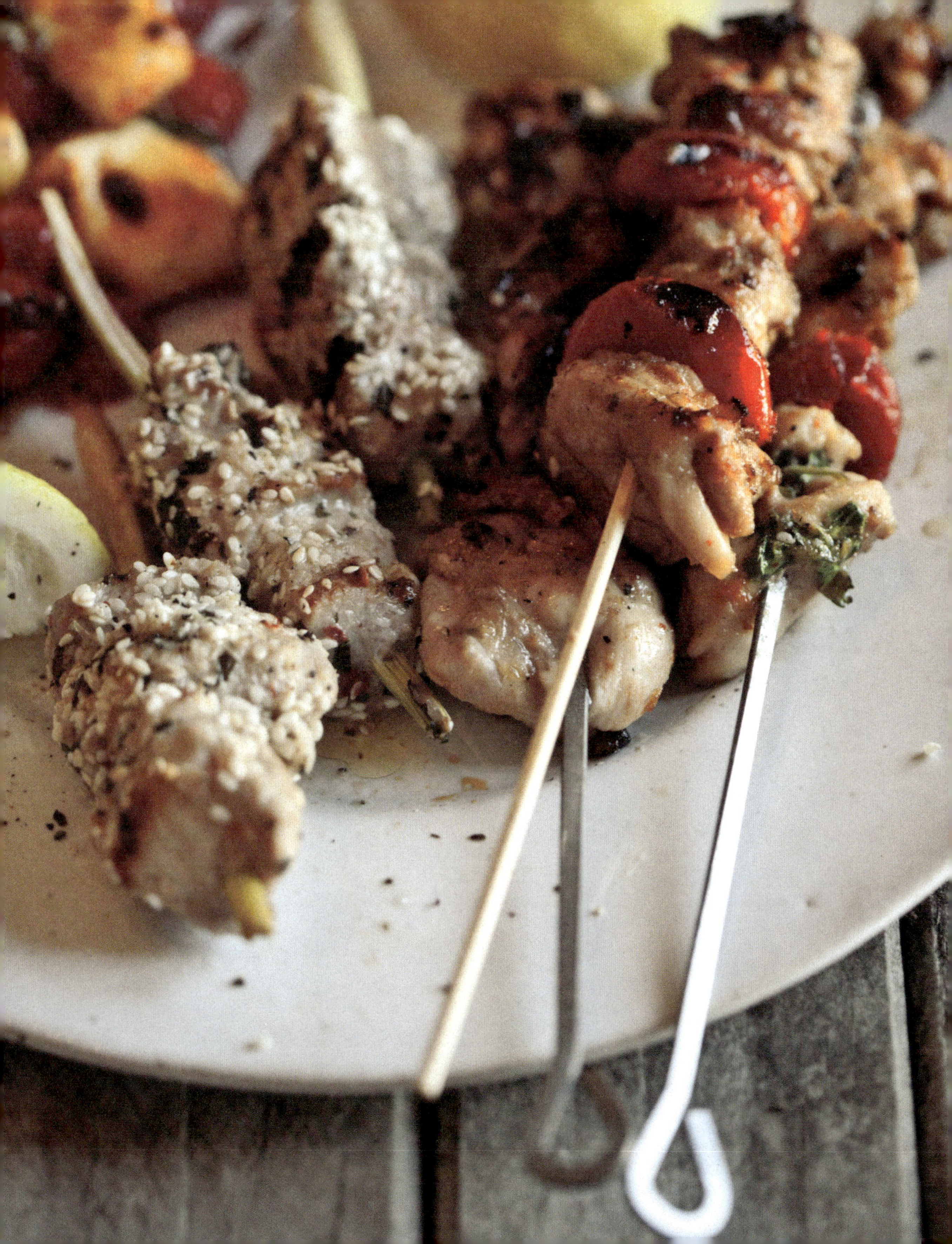

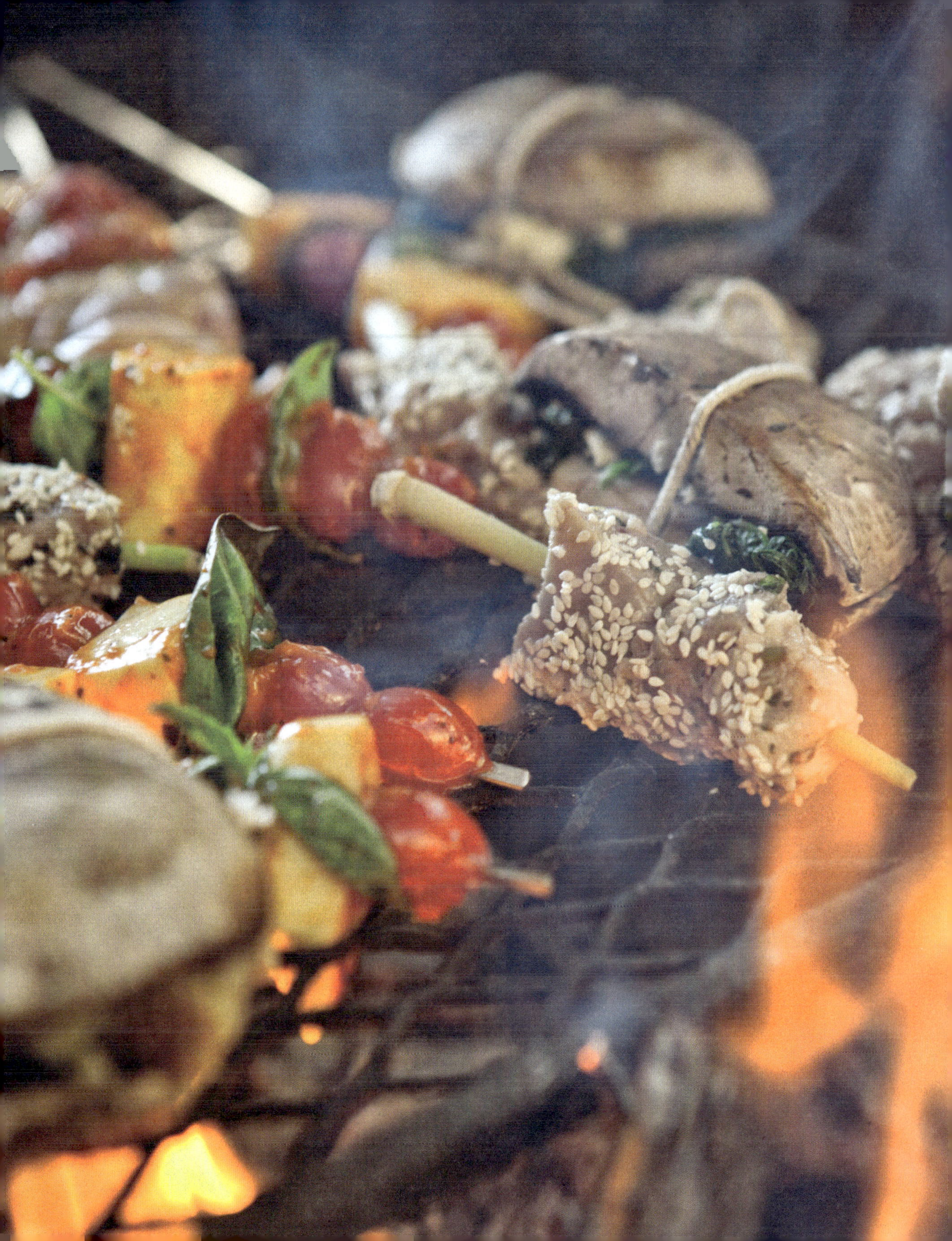

THE VEGETARIAN GOAT

You're going to do pretty much the same with these kebabs as you did with the others. Chuck all the ingredients into a bowl and mix them up with your hands. Let the mixture marinate for at least an hour in the fridge. The Haloumi must be as cold as possible so that it keeps its shape better. Alternate the cubes of Haloumi with the cherry tomatoes when skewering. When you braai these, you've got to keep turning, otherwise the haloumi is going to melt, and all you'll get to eat is the sticky cheesy mess left on the grid (which actually doesn't sound half bad).

You'll need:
> Haloumi – cubed
> cherry tomatoes – whole
> black olives – smashed
> lemon
> crushed black pepper
> basil – chopped

HOT AND SOUR TUNA

Grab another big bowl, add the tuna, a generous drizzle of sesame and peanut oil, a good squeeze of lemon and lime and chuck in the garlic, ginger, chilli, chilli flakes and mint. Mix it around so that all the flavours cover the tuna. Just before you're ready to cook, cut the lemon grass into skewers. (If you can't get your hands on lemon grass, just use normal skewers.) Once you've skewered the tuna, roll it in sesame seeds and the kebabs are ready to braai. The rule of fresh tuna: never overcook it – aim for about 30-60 seconds a side. The tuna must be sealed on the outside and sashimi on the inside.

You'll need:
> a big chunk of yellow fin tuna – cubed
> sesame oil
> peanut oil
> lemon
> lime
> a couple of cloves of garlic – crushed
> a big piece of ginger – roughly chopped
> roughly chopped chilli
> a pinch of dried chilli flakes
> mint – chopped
> sesame seeds
> lemon grass

★ SKEWERS

If you're using wooden skewers, soak them in water first so they don't catch fire. Another note on skewers. If you are using metal ones, remember that they conduct heat so they'll cook the kebabs from the inside out as well – that is, they'll cook faster.

THAI SEAFOOD SALAD

Just a quick word of warning: when you get black mussels off the coast, always check with the locals whether or not there's a red tide. There's nothing worse than having seafood poisoning on your weekend away or, even worse, making your friends sick on their weekend away.

Preheat a flat-bottomed potjie. Add your mussels and a generous splash of wine, put the lid on and let them steam until they open, which should take about 5 minutes, time enough for you to have a glass. Be careful not to overcook them, because if you leave them too long they're going to become toughish.

For four you'll need:
› 24 or so West Coast mussels
› 12 or so prawns
› white wine

Remove the potjie from the heat and let it cool down a bit. Once you can touch the mussels without speaking in tongues, it's time to clean them. Chuck all the ones that are still closed into the sea – chances are they were already dead – and then clean the remaining mussels by pulling them out of their shells and removing the beard. Put them in a separate bowl. Get your friends to start making the dressing while you get busy with the prawns.

You're going to use about 3 prawns per person, deveined and cleaned, but still in their shells. Whack them straight on to the fire. Once they start changing colour from translucent to red, you know they're almost done. Taste one. If it's cooked, take them all off.

BEWARE

The worst thing you can do is overcook prawns – they become floury. Once they're done, peel and set aside and don't bother with a marinade – the salad dressing is going to take care of the flavour.

★ **For the dressing:**
> 6 cloves of garlic
> a knob of peeled ginger
> a small handful of brown sugar
> sesame oil
> a splash of soya sauce
> 2 limes

★ **For the salad:**
> a handful of rocket
> a handful of tatsoi
> a handful of pak choi
> a handful of pepper lettuce
> a handful of baby beetroot leaves
> a handful of mange tout
> about 3 red chillies – finely chopped, seeds and all
> 2 mangoes

To make the dressing

Chuck the garlic and the ginger into a mortar and pestle with a tablespoon or so of brown sugar and bang it a bit to create a garlic and ginger mush. The sugar provides some roughage and resistance to really get the mush going. Next, to give the dressing a lovely dark nutty flavour, add a good splash of sesame oil (anything from 2 tablespoons to 8 – enough to lubricate the salad leaves – but more of that later). Add the juice of 2 limes and a splash of soya sauce. The lime is going to add that nice sharp flavour that's usually associated with Thai food and the soya will provide the saltiness. Finally, sprinkle in a bit more brown sugar to mellow down the bite of the garlic and lime.

Mix it all together. Taste. Make sure you're happy. It should be a sweetish-sourish-biting dressing.

Now for the rest

Once your mussels and prawns have cooled down, take the biggest salad bowl you have and toss together your leaves, mange tout and chilli. Drizzle with generous amounts of the dressing and mix together with your hands. This way the flavour of the dressing will only coat the leaves. Next, peel and slice your mangoes into nice chunky pieces and add to the bowl and, lastly, add the mussels and prawns. Give it one more swirl with your hands and eat with a nice braaied West Coast Snoek.

Some of you might be thinking, Why the chilli and the mango? Truth is, the chilli is going to provide an unexpected bite (the Bonello surprise) and the mango is a delicious contrast to that heat. This sweet-sour-biting salad is and will always be one of my firm favourites.

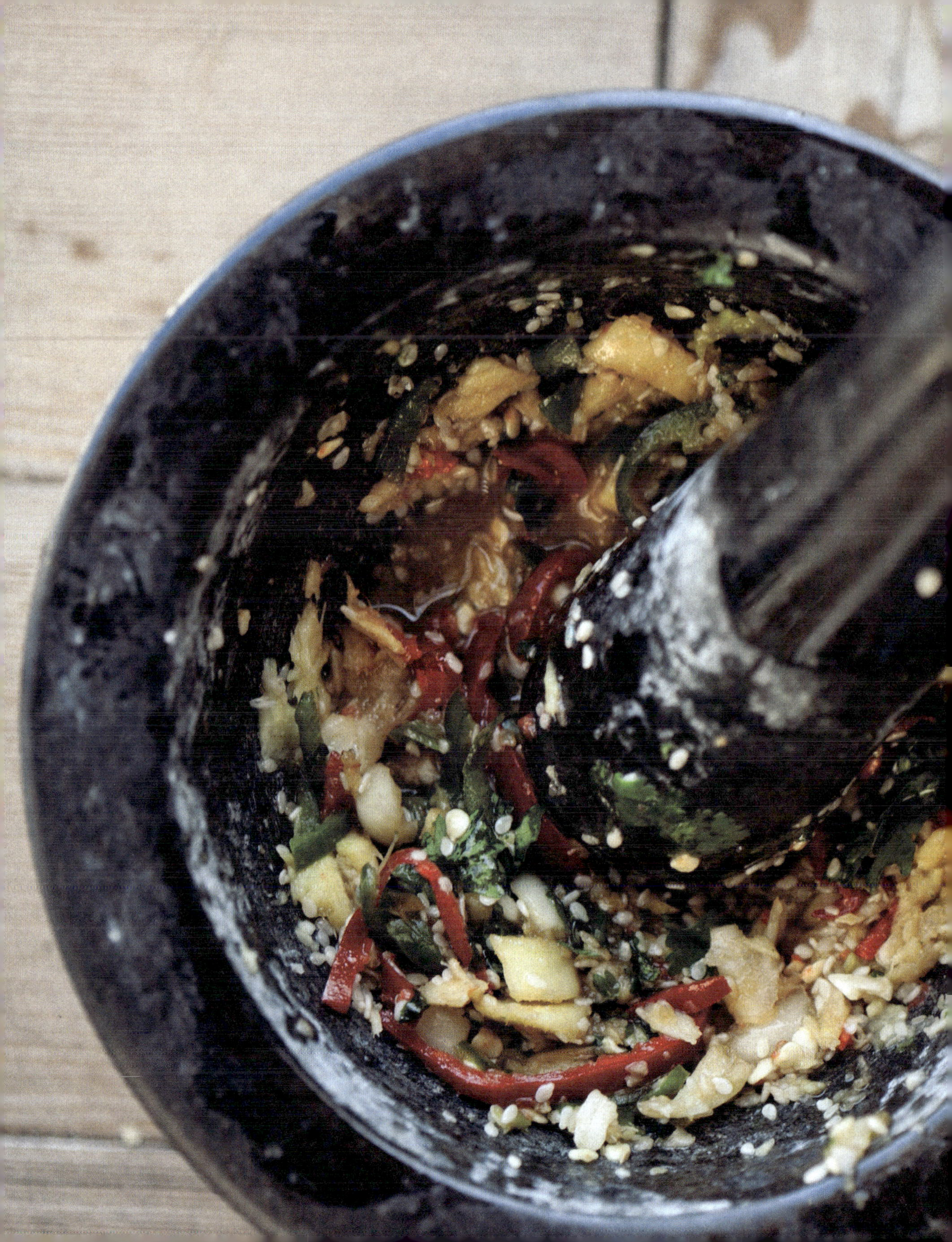

SALAD DRESSING WITH A BITE

A naked salad is just not decent. This angry-but-beautiful dressing adds a love bite to a bowl full of an Oriental-style salad of leaves, sprouts, peppers, courgettes, lentils, chickpeas, mange tout and basil.

Start with the largest, heaviest mortar and pestle you can find. Into it throw peeled garlic, chunks of peeled ginger with the ugly knobbly bits cut off, loads of sliced chillies (leave the seeds in for extra heat), coriander, peanut oil, soya sauce, sesame oil (which imparts amazing deep, dark, nutty flavours), sesame seeds, brown sugar and lemon juice.

Pound everything together until you have a nice smooth-ish dressing. Pour over the salad just before serving.

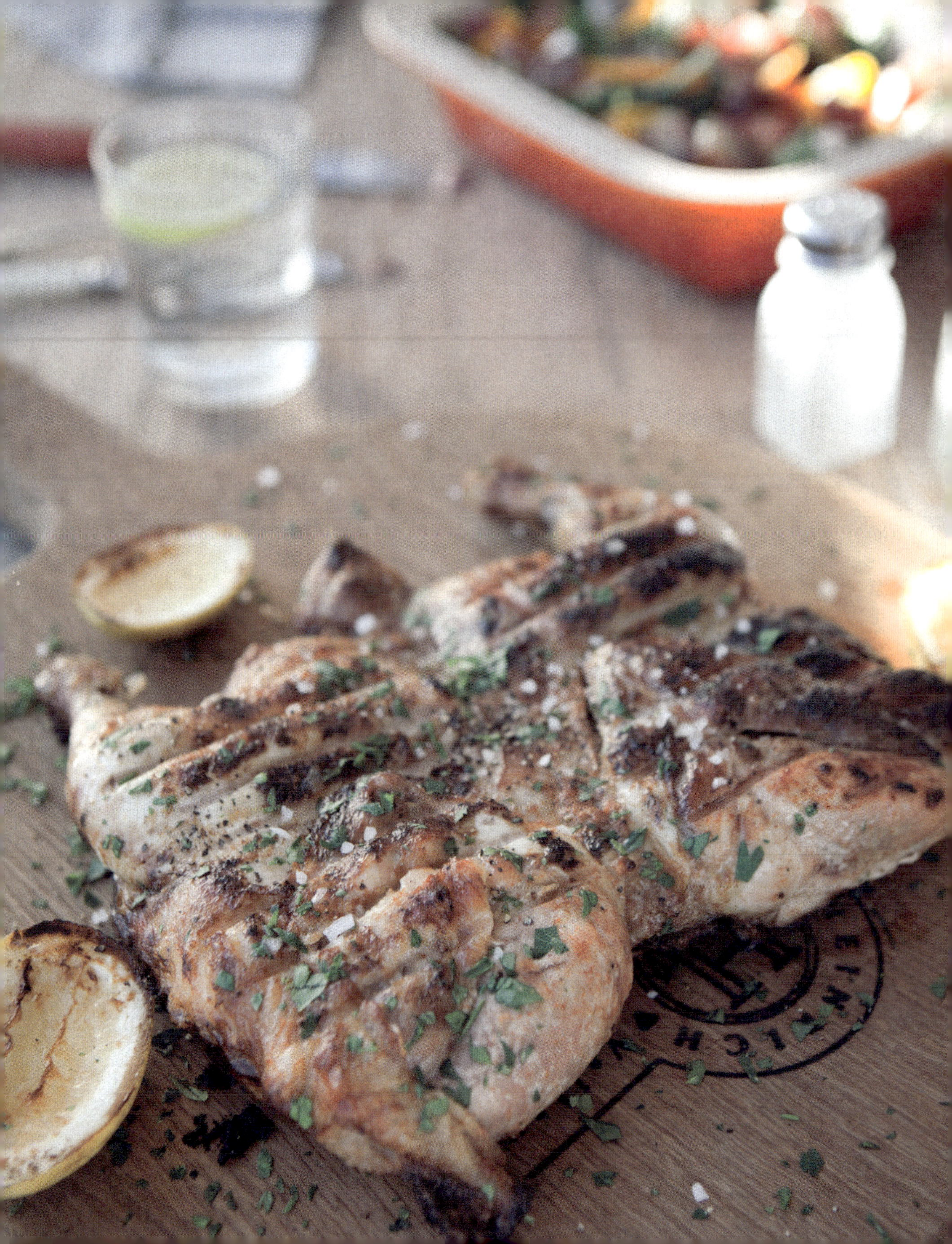

BUTTERMILK AND PAPRIKA
SPATCHCOCK CHICKEN

The acidity in buttermilk is a natural tenderiser, so if you decide to make this get ready to taste the most tender bird (think of your first girlfriend) you'll ever have eaten. Another bonus of this recipe is that a Spatchcock chicken cooks a lot faster than a roast one, which means you've just cut your normal chicken braaiing time in half, and that means you get to watch the preamble before the rugby match instead of cutting in 15 minutes into the game.

Place your chicken in a large bowl. Mix together the buttermilk, paprika and salt and pepper and pour over the chicken until it's covered. Cover the bowl with cling film and let it sleep in the fridge overnight to marinate.

When the cock crows, get up and shuffle to the kitchen. If it's a Saturday, it's probably almost time for lunch and rugby. Remove the chicken from the buttermilk marinade, and pat it dry with paper towel. Sprinkle with salt and pepper to taste. When the fire's ready, it's time to braai.

Turn the bird every so often to avoid ending up with charcoal chicken and you'll know it's cooked if you stab the thickest part of the chicken (the thigh or breast) and the juice runs clear.

★ Serve with lemon wedges, warm tomato salad (page 164) and kassie bread (page 45). *Lekker*.

You'll need:
› 1 chicken – spatchcocked
› buttermilk – enough to cover the chicken
› a good pinch or three of paprika
› salt and pepper to taste

WARM TOMATO SALAD

★ *Sometimes we forget that tomatoes don't always have to be raw for a salad. In fact, they're really delicious when they've been cooked up in olive oil and garlic and their sugars get going...*

So the first-up thing you've got to do is slice up a couple of cloves of garlic and a handful of spring onions and roughly chop up the tomatoes, skin and all. Season with salt and freshly crushed pepper and pan-fry in loads of olive oil (and I mean loads) until the tomatoes start sweating out all those beautiful sweet flavours and the olive oil starts taking on a rosy glow. As soon as it's done, set aside to cool down.

The next thing you're going to do is blanch the green beans and mange tout in some boiling salted water. The idea with blanching is not to overdo it, so boil them for about 2 minutes till they've got some flavour but are still crisp. Take them off the heat and immediately chuck them in cold water to stop the cooking process (this is called 'refreshing'). This way you won't end up with floppy, lifeless vegetables and they'll keep all their nutrition, natural goodness and crunchiness.

When the tomatoes have cooled down, chuck the rocket, tomatoes, green beans, and mange tout into a large salad bowl, then add a generous amount of Danish feta and toss around till everything is coated in the tomato-olive oil.

You'll need:
- a couple of cloves of garlic
- a bunch of spring onions
- about 10 very ripe tomatoes (Rosa, if possible)
- crushed salt and black pepper to taste
- good quality olive oil
- 2 handfuls of green beans – topped and tailed
- 2 handfuls of mange tout
- 2 or 3 big handfuls of wild rocket
- Danish feta

As they say in Afrikaans: *SMAAKLIK.*

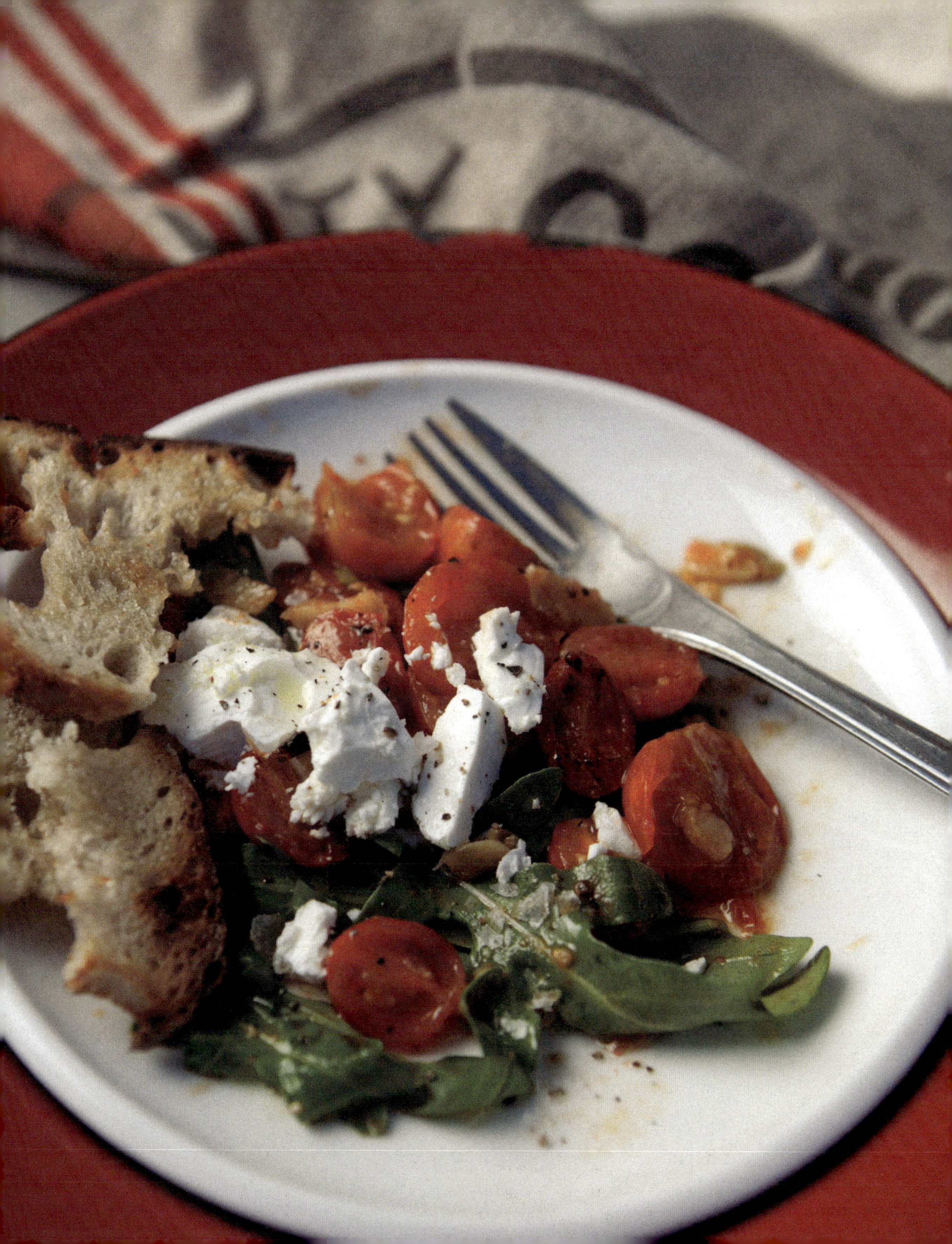

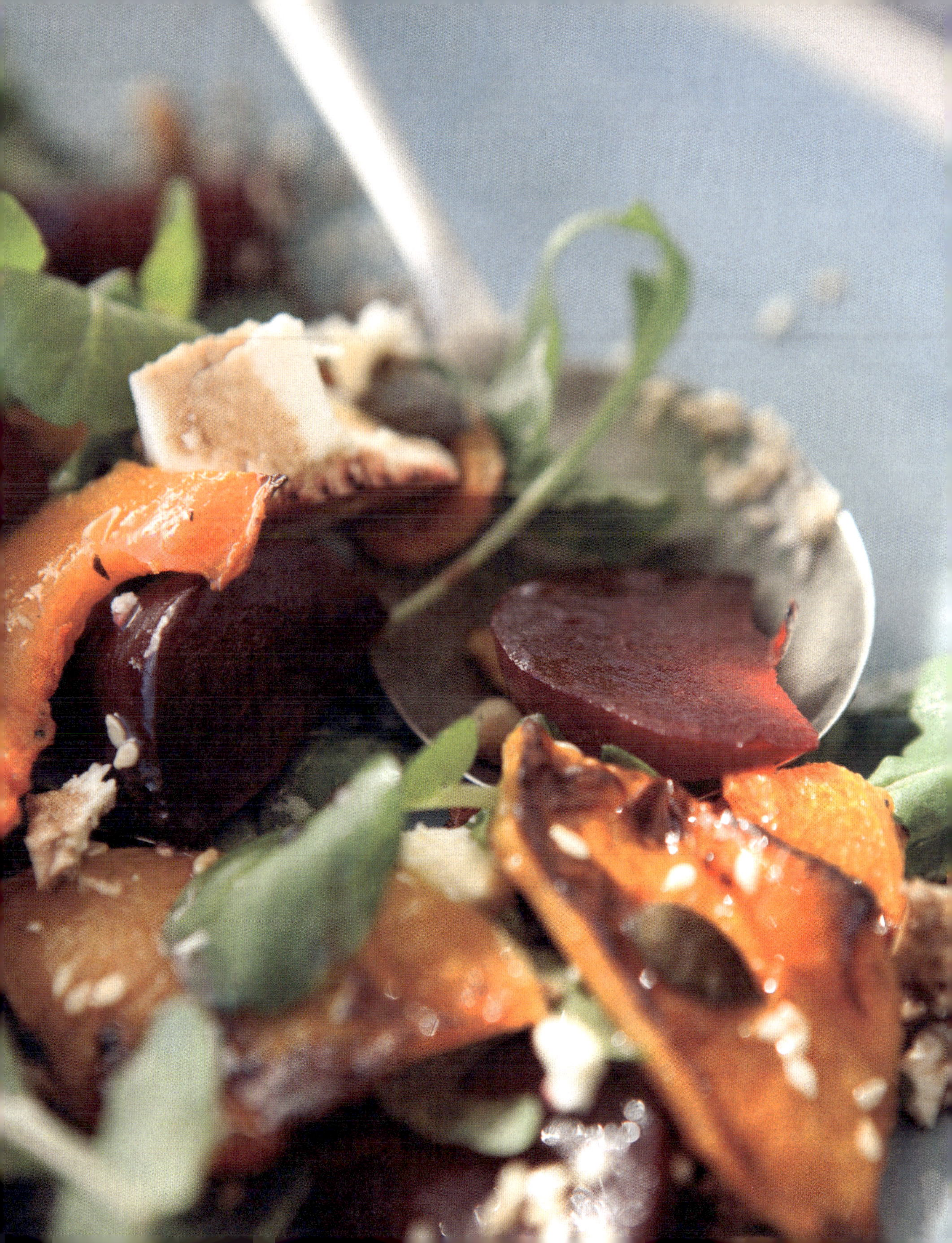

GENIE'S ROASTED BUTTERNUT AND BEETROOT SALAD

Sometimes when I get home from work, the last thing I feel like doing is cooking or making dinner. My missus, Eugenie, will often make this killer salad. The crunch of the nuts and beetroot, contrasting with the peppery bite of the rocket and watercress and the sweetness of the butternut and saltiness of the feta, makes this one of my firm favourites, and that's a good thing, because Genie makes it all the time.

You'll need:
- whole medium-sized butternut
- 5-6 garlic cloves – peeled
- drizzle of olive oil
- 4 or 5 medium-sized beetroots
- palm full of pine nuts
- small palm full of sesame seeds
- small palm full of pumpkin seeds
- handful of smooth Danish feta cut into smallish chunks
- double handful of watercress
- double handful of rocket
- drizzle of balsamic glaze

Peel the butternut, cut it in half, scoop out the seeds and cut it into cubes about 1 cm x 1 cm. Chuck them on to a baking tray with the garlic, drizzle with olive oil and roast in the oven at 180°C until the garlic is soft and the butternut cubes start caramelising and browning at the edges. Take the garlic and butternut out of the oven and let them cool down.

While the butternut and garlic are in the oven, wash and then boil the beetroot for about 40 minutes. It should be cooked but still crunchy (think al dente). Cut off the tips, remove the skins and cut it into quarters and then into smallish chunks.

In a non-stick pan, dry toast the pine nuts and all the seeds and until they're brown and start trying to jump out of the pan.

★ Finally, slice the roasted garlic finely and then toss all the ingredients in a salad bowl. Drizzle with olive oil and balsamic glaze and toss with your hands to get the goodies all mixed up. EAT!

OLIVE OIL

It's ironic that one of the ingredients I most love cooking with (other than garlic, salt and pepper) has been compared to mother's milk because of the Omega 3 and 6 it contains. Incidentally, it has exactly the same ratio of these essential fatty acids as mother's milk, so it comes as no surprise that olive oil is known as the most nutritious vegetable oil around.

> Look, it's easy to take a short cut and opt for a cheap olive oil blend, just like you would rather save some bucks and buy a blended wine, but the problem is, just as cheap wine will ultimately give you a hangover from hell, the dish you're cooking will inevitably be as good (or as bad) as the olive oil you choose to cook with.
>
> So next time you buy olive oil make sure you get the Extra Virgin kind. It tastes much better and has loads of health benefits because of the cold extraction process. Also, before handing out your hard-earned cash, check that there's an expiry date somewhere on the bottle – if there isn't, chances are you're wasting your money.

★ A SPLASH A DAY . . .

If you consider that olive oil is the only vegetable oil that's okay for humans to consume straight after it's been pressed because it's completely natural and doesn't need any refining, it makes sense that it's good for you. Some of the health benefits include lowering the risk of getting breast, colon or gastric cancer. Plus, if you're getting older and start getting forgetful, olive oil is said to help maintain optimal brain function – so the chances are smaller that you'll misplace your car keys, wife, credit card or other valuables.

★ DON'T SPIT. SWALLOW

When you taste olive oil, the first thing you're going to do is smell it – it will tell you a lot about the oil's character. The rest is pretty much the same as wine tasting (a lot of swirling, sipping and slurping), but the big difference is that you're not going to spit. When you swallow the oil, you'll notice a peppery sensation in your throat. The longer that sensation lasts, the better quality olive oil it is.

> Olive oil on its own might not be your cup of tea, but if you're going on a bender with your mates, a shot of olive oil is just the thing you need to line your stomach and protect it against any abuse it'll endure during your playtime.

★ COOKING

If you use olive oil for cooking, you've got to keep in mind that it expands when it heats up. One teaspoon of olive oil is about the same as one tablespoon of normal cooking oil. The better the quality of olive oil, the better your dish will taste.

Olive oil isn't just for cooking. Try drizzling some olive oil into a dipping bowl, add a couple of splashes of balsamic and serve with a selection of breads, cheese, olives, cherry tomatoes and wine.

★ STORING

Extra Virgin Olive Oil is light-sensitive, so treat it like a hungover friend and keep it in a dark cool place. It's also a bad idea to store it next to the stove, because it doesn't like warm temperatures and you've also got to make sure it's sealed properly – oxygen isn't popular either. If you don't store it correctly, chances are the oil will become rancid. You'll know this has happened if the oil has a buttery taste.

Handy uses for olive oil (other than eating)

So if you're flat out and have no patience or *lus* to go to a chemist, hardware, seamstress or doctor, it's great to know that your trusty bottle of olive oil might just do the trick.

I did some research and these are some of the things you can do with olive oil. Let's say you're late for work and you realise you're out of shaving cream and you've got an important meeting. Don't worry. Use some olive oil instead – it will help you get (or avoid) a close shave. Or if you suffer from frizzy hair syndrome and you're tired of people mistaking you for Mick Hucknall, rub some olive oil through your locks after washing. Not too much though – you don't want to end up looking like Donald Trump either! Squeaky door or bed and no Q20? Olive oil. Jeans zipper stuck? Don't panic and try to cut them off your body. Just lubricate the zipper with olive oil and you'll be out of your pants in no time. Olive oil is also said to relieve colds and snoring. Let me know if you have any other uses for it – apart from cooking, of course.

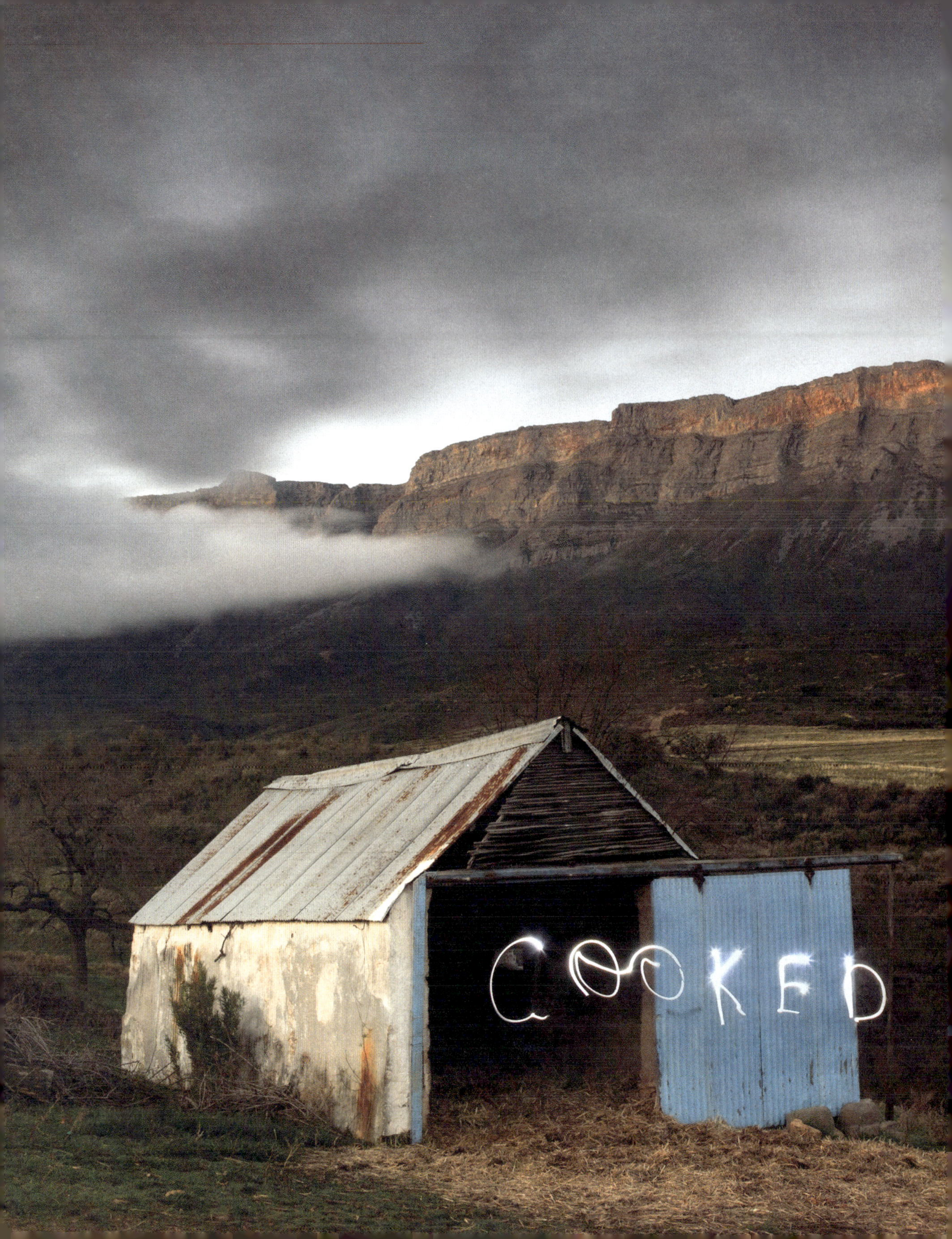
COOKED

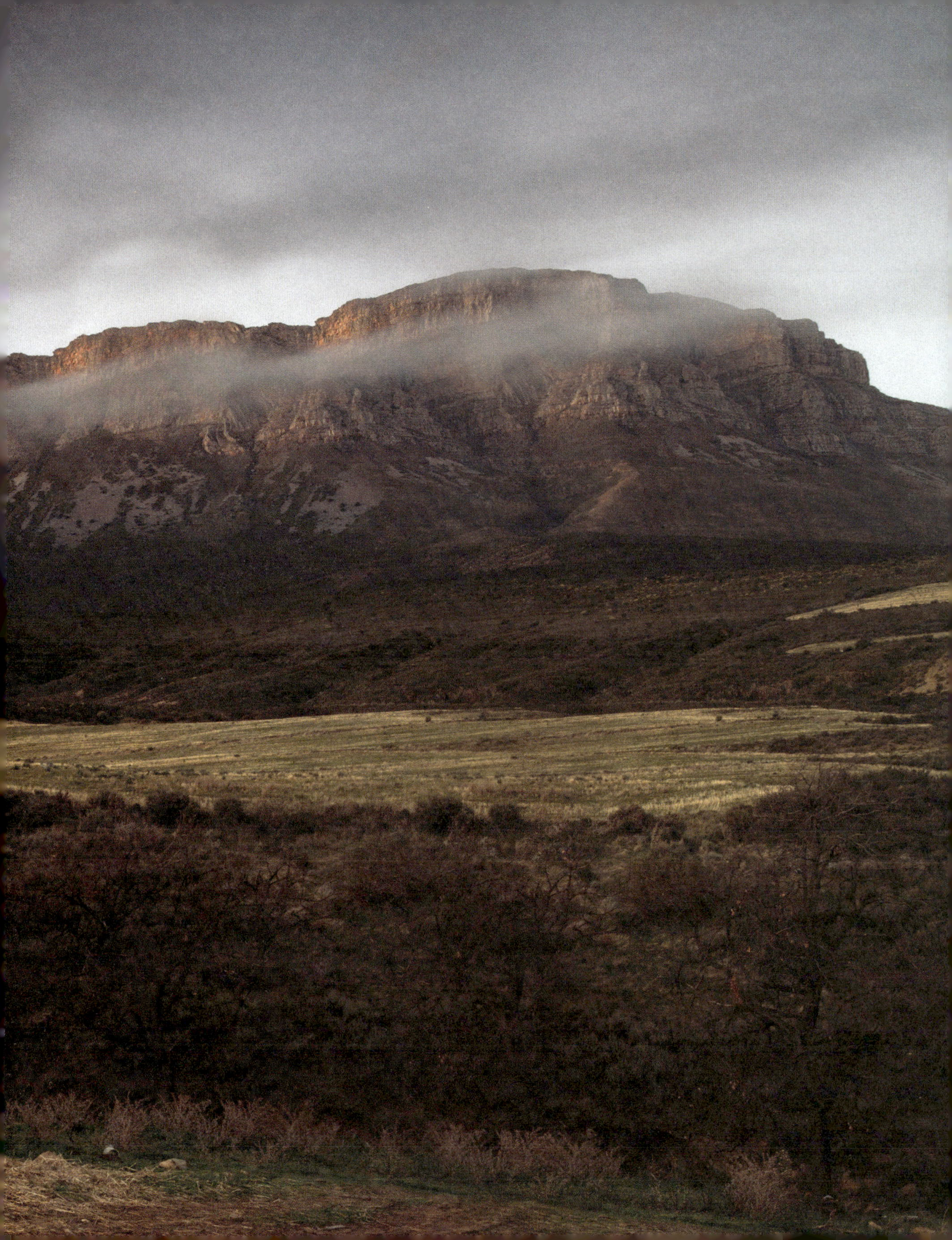

GARTH'S TART

I wish I could say I'm referring to Garth's ex-girlfriend here, but I'm actually talking about his world-famous peppermint crisp tart, which he made for me when we were in Namibia. I often get emails from *Cooked* fans begging for this sweet recipe, so I finally got Garth to make it again, and this time I took notes.

> ★ It's a really easy pudding, but get ready to be smooched by a bunch of tarts once they've had their fill. This one is definitely for the ladies.

First up, whip up your cream until it's nice and thick, then add your caramel and condensed milk and fold it all together.

Next, pour milk into a flat-bottomed bowl and, one by one, soak your biscuits (not for too long – they mustn't collapse into a soggy mess) and tile them into a wide-bottomed pudding dish.

Pour over a layer of the cream mixture and smooth it out with a wooden spoon or spatula. Grate some peppermint chocolate over the cream filling and keep repeating the layers (biscuit, cream, peppermint choc), until you've run out of ingredients.

Put it in the fridge to set for 45 minutes, and serve.

★ If you feel like something more adult-orientated, you can soak the biscuits in a crème-based liqueur like Amarula instead of milk.

You'll need:
- 500 ml fresh cream
- 1 tin caramel
- 1 tin sweetened condensed milk
- coconut biscuits – good old Tennis Biscuits do the trick
- milk
- a couple of Peppermint Crisp bars

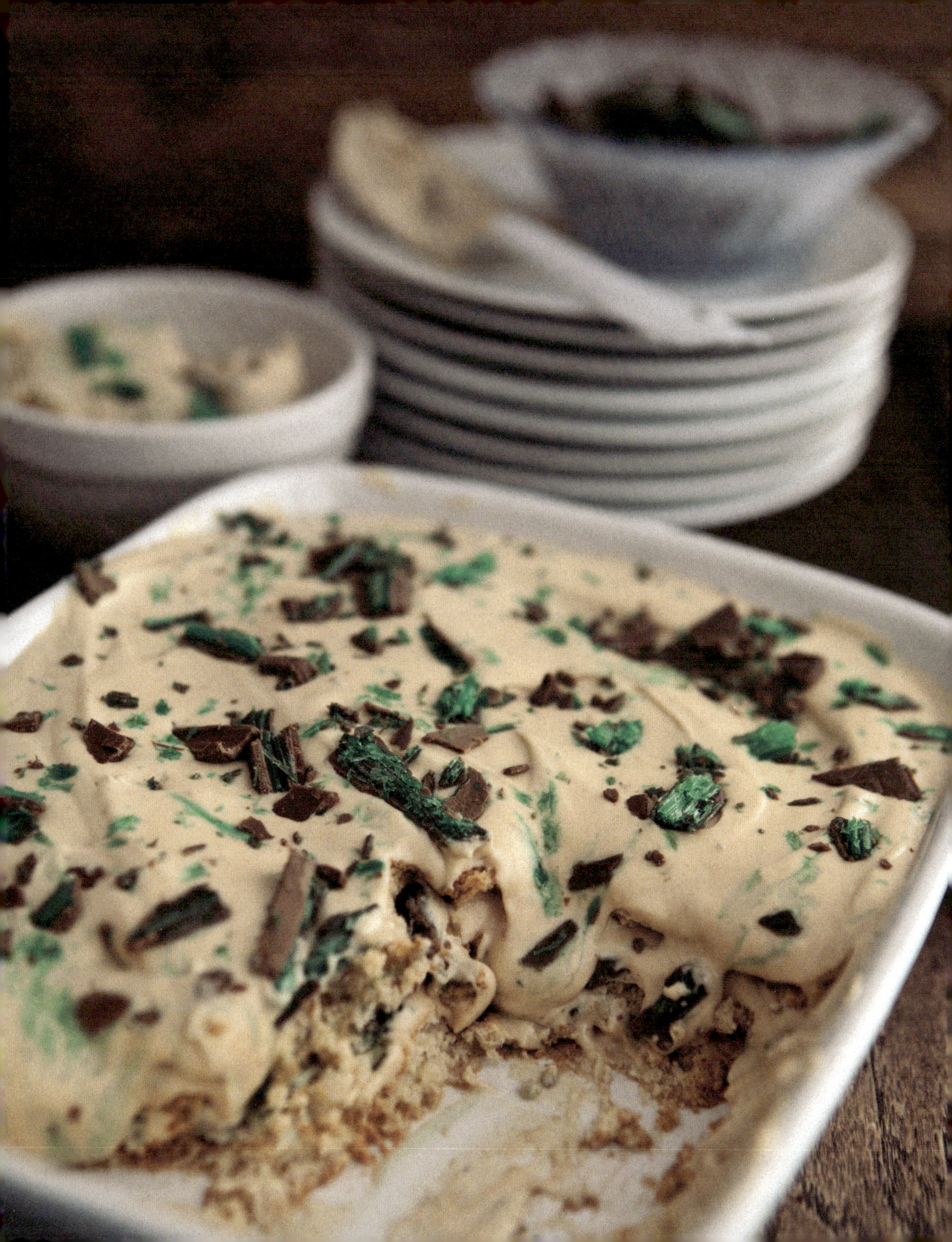

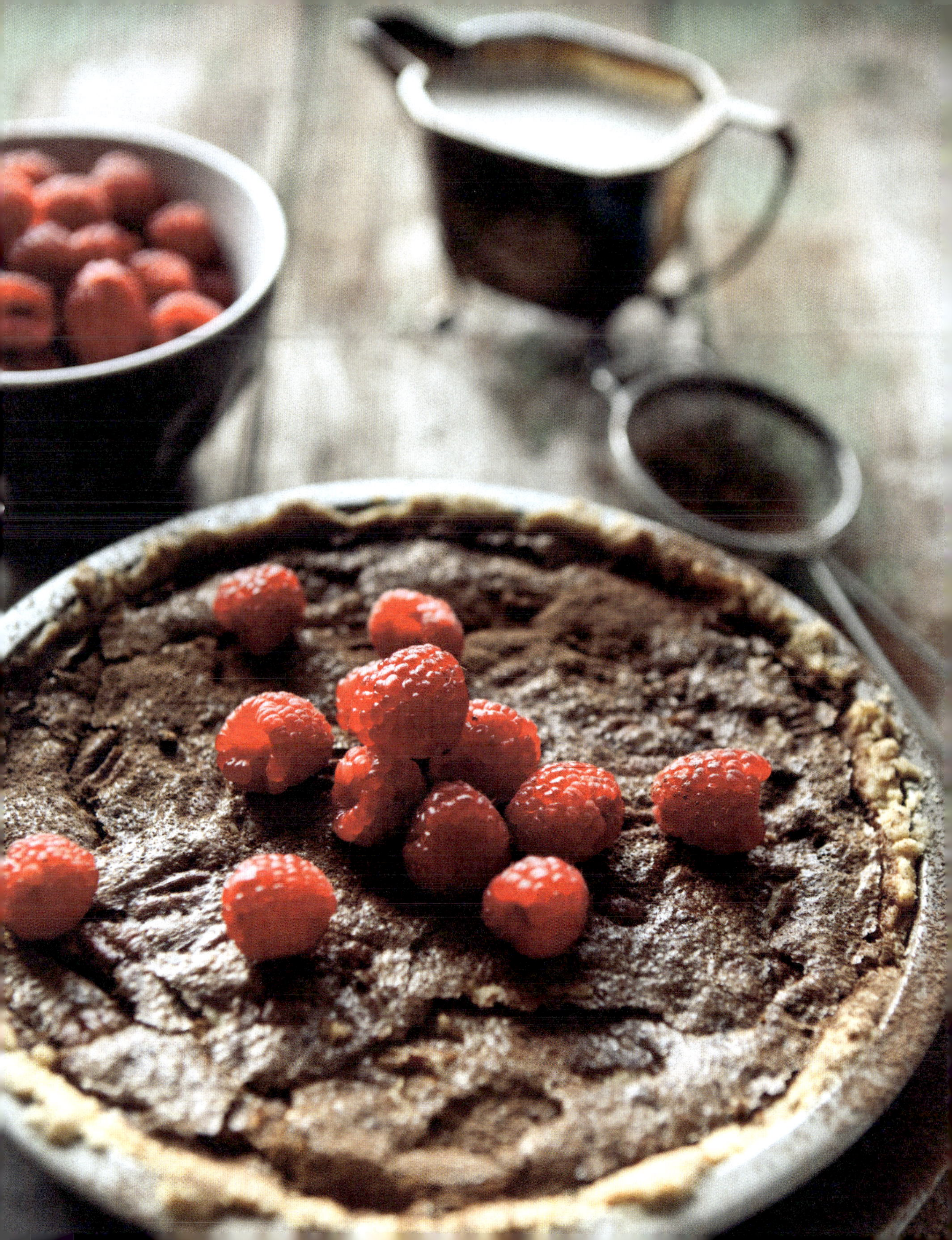

MESSY CHOCOLATE AND BERRY PIE

This is my spin on a recipe given to me by Alfred Henry, but like most things in life I've changed it and made it my own. It's my take on the classic Mississippi Mud Pie born in America in the 1970s and it's got to be the ultimate dessert sin. It's loaded with chocolate, butter, cream and syrup . . . and if you're me, it's definitely an everyday kind of pie.

For the pastry you'll need:
› 150 g butter
› 370 g flour
› 75 g brown sugar

And for the mess:
› 3 free-range eggs
› 250 g treacle sugar
› 150 g butter
› 40 g dark chocolate
› 2 teaspoons good quality instant coffee powder
› 6 tablespoons cocoa powder
› a handful of pecan nuts – crushed
› 2 tablespoons sour cream
› 3 tablespoons golden syrup
› 1 teaspoon vanilla essence
› whipped cream
› fresh berries

★ *One big note: use the best chocolate, coffee and cocoa powder you can afford – you want those beautiful deep dark flavours to come out. Cheap stuff tastes cheap.*

The S(ch)weet Pastry
(you can use store bought, but it's always nicer to make your own)

Chuck the flour and butter into a large bowl and mix it with your hands. Once you have a nice crumbly dough, add the brown sugar and combine loosely, taking care to not compress the dough too much. You might think you've used enough butter, but the fun isn't over yet. Grease a 23 cm baking tin. Then take a ball of dough and press it down into the tin and up the sides until it's about 2-3 mm thick. Whack it in a pre-heated oven at 180°C and blind bake for about 5 minutes until the pastry has set. It'll still work if you don't do this, but the pastry won't be crunchy crumbly.

For the Mess

Whisk the eggs and sugar to form a sabayon (which is really just a fancy word for a foamy mixture – think almost like custard). It doesn't matter if the sugar isn't completely dissolved. Take a non-stick saucepan and chuck in the butter. When it's melted, add the chocolate, coffee and cocoa powder. Stir around until everything has melted and it's been properly mixed, then add the crushed pecan nuts. Steer clear of friends with sticky fingers and set it aside.

Take the whisked egg/sugar combination and add the sour cream and the syrup and vanilla essence. Mix well.

The last part of this messy process is to combine the chocolate and the egg mixture to form a thick mousse.

Pour into the pastry-lined tin and bake for 40 minutes until the mixture puffs up and forms a crust. Now comes the really tricky part. You've got to hide the pie somewhere – it needs time to rest and cool down on a wire rack but putting it on a windowsill with an open window is not a good idea when aforementioned friends with sticky fingers are around.

Once it's cooled down, top with fresh berries and serve with a dollop of whipped cream. In my house, this messy pie never lasts more than a day.

MESSY CHOCOLATE SUSHI

I doubled up on my Messy Chocolate and Berry Pie ingredients, because I had a sinful idea floating in my head.

This is what you do

Make a batch of the pastry and the filling for the Messy Choc and Berry pie (page 175).

Take a roasting pan (the biggest you have) and line it with baking paper, making sure it hangs over the sides, then take a ball of the sweet pastry dough and flatten it on to the paper. Pour over the chocolate mess, but make sure you leave the edges uncovered. Bake for about 40 minutes then take it out and let it cool down to a medium heat. Now for the sushi trick. Roll it all up like you would a Swiss Roll, twist the ends of the paper to seal (think boiled sweets) and whack it in the freezer. And, please, the baking paper must be on the outside, not rolled up into the inside.

The next morning, take your family for a really long walk, but leave the chocolate sushi in a cooler box in the car. When you're done (if you are going to eat this, you should have at least done an hour of hard walking), surprise your family with a picnic (with Messy Chocolate Sushi as the star). Slice up the roll into sushi sized circles. Enjoy as is or topped with vanilla ice cream.

> ★ This dessert is meant to be treacly chocolate and the texture should be like toffee. Two things are going to happen. One is you're going to start talking Bushman (clicking your tongue on the roof of your mouth). The second thing is that you're about to embark on a serious sugar high (like when you were a kid). It's probably a good idea to go for another walk.

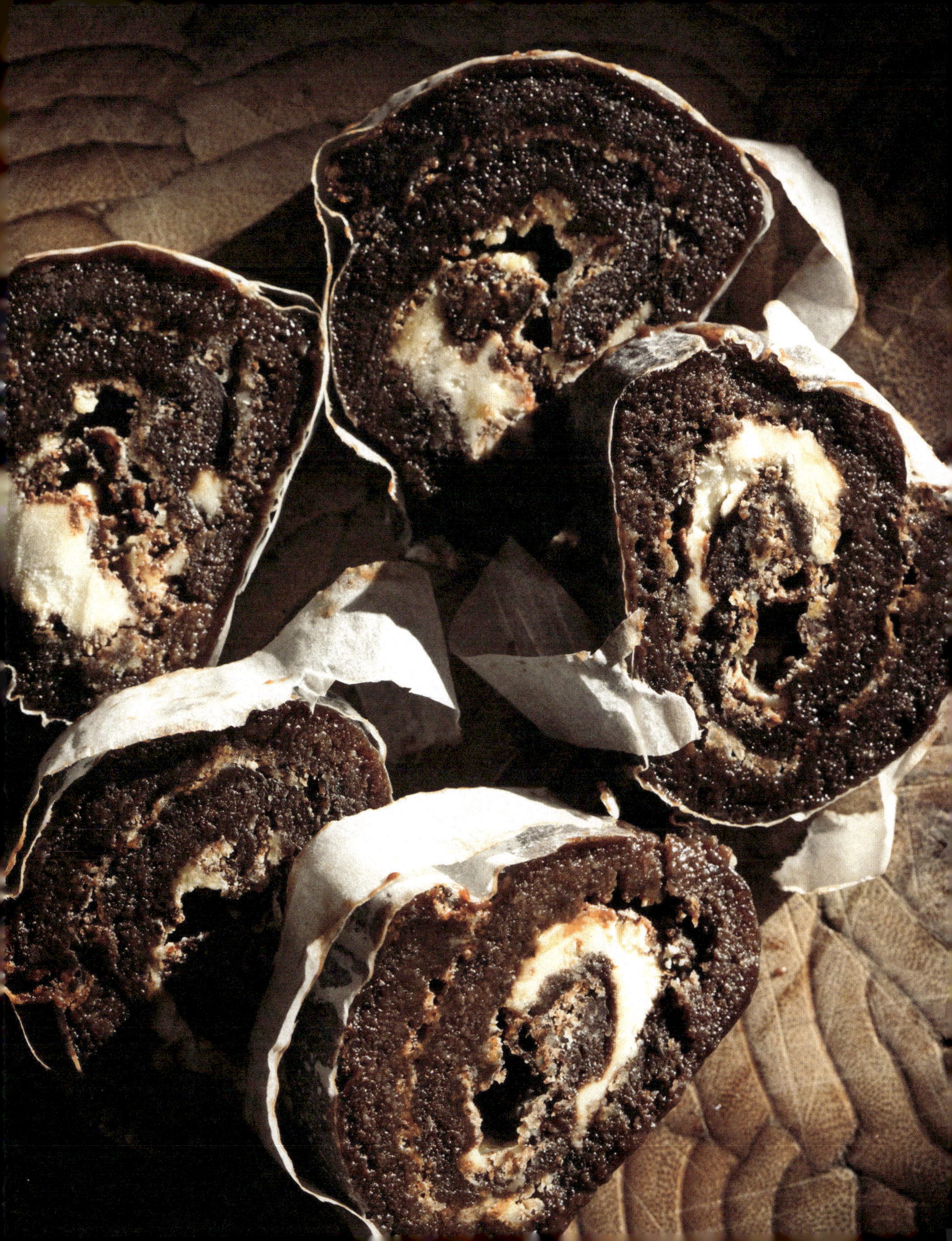

MELKTERT

If you're a South African, you love melktert. Fact. It runs in our blood and is synonymous with watching the rugby and eating braaivleis. Even while reading this you're probably conjuring up that nostalgic feeling you get when you see an old Aga stove or when you page through photo albums filled with trinkets and photos of your childhood.

Chances are you have a secret family recipe for the perfect crust and smoothest filling that you whip up for special Sunday lunches. And chances are you keep that recipe under lock and key. Sorry to say, this is not that kind of melktert. In fact, this isn't a tert that you'd want to introduce to your new mom-in-law. This is the kind of tert you're going to give your mates after a killer day in the great outdoors as a reward for being your friends.

All you need is

2 tins of sweetened condensed milk / ground cinnamon / half a bottle of vodka

(If you've been kuiering all day finding a discarded half bottle shouldn't be a problem. But if it is, grab a new one and decant half and save it for later, or inject it into oranges or watermelon)

Open your condensed milk tins, pour the contents into your vodka bottle, and shake it up to the beat of your favourite song. Let it chill in the freezer until it's thick and syrupy and the sun is just at the right spot. If your mates actually give you the time to pour it into shooter glasses, do that, sprinkle on some grated cinnamon and swallow. Otherwise, pass the bottle around, glug it down and enjoy.

Warning

The sweetness of the condensed milk will give you a huge sugar rush and when that amount of sugar is mixed with alcohol, you should get ready to party until the sun comes up (again).

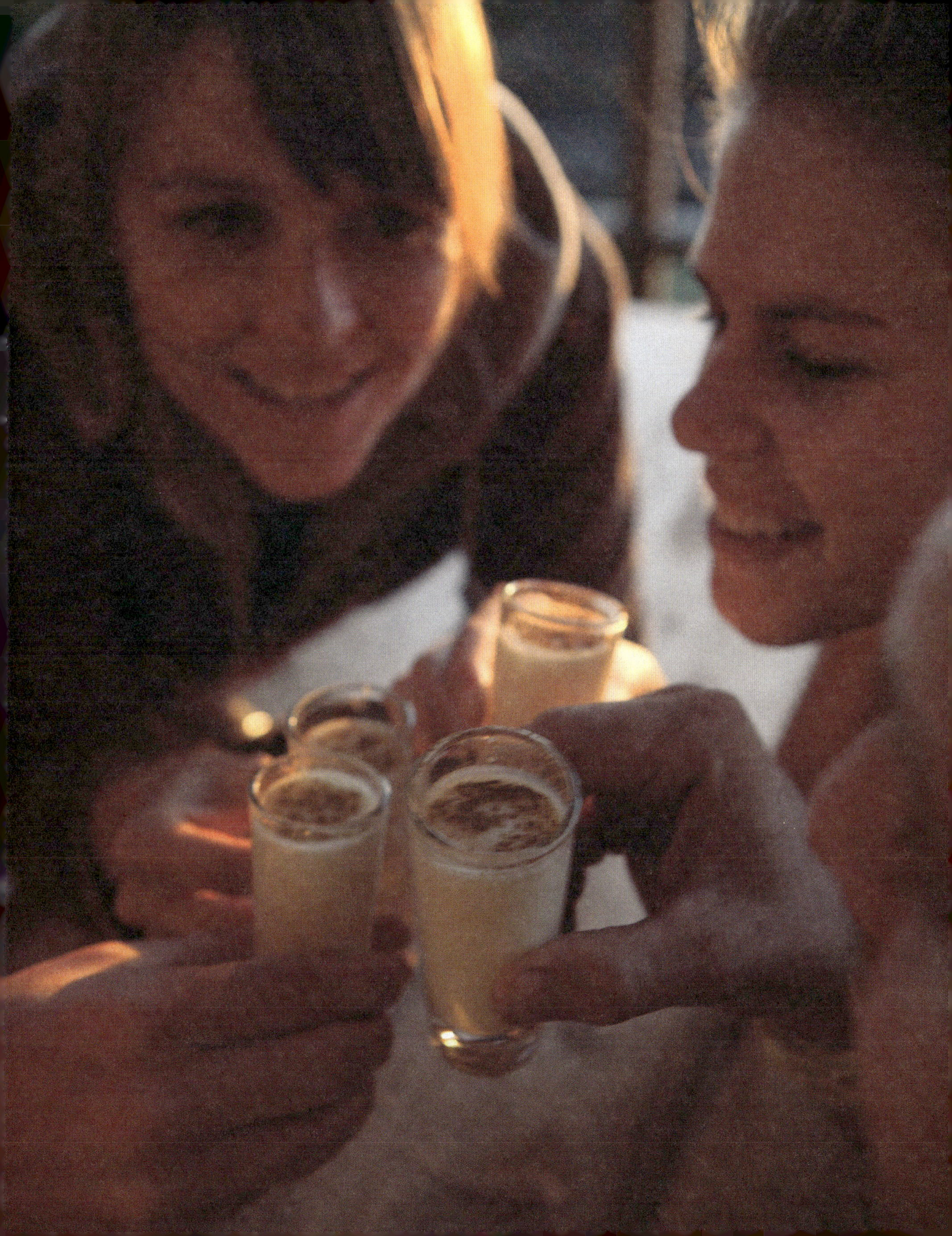

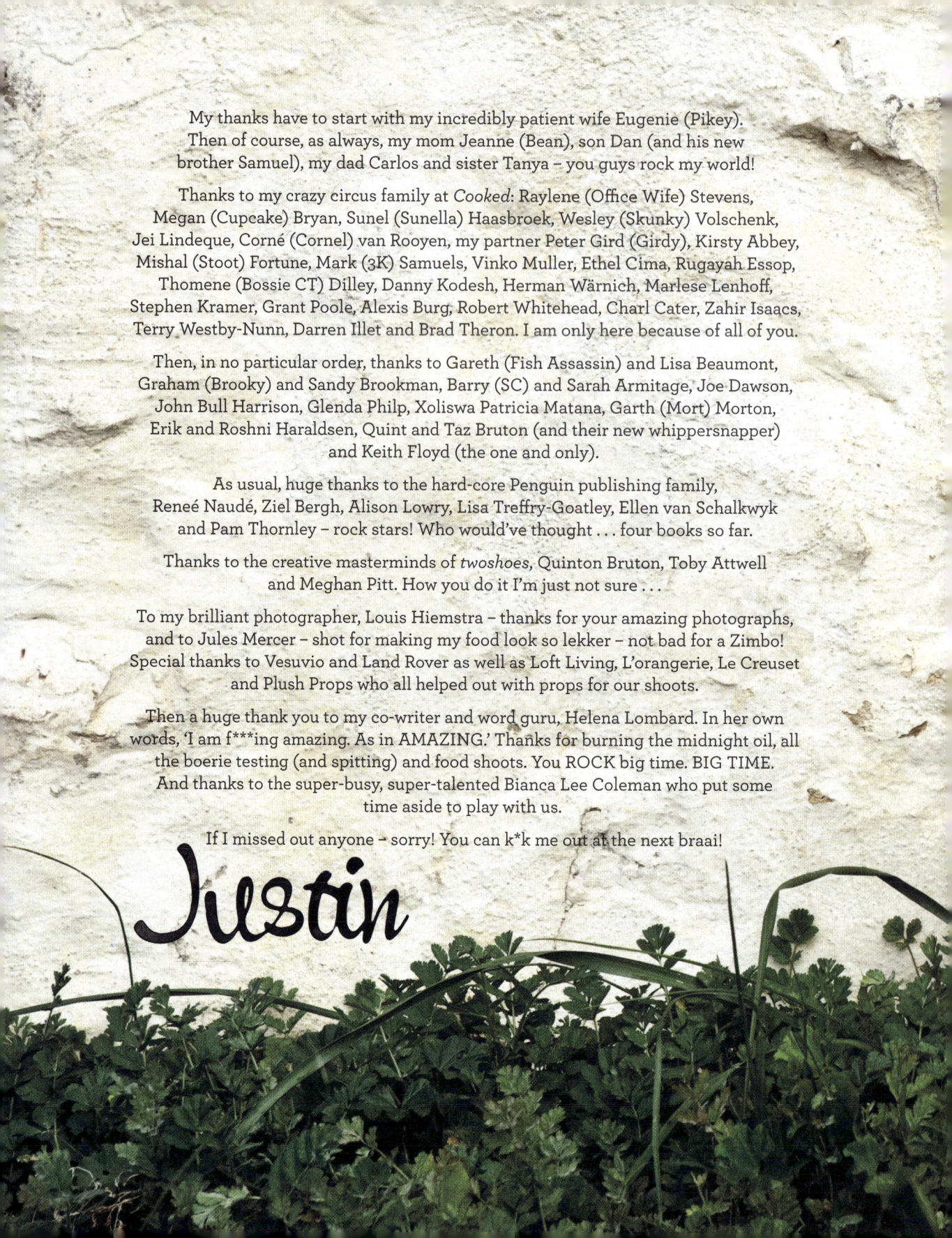

My thanks have to start with my incredibly patient wife Eugenie (Pikey). Then of course, as always, my mom Jeanne (Bean), son Dan (and his new brother Samuel), my dad Carlos and sister Tanya – you guys rock my world!

Thanks to my crazy circus family at *Cooked*: Raylene (Office Wife) Stevens, Megan (Cupcake) Bryan, Sunel (Sunella) Haasbroek, Wesley (Skunky) Volschenk, Jei Lindeque, Corné (Cornel) van Rooyen, my partner Peter Gird (Girdy), Kirsty Abbey, Mishal (Stoot) Fortune, Mark (3K) Samuels, Vinko Muller, Ethel Cima, Rugayah Essop, Thomene (Bossie CT) Dilley, Danny Kodesh, Herman Wärnich, Marlese Lenhoff, Stephen Kramer, Grant Poole, Alexis Burg, Robert Whitehead, Charl Cater, Zahir Isaacs, Terry Westby-Nunn, Darren Illet and Brad Theron. I am only here because of all of you.

Then, in no particular order, thanks to Gareth (Fish Assassin) and Lisa Beaumont, Graham (Brooky) and Sandy Brookman, Barry (SC) and Sarah Armitage, Joe Dawson, John Bull Harrison, Glenda Philp, Xoliswa Patricia Matana, Garth (Mort) Morton, Erik and Roshni Haraldsen, Quint and Taz Bruton (and their new whippersnapper) and Keith Floyd (the one and only).

As usual, huge thanks to the hard-core Penguin publishing family, Reneé Naudé, Ziel Bergh, Alison Lowry, Lisa Treffry-Goatley, Ellen van Schalkwyk and Pam Thornley – rock stars! Who would've thought . . . four books so far.

Thanks to the creative masterminds of *twoshoes*, Quinton Bruton, Toby Attwell and Meghan Pitt. How you do it I'm just not sure . . .

To my brilliant photographer, Louis Hiemstra – thanks for your amazing photographs, and to Jules Mercer – shot for making my food look so lekker – not bad for a Zimbo! Special thanks to Vesuvio and Land Rover as well as Loft Living, L'orangerie, Le Creuset and Plush Props who all helped out with props for our shoots.

Then a huge thank you to my co-writer and word guru, Helena Lombard. In her own words, 'I am f***ing amazing. As in AMAZING.' Thanks for burning the midnight oil, all the boerie testing (and spitting) and food shoots. You ROCK big time. BIG TIME. And thanks to the super-busy, super-talented Bianca Lee Coleman who put some time aside to play with us.

If I missed out anyone – sorry! You can k*k me out at the next braai!

Justin

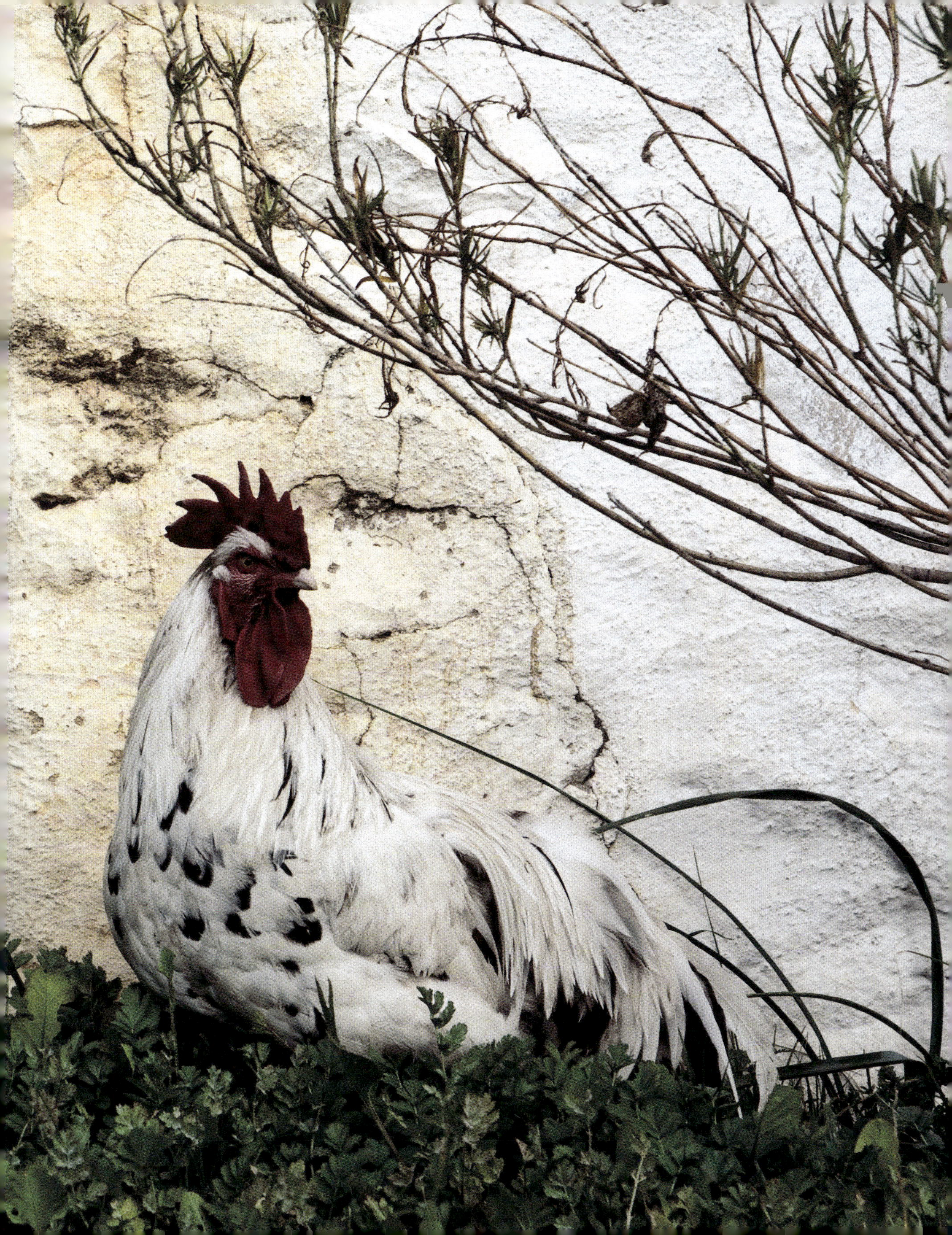

A
Anchovy Butter *47*
Apple Crumble, Bottomless *80*

B
Basil Pesto *150*
Beef
  Fillet, Smoked in a Kassie *42*
  Fillet, Stuffed *68-71*
Biltong *48-51*
Biltong, Leek & Asparagus Quiche *52*
Boerewors *58-59*
Bread, Baked in a Kassie *45*
Breads
  Basic Bread Dough *45*
  Juanita's Potato Bread
  Kassie Flat Bread *45*
  Stick Breads, Stuffed *148-151*
Breakfast in One Pan *130*
Bunny Chow *92*
Burgers, Really Scrumptious *138*
Butternut & Beetroot Salad *167*
Butters, Flavoured *46-47*

C
Calamari. *See Lula*
Chicken in Crusty Bread *112*
Chicken Herb Rub *41*
Chicken in a Kassie *41*
Chicken Satay Kebab *154*
Chicken, Spatchcock *163*
Chocolate & Berry Pie, Messy *175*
Chocolate Sushi, Messy *176*
Crab in Pumpkin Leaves *102*

D
Desserts
  Apple Crumble *80*
  Chocolate & Berry Pie, Messy *175*
  Chocolate Sushi, Messy *176*
  Melktert *178*
  Tart, Garth's Famous Peppermint *172*
Dipping Butters *46-47*

F
Fillet, smoked in a Kassie *42*
Fillet, Stuffed *68-71*
Fish & Seafood
  Crab in Pumpkin Leaves *102*
  Curried Fish. *See Kerrie Vis*
  Fish Parcels (en papillote) *95*
  Hottentot, Braai'd *22*
  Kreef Chowder *16-19*
  Lula in Água Negra *116*
  Mussels, Black *28*
  Mussels, Thai, on Pot Bread *86*
  Periwinkle *27*
  Sardines Baked in Salt *119*
  Seafood Salad, Thai *158-159*
  Trout, 3 Ways *96-99*
  Tuna Kebab *157*
  Yellow Fin Tuna, Seared *13*
Fish Parcels (en papillote) *95*
Fritters
  Corn *152*
  Pear & Blue Cheese *152*
  Sweet Potato & Chorizo *152*
  Zucchini & Beetroot *152*
  Zucchini & Parmesan *152*

G
Gazpacho *141-143*
Gnocchi *57*
Green Sauce. *See Salsa Verde*

H
Honey & Soya Sauce *13*
Hottentot, Braai'd *22*

K
Kassie, The *37-39*
Kebabs
  Chicken Satay *154*
  Tuna *157*
  Vegetarian *157*
Kerrie Vis *32*
Kreef Chowder *16-19*

L
Lamb
- Bunny Chow *92*
- Smileys *63*
- Tomato Lamb Potjie *54-57*

Lula in Água Negra *116*

M
Marmite Butter *46*
Mayonnaise *13*
Melktert *178*
Mushroom & Smashed Baby Potato Salad *66*
Mushrooms, Stuffed *73*
Mussels, Black *28*
Mussels, Thai, on Pot Bread *86*

O
Olive Oil *169-169*
Onion, Caramelised & Kalahari Truffle
(stuffing for fillet) *69*
Ostrich Peppercorn Fillet *65*

P
Pancakes, Fruity *120*
Periwinkle *27*
Pies on the Braai *132-135*
- Chicken, Pea & Beer Filling *132*
- Mussel & Prawn Filling *135*
- Spinach & Feta Filling *132*

Potato Bread, Juanita's *77*
Potato Potjie *79*
Potato Skins, Crispy *57*
Poultry
- Chicken in Crusty Bread *112*
- Chicken in a Kassie *41*
- Chicken Satay Kebab *154*
- Chicken, Spatchcock *163*

Prego Roll *109*

R
Rosemary & Orange Zest *46*

S
Salads
- Butternut & Beetroot *167*
- Mushroom & Smashed Baby Potato *66*
- Seafood, Thai *158-159*
- Tomato, Warm *164*

Salsa Verde/Green Sauce *150*
Sardines Baked in Salt *119*
Sauces, Dressings & Rubs
- Basil Pesto *150*
- Chicken Herb Rub *41*
- Honey & Soya Sauce *13*
- Mayonnaise *13*
- Peppercorn Rub *42,65*
- Salsa Verde/Green Sauce *150*
- Salad Dressing with a Bite *161*
- Tomato Sauce, Sweet *116*

Smileys *63*
Smoothies
- Blueberry & Pomegranate *125*
- Gooseberry, Banana & Melon *125*
- Peanut Butter, Honey and Vanilla Ice Cream *125*

Soups
- Gazpacho *141-143*
- Vicious Wa! (Vichyssoise) *144*

Spinach, Creamy (stuffing for fillet) *69*
Stick Breads, Stuffed *148-151*

T
Tart, Garth's Famous Peppermint *172*
Tomato Lamb Potjie *54-57*
Tomato Salad, Warm *164*
Tomato Sauce, Sweet *116*
Trout, 3 Ways *96-99*
Tzatziki *138*

Y
Yellow Fin Tuna, Seared *13*